Thomas Paine

Sir Alfred Ayer was born in 1910 and educated at Eton College and Christ Church, Oxford where he later became a Lecturer and Student in Philosophy. During the war he served in the Welsh Guards and Military Intelligence. He was Grote Professor of the Philosophy of Mind and Logic in the University of London, 1946–59, and Wykeham Professor of Logic in the University of Oxford, 1959–78. His numerous distinctions include honorary doctorates from the Universities of Brussels, East Anglia, Durham, London, Trent (Ontario) and Bard (USA). He has an honorary Fellowship of University College London, is an honorary member of the American Academy of Arts and Sciences, honorary Fellow of Wadham College and New College and honorary Student of Christ Church. He has been a Fellow of the British Academy since 1952, is a Chevalier de la Légion D'Honneur and a member of the Order of Cyril and Methodius, First Class (Bulgaria). He was knighted in 1970. His numerous publications include a study of Voltaire, published by Faber in 1988.

Thomas Paine

A. J. Ayer

faber and faber

LONDON · BOSTON

First published in Great Britain in 1988
by Martin Secker & Warburg Ltd
This paperback edition first published in 1989
by Faber and Faber Limited
3 Queen Square London WC1N 3AU

Printed in Great Britain by
Cox & Wyman Ltd, Reading, Berkshire
All rights reserved

© A. J. Ayer, 1988

*British Library Cataloguing in Publication Data
is available*

ISBN 0-571-15444-1

To
Rebecca, Gully and Peter Foges

Contents

Preface

There have been many biographies of Thomas Paine but I believe that this is the first attempt that has been made to combine a sketch of his life and character with a critical examination of his political and religious standpoints. In dealing with his politics, I have allowed myself the luxury of devoting separate chapters to the political philosophers who created the theoretical climate in which he practised, and to the evaluation of the status of Edmund Burke, whose attack on the French Revolution provoked Paine into writing his famous *Rights of Man*. I hope that these excursions will be found to have some interest in themselves.

Next to the seminal work of Moncure Conway, to which I make frequent acknowledgements in my text, I have drawn most heavily upon the research of Professor A. Owen Aldridge, in particular his book *Thomas Paine's American Ideology*, which was published in 1984 by the University of Delaware Press. I first learned of this book through a review of it in *The New Humanist* by my friend Michael Foot, to whom I am particularly grateful both for drawing my attention to H. N. Brailsford's essay on Thomas Paine, and for his own appreciation of Paine in his book *Debts of Honour*. I owe thanks also to Mr A. C. Goodwin, curator of the Ancient House Museum at Thetford, for his information concerning the recent Paine exhibition and other points of historical interest.

Finally, I wish to express my thanks to Miss Barley Alison and Mr Peter Grose who encouraged me to write the book, to Stephen Cox, for his editorial assistance, and once again to Mrs Guida Crowley for typing my manuscript and helping me to correct the proofs.

A. J. AYER

I

The Years of Obscurity

Thomas Paine was born on 29 January 1737 in the old English country town of Thetford in Norfolk. His family name was Pain and he himself usually spelt it in this way for the first half of his life, insisting on the final 'e' only when he emigrated to America in 1774. Nevertheless, as he became historically famous as Thomas, or Tom, Paine, I shall so refer to him from the start.

Thomas Paine's father, Joseph Pain, was a Quaker who kept a shop in Thetford as a staymaker, in modern terms a maker of women's corsets. In June 1734, he married Frances Cooke, a woman eleven years his senior, the daughter of a Thetford attorney. In George Chalmers's hostile *Life of Thomas Paine*, published in 1791 under the pseudonym of 'Francis Oldys', she is described as a woman of 'sour temper and eccentric character'. Whether this description is accurate or not she appears to have had little influence upon her son, who was, however, closely attached to his father. The couple had a second child, a girl who died young. Frances Cooke was an Anglican and the marriage took place in a parish church. Tom Paine was consequently baptized, and later admitted to confirmation by the Bishop of Norwich. Nevertheless he was mainly brought up as a Quaker, apparently without opposition from his mother.

Joseph Pain ran a small farm besides his staymaking business and he made enough money to be able to send his son to the local grammar school, where he remained from his sixth until his fourteenth year. Surprisingly he learned no Latin there, let alone Greek, but was taught history, mathematics and science. We shall see that he had a scientific bent and at a later period he might well have started to be trained as an engineer.

As it was, he returned to his father's shop to pursue his apprentice-ship as a staymaker. Three years later, at the age of sixteen, he ran away to Harwich with the object of enlisting as a seaman on the privateer *The Terrible*, commanded by a Captain Death. His father pursued him and reached him in time to prevent his enlistment. He returned to his trade at Thetford for a further three years but continued to nourish his romantic vision of a naval career. The result was that when England went to war with France in 1756, the outbreak of the Seven Years' War, Tom Paine again ran away to sea and this time succeeded in joining the crew of the privateer *The King of Prussia*, under the command of Captain Mendez. It would seem that the actual conditions of a seaman's life in the mid-eighteenth century did not match Paine's expectations, for he served on *The King of Prussia* for no longer than a year.

Though this was the whole of Paine's experience as an active seaman, he frequently allowed himself to assume, in his later writings, the character of a naval expert, though admittedly one more concerned with finance than with tactics. It is interesting that when he does support an argument with a reference to an actual naval engagement he cites not *The King of Prussia* but *The Terrible*, on which he never served. In an attempt to show in *Common Sense*, written in 1775, that the ability of the American colonies to build a fleet that will be a match for Britain's will not be frustrated by their lack of trained seamen he argues that not more than a fourth of those who man a ship need be sailors. The only evidence he gives for this implausible proposition is that

> The Terrible privateer, Captain Death, stood the hottest engage-ment of any ship last war, yet had not twenty sailors on board, though her complement of men was upwards of two hundred. A few able and social sailors will soon instruct a sufficient number of active land-men in the common work of a ship.[1]

It is not known how Paine contrived, in time of war, to serve for so short a period on *The King of Prussia*. He resumed staymaking but did not return to Thetford. He went to work instead for a staymaker called Morris who kept a shop in Hanover Street, London. On his own showing, Paine took advantage of his living, for the first time, in London to pursue his scientific interests. He attended 'philosophical lectures' and managed to make the acquaintance of at least one future Fellow of the Royal Society, Dr Bevis, an astronomer.

[1] Paine, *Common Sense*, Penguin Classics, p. 104.

One might have expected Paine to do his utmost to prolong his stay in London but either he fell out with his employer, or the restlessness which had taken him away from home again overcame him, so that he kept his job with Morris for no more than a year. In 1758, he went to work for a Mr Grace in Dover, and in the following year he moved nearby to Sandwich, where he set up in business on his own as a master staymaker. It is not known how he obtained the capital. In September of 1759, he married Mary Lambert, a maid in the house of a local woollen draper.

At the time of his marriage Tom Paine was twenty-two years old. By most accounts, he was a handsome man, at least five foot nine inches in height, which was reckoned tall in those days, slim, well proportioned, with strong features, a mass of dark wavy hair, a high forehead and bright blue eyes. His portrait by George Romney, painted in 1792, shows that he kept his looks into late middle age. He was not a dandy but the innuendoes of his critics that he was slovenly in his appearance seem not to have been justified. His addiction to drink, which is not disputed, was not yet in evidence.

Whatever his skill in staymaking, Tom Paine was not a gifted man of business and his venture in Sandwich failed almost immediately. He moved with his wife to Margate where she died within a year of their marriage. A natural inference would be that she died in childbirth, but there is no record of this nor is any other cause of her death known. There is no reference to her in any of Paine's published writings or in any of his correspondence that survives.

This marriage did, however, have one important effect on Paine's career. Mary Lambert's father had been a customs officer or exciseman, as it was then commonly known, and Paine decided to adopt this profession. It promised him neither prosperity nor prestige but it would at least afford him an escape from staymaking, an occupation in which by then he can hardly have had much hope of achieving any lasting satisfaction.

Accordingly, Paine returned to his father's house in Thetford in 1761, to prepare himself for admission to the Excise. He needed a personal recommendation to enter the service, and obtained one in time to become a supernumerary officer on 1 December 1762, with the responsibility of examining brewers' casks at Grantham in Lincolnshire. It was not until August 1764 that he was promoted to being a regular officer, being allotted the more dangerous duty of patrolling a section of the Lincolnshire coast on horseback, with the object of intercepting smugglers. He escaped being harmed by the smugglers only to be dismissed from the service in August 1765 for the misdemeanour of stamping a consignment of goods which he admitted that he had not examined. There has never been any suggestion that he was bribed. His offence, which was quite common, was due to the fact that more work was expected of excisemen than they could conscientiously carry out.

Having no other resources, Tom Paine returned to staymaking and accepted employment under a master at Diss in the neighbourhood of Thetford. He had, however, reason to hope that he would be allowed back into the Excise and a humble letter of apology, written in July 1766, procured his reinstatement. Unfortunately, there was no immediate vacancy in the service for him to fill.

Rather than continue to be employed as a staymaker until a suitable vacancy arose, Paine made his way to London and for the remainder of 1766 taught English at what would appear to have been an elementary school, for a salary of £25. In January 1767, he moved, presumably to a better position, at a school kept by a Mr Gardiner in Kensington. In Chalmers's hostile biography it is asserted both that Paine was disliked by the boys for his strictness and that he forsook the school after three months in order to become an itinerant preacher. There is no supporting evidence for either statement and the second at least is improbable. Even if he had not been deterred by the risk of preaching deism, his doing so would have created a stir of which some record would have remained. It is, indeed, more likely, especially in view of the appeals to scripture that we shall discover in his *Common Sense*, that he had not yet turned against theism, but there is no warrant at all for supposing him to have been a religious enthusiast. The fact is that we have no reliable evidence at all about the way in which Paine lived in London in 1767 or the acquaintances that he made. All that we learn from Paine himself is that he was not then interested in politics.

Having courageously refused the offer of a post in Cornwall, Paine was appointed Officer of Excise at Lewes near the Sussex coast on 11 February 1768. It was an important but also a dangerous post, as smuggling was almost a recognized profession in Lewes and Officers of Excise were not popular. Fortunately for himself Paine was accepted as a lodger in the house of Samuel Ollive, a tobacconist who was then one of the two 'Constables' who were chiefly responsible for what we should now call local government. They were assisted by two so-called Headboroughs, and both sets of officials received their powers from an organization called 'The Society of Twelve' of which Paine somehow became a member. He was also admitted to the Vestry of St Michael's church. At that date Vestries, at least in country towns like Lewes, had not yet acquired the power and responsibilities that were later to render them the prototypes of borough councils. They were mainly concerned with the administration of public charities. What is remarkable is that Paine was so quickly introduced into the inner circle of local government in Lewes.

No doubt it was mainly due to the strength of his personality. By now he was thirty-one years old and had begun to take a lively interest in politics. He joined a social club which met regularly at the White Hart Inn and took a prominent part in its debates. There is no evidence that he had yet become a Republican, but he sided strongly with the Whigs and is reported to have received three guineas for writing an election song on behalf of the Whig candidate at New Shoreham. He is said to have been a forceful and witty speaker, vehement in the expression of his views, and reluctant to make any concessions to his opponents in argument.

In July 1769 Samuel Ollive died, leaving a widow, three sons and a daughter, Elizabeth, who had been born on 16 December 1749. Tom Paine left the house but went into partnership with Mrs Ollive in what had become a business of selling groceries as well as tobacco. He returned to live in the house after he married Elizabeth on 26 March 1771. Surprisingly, he is described on the marriage certificate as a bachelor. This might be taken to imply that he concealed the fact of his previous marriage from the Ollives, though there seems to be no good reason why he should have done so.

Thomas Paine had come to feel that he had the right, or even the duty, to speak for his fellow excisemen and in 1772 he composed and published a pamphlet setting out their grievances, mainly on the score of pay. Though officers of his standing carried a heavy load of responsibility, they were paid only £50 a year and Paine alleged that this was effectively reduced to £32, since it cost them £18 to maintain a horse. He argued, persuasively, that the revenue was actually diminished by this parsimony, since their low wages made the excisemen less zealous in the conduct of their duties and also more susceptible to accepting bribes.

Paine printed four thousand copies of his pamphlet and priced it at three shillings a copy. Though some of his fellow officers contributed to the cost of publication, the bulk of it fell on Paine himself and it can be taken for granted that he suffered a financial loss. In the winter of 1772–3 he was in London distributing copies of the pamphlet to Members of Parliament, and other prominent persons including Oliver

Goldsmith, with whom he made friends at least to the extent of their taking a drink together.

The pamphlet, though clearly written and well argued, did not induce the authorities either to lighten the duties of the Officers of Excise or to increase their wages. It may have cost Paine his job, though the official reason given for his dismissal on 8 April 1774 was that he had left his post without the Board's leave and that he had gone off on account of the debts which he had contracted.

This second charge refers to yet another failure in Paine's commercial career. He had just gone bankrupt and had been forced to sell his household goods, and the contents of his shop. He managed to satisfy his creditors, but his comment 'Trade I do not understand' is one that he might have taken to heart some time before. What is curious is that he never hesitated in his later writings to make confident pronouncements at least about governmental trade.

Two months after Paine's failure in business, in June 1774, he and his wife separated. The cause has never been made known. Thomas, 'Clio', Rickman, who became a friend of Paine's and published a eulogistic biography of him in 1819, states that Paine was not impotent but that nevertheless the marriage was not consummated. Rickman was born in Lewes but only in 1761 so that he was not a contemporary witness. He claims to have obtained his information from a Lewes doctor. The parting seems to have been amicable, in that Elizabeth, who eventually set up house with one of her brothers and lived until 1808, the year before Paine himself died, could never be induced to denounce him to his detractors, and, according to Rickman, Paine occasionally sent her sums of money anonymously. He also resigned his rights over her property, signing a document in which he permitted her to carry on such trade and business as she should think fit, 'as if she were a femme sole', and promised not to lay claim to any money that she might receive from the sale of the house or any other goods that she might acquire.

It would have been a matter of principle for Paine not to take advantage of the law which subordinated wives to their husbands in respect of property. Nevertheless it cannot be said that he comes entirely well out of this affair. Initially, he left his wife almost wholly unprovided for. By obtaining her consent to a legal separation rather than a divorce, he prevented her from remarrying. Even if he did occasionally send her sums of money, and that anonymously, he took hardly any further interest in her. In 1800 she was able to state in a legal document that 'Thomas Paine had many years quitted this Kingdom and resided (if living) in parts beyond the seas, but had not since been heard of by the said Elizabeth Pain, nor was it known for certain whether he was living or dead'.

There is no evidence that Paine entered into any other liaison. His correspondence, especially in later life, shows him not to have been uneasy in the company of women, but the obvious implication is that he was not much interested in sex.

It is not known how Paine earned a living when he came to London in June 1774. He renewed his acquaintance with his scientific friends and one of them, George Lewis Scott, who was also a member of the Excise Board, introduced him to Benjamin Franklin. Long a famous man, Franklin aged sixty-eight, had first come to London in 1757 as an agent for the American colonies and returned there in 1764. Though Paine was to claim when he reached America that he had always had an inclination to see the western side of the Atlantic, since he had picked up and read as a schoolboy a natural history of Virginia, it was probably Franklin who persuaded him to emigrate. Franklin supplied him with a letter of introduction to his son-in-law, Richard Bache, in Philadelphia. It was not and at that time had no reason to be a particularly warm recommendation; rather the sort of testimonial that one supplies to a second-class pupil.

The bearer Mr. Thomas Pain is very well recommended to me as an ingenious worthy young man. He goes to Pennsylvania with a view of settling there. I request you to give him your best advice and countenance, as he is quite a stranger there. If you can put him in a way of obtaining employment as a clerk, or assistant tutor in a school, or assistant surveyor, (of all of which I think him very capable,) so that he may procure a subsistence at least, till he can make acquaintance and obtain a knowledge of the country, you will do well, and much oblige your affectionate father.

Paine set out for America in the last week of September, the voyage taking him just over two months. There was an epidemic of scurvy on the ship. Paine caught the disease and very nearly died. When he was well enough to present his letter of introduction, Richard Bache quickly found him a job as a tutor, from which Paine almost immediately escaped into journalism. At one of the several taverns at which informal debates took place, as at the White Hart at Lewes, Paine met Robert Aitken, a printer who was starting a new monthly periodical called the *Pennsylvania Magazine*, and was invited to write an introduction to the first number. This took the form of an argument in favour of the superiority of the modern to the ancient world, with special reference to America. 'Those who are conversant with Europe,' he wrote, 'would be tempted to believe that even the air of the Atlantic disagrees with the constitution of foreign vices; if they survive the voyage, they either expire on their arrival, or linger away in an incurable consumption. There is a happy something in the climate of America which disarms them of all their power both of infection and attraction.'

Aitken was sufficiently pleased with Paine to make him managing editor of the magazine and Paine repaid him by increasing its list of subscriptions from six hundred in January 1775 to fifteen hundred in March. He wrote his own contributions under pseudonyms, most often 'Atlanticus' or 'Amicus'. Aitken had undertaken in his prospectus to avoid matters of religious and political controversy, so that Paine had to confine the expression of his radicalism to social issues. He did, however, allow himself to allude to the colonial question in some lines of verse. He was a much better writer in prose.

> But hear, O ye swains ('tis a tale most profane),
>   How all the tyrannical powers,
> King, Commons, and Lords, are uniting amain
>   To cut down this guardian of ours.
> From the east to the west blows the trumpet to arms,
>   Thro' the land let the sound of it flee,
> Let the far and the near – all unite with a cheer,
>   In defense of our *Liberty tree*.

He also published an article in which he criticized the thoroughgoing pacifism of the Quakers. 'I am thus far a Quaker,' he wrote, 'that I would gladly argue with all the world to lay aside the use of arms, and settle matters by negotiation, but unless the whole will, the matter ends, and I take up my musket and thank heaven he has put it in my power.' This is a proposition to which almost everyone nowadays pays nominal assent, although there does not appear to be any widespread disposition to lay aside the use of arms.

The most interesting of Paine's contributions to the *Pennsylvania Magazine* is a short piece in which he undertakes to publish a plan for raising a fund to assist young people at the outset of their careers and another fund for the support of persons in their old age. He fulfilled this undertaking over twenty years later in a pamphlet the contents of which were fully summarized in its title.

Agrarian justice, opposed to agrarian law, and to agrarian mo⎿
poly, being a plan for meliorating the condition of man, by creating
in every nation, a national fund to pay to every person, when arrived
at the age of twenty-one years, the sum of fifteen pounds sterling, to
enable him or her to begin the world! And also, ten pounds sterling
during life to every person now living of the age of fifty years, and to
all others when they shall arrive at that age, to enable them to live in
old age without wretchedness, and go decently out of the world.

This is Paine at his best and a remarkable anticipation of the humane
principles of the Welfare State. We shall see later on how far he was
ready to go in this direction.[1]

The first article which Paine published in America under his own
name appeared in a newspaper called the *Pennsylvania Journal* on 24
November 1775. Written in collaboration with Thomas Prior, an
officer in the Continental Army, it explains a process for making
saltpetre to be used for ammunition. Further details of this method of
what Paine called 'extracting' one of the secrets of nature were
furnished in the next issue.

It is probable that a letter signed 'A Lover of Order' which appeared
in the same issue as the first of these articles was also written by Paine.
It consisted in an attack on the Pennsylvania Assembly for instructing
its delegates to the Continental Congress to 'dissent from, and utterly
reject, any propositions, should such be made, that may cause, or lead
to, a Separation from Our Mother Country, or a change of the form of
this Government'. Paine's argument was that the Assembly was
exceeding its powers. 'The Delegates in Congress are not the Delegates
of the Assembly but of the People, – of the Body in Large.' The
implication was that the delegates should express the views of the
People, though Paine did not say how this was to be effected.

This letter was seen, no doubt correctly, as a veiled plea for
independence and produced two rejoinders, to one of which Paine is
thought to have replied under the pseudonym of 'A Continental
Farmer', probably an allusion to the pseudonym 'Pennsylvanian
Farmer' employed by John Dickinson, the most prominent enemy to
independence in the Pennsylvania Assembly. Apart from adding actual
criticism of the instructions which the Assembly had issued to its
delegates, and repeating his argument that it was misusing its
authority, Paine's main point was that when it came to such a question,

[1] See ch. 6.

the Assembly should abandon the limited outlook shown by its claiming to speak 'in behalf of this colony'. 'I despise,' he wrote, 'the narrow idea of acting PROVINCIALLY, and reprobate the little unworthy principle, conveyed in the following words, "In behalf of this colony", and the more so, because by a late resolve, all Colony distinctions are to be laid aside. 'TIS THE AMERICAN CAUSE, THE AMERICAN CONGRESS, THE AMERICAN ARMY, &c, &c, Whom God preserve.'

In less than a month Paine was to publish the pamphlet *Common Sense* which turned the tide of American opinion in favour of independence. It may be instructive to outline the historical circumstances which helped to make this possible.

When Thomas Paine arrived in Philadelphia in November 1774, relations between the British government and its thirteen American colonies had been rapidly deteriorating for over a decade. The starting point of this decline was the conclusion in 1763 of the Seven Years' War, which had been partly fought upon the American continent. Here England had been signally victorious, acquiring not only the whole of French Canada but nearly all the territory east of the Mississippi except Louisiana. These victories had, however, been costly both in men and money and the costs did not end with the ending of the war. The enlarged empire had to be defended. This would be an expensive business, and it seemed only reasonable to George Grenville, who had just become King George III's First Minister, that the colonists should bear their part of the expense. He estimated that a standing army of ten thousand men would be needed to protect the American empire and that their maintenance would cost £300,000 a year.

To avoid trouble with the Indians, Grenville laid an embargo on any further settlement west of the Appalachian Mountains. This was infuriating to the colonies, whose population had increased in the past sixty years from about a quarter of a million to over a million and a half, thereby affording encouragement not only to land speculators but to the pioneering spirit which both in fact and fiction has animated Americans throughout their history. But what annoyed the colonists still more was the set of financial measures which Grenville imposed on them in the course of the next two years. The Navigation Acts, which required that all goods imported to America should be heavily taxed, unless they were shipped by way of England, were reinforced. The so-called Sugar Act imposed further duties and restrictions on American trade. The Quartering Act threw the cost of supplying British troops in colonial barracks on to the local governments.

The Stamp Act imposed a duty on all newspapers, advertisements and legal documents. It was at a conference in New York, attended by delegates from nine colonies, that the famous protest against taxation without representation was made.

The Stamp Act was indeed repealed by Rockingham in his short-lived ministry of 1765–6 but the advent of Charles Townshend as Chancellor of the Exchequer in 1766 made things worse. He imposed duties on glass, lead, tea and paper and took steps to see that they were paid. Again the reaction was not limited to verbal and written protests, though they were abundant. There was a boycott of English goods, and Englishmen, especially officers, and their property were subjected to violence. The British government foolishly replied in kind. They already had garrisons in America but kept them mainly on the frontiers. In 1768 they sent troops into Boston. In 1770 a riot which started with an English sentry's being snowballed ended in shooting, whereby three Americans were killed. Samuel Adams labelled it 'The Boston Massacre'.

The leading American colonists were respectable merchants and lawyers, who had a strong sense of their rights, but no taste at all for riots, and the effect of the Boston Massacre was to make them consider that a compromise with England, on terms favourable to themselves, might be preferable to a declaration of independence which might result in bestowing more political power on the less prosperous members of American society. The British government, for its part, decided that it had gone too far. The Townshend duties were abandoned except for the duty on tea, and for some three years the counsels of moderation prevailed on both sides.

It was tea that broke the truce. To rescue the East India Company from impending bankruptcy, the British government granted it a monopoly of the tea trade in America. This was politically offensive to the colonists and injurious to the colonial shippers. Their protest culminated in the famous Boston tea party on 16 December 1773 when a group of white men, disguised as Indians, boarded the Company's ships in Boston harbour and, watched by a large and enthusiastic crowd, threw 342 chests of tea into the sea.

Lord North, who had become George III's First Minister, reacted as though he had received a personal affront. He altered the Charter of Massachusetts to give the Governor more power, strengthened the Quartering Act, and closed the port of Boston until the tea was paid for and an assurance given for the payment of all other English customs duties.

Thomas Paine

These measures, denounced by their victims as 'the Intolerable Acts', provoked great resentment not only in Massachusetts but throughout all the colonies. The first Continental Congress met in Philadelphia in September 1774 and was attended by representatives of all the colonies except Georgia, where the Governor had managed to prevent any from being selected. The Congress issued a strong manifesto of rights, foreshadowing the preamble to the Declaration of Independence. More practically, it resolved that no goods of any kind were to be imported from England after 1 December and that if this did not cause the British government to mend its ways, no American exports were to go to England after 10 September 1775.

Not all English politicians desired to meet this challenge. Chatham, speaking in the House of Lords, espoused the case of the Americans and urged the government to allay their grievances, on grounds both of principle and of prudence. Edmund Burke made the same plea in several eloquent speeches in the House of Commons. Something stronger than moral support was advocated by Radicals, both in and out of Parliament. But this had only the effect of stiffening the attitude of Lord North's government. Its response was to blockade the whole of New England.

This led almost immediately to the outbreak of war. Some colonists of Massachusetts set about assembling military supplies at Concord. On 18 April 1775 Paul Revere earned himself a place in history by riding through the night from Boston to warn his countrymen that General Gage, the military Governor of Massachusetts, was sending troops against them. There were skirmishes at Lexington and Concord and a bloody retreat by the British, who suffered very heavy casualties on the road to Boston.

It was consequently in a changed climate that the Second Continental Congress met at Philadelphia in May 1775. The number of delegates who were in favour of independence had grown but they were still far from being in the majority. It was the publication of Tom Paine's pamphlet on 10 January 1776 that turned the scale. Massachusetts was the first colony to instruct its delegates to vote for independence. Other colonies gradually followed suit. Pennsylvania, held back by John Dickinson, was one of the last to come round. Early in June the delegates from all the States except New York voted for independence. The final draft of the Declaration of Independence was adopted on 4 July.

As we shall see, Tom Paine was a brilliant journalist. His style of writing was clear and forceful, adorned with striking images. Some of his radical proposals were far in advance of his time. He did not, however, make any original contribution to political philosophy. The foundations of his political theory had already been laid and he wrote for an audience which was familiar with them. It will be worth our while to devote some space to examining what these foundations were. The two concepts which particularly call for our attention are those of the social contract and of natural rights.

The Precursors

The distinction between natural and civil rights was a commonplace of seventeenth- and eighteenth-century political thought. For Thomas Hobbes, 'The right of nature, which writers commonly call *jus naturale*, is the liberty each man hath to use his own power, as he will himself, for the preservation of his own nature: that is to say of his own life: and consequently of doing any thing, which in his own judgement and reason, he shall conceive to be the aptest means thereunto.'[1]

Hobbes looks upon this right as comporting a duty, which is incumbent upon oneself. He speaks of there being 'a precept or general rule, found out by reason, by which a man is forbidden to do that which is destructive of his own life, or taketh away the means of preserving the same; and to omit that by which he thinketh that it may be best preserved'.[2]

Misleadingly, Hobbes refers to this precept as a law of nature, obliging every man to preserve peace so long as he can reasonably hope to do so, entitling him to resort to war when this hope fails, and entailing what he calls the first and fundamental law of nature, namely, 'to seek peace and follow it', together with 'the sum of the right of nature; which is, by all means we can, to defend ourselves'.[3] From this first law a second, of crucial social importance, is supposed immediately to follow: 'that a man be willing, when others are so too, as far forth as for peace and defence of himself he shall think it necessary, to lay down this right to all things; and be contented with so much liberty against other men, as he would allow other men against himself'.[4]

[1] Hobbes, *Leviathan*, ch. XIV.
[2] ibid.
[3] ibid.
[4] ibid.

In the following chapter,[1] Hobbes goes on to list some fifteen other 'laws of nature', of which the most significant are 'that men perform their covenants made', that when it comes to revenge or retribution 'men look not at the greatness of the evil past, but the greatness of the good to follow', with the important consequence that 'we are forbidden to inflict punishment with any other design than for correction of the offender or direction of others', that 'every man acknowledge other for his equal by nature', that controversies be decided by arbitration, and that judges, including arbitrators, deal equally between those who come before them. Less clear than the rest is a so-called law of equity, affording 'equal distribution to each man of that which in reason belongeth to him', for we are not supplied with a criterion for the rational apportioning of property. Hobbes goes so far as to say 'that such things as cannot be divided, be enjoyed in common, if it can be; and if the quantity of the thing permit, without stint; otherwise proportionably to the number of them that have right', but he gives no examples, nor does he explain how right is determined in such instances, except when it is made a matter of agreement. He does indeed say that in the case of things which can neither be divided nor enjoyed in common, the law of equity requires that the entire right, or the first possession, when it has been agreed that the use is to be alternate, is to be determined by lot. What is perplexing is that he goes on to identify what he calls natural lot with 'primogeniture' or 'first seizure'. Going by the general tenor of his remarks in this section, I am inclined to think that he did not here intend the word 'primogeniture' to carry its usual implication of the right's passing exclusively to the eldest son.

I wrote earlier of Hobbes's use of the word 'law' in this context as being misleading. He himself acknowledges this by referring to these 'laws of nature' as dictates of reason and adding that while men are accustomed to call them by the name of laws they do so 'improperly'. 'For,' he adds, 'they are but conclusions, or theorems, concerning what conduceth to the conservation and defence of themselves; whereas law, properly, is the word of him that by right hath command over others.'[2] He has already equated these theorems with moral principles, remarking that 'the science of them is the true and only moral philosophy', and he makes a perfunctory attempt to legitimize the popular conception of them as laws by suggesting that they can be viewed as God's commands.

In calling this attempt perfunctory, I am not endorsing the view held

[1] ibid., ch. XV.
[2] ibid.

by some of his contemporaries that Hobbes was an atheist. This is a question that I shall not attempt to decide. It is rather that I consider Hobbes far too acute a philosopher to have been duped by the fallacy, already exposed by Plato in his dialogue *Euthyphro*, that morals can be grounded on authority, however powerful the authority be thought to be. This is not to say that if there were a Supreme Being he could not be good; only that his goodness could not be a logical consequence of his supremacy. A theist would be very foolish if he took the assertion that such and such a state of affairs was good to mean no more than that God commanded it; for then so far from paying a tribute to his deity by calling him good, he would be treating the attribution of goodness to him as a simple tautology. Worse still, if the Supreme Being happened to be daemonic, our theist would be committed to the moral endorsement of his devilish commands.

In fact it appears that Hobbes took the view, advanced in the present century by Moritz Schlick and Bertrand Russell, that morality is yoked with desire. In his own words, '*good* and *evil* are names that signify our appetites and aversions'.[1] For one who abided in what Hobbes called the condition of nature, that is to say, a condition in which his and other men's conduct was not regulated by the enforcement of civil laws, the criteria of good and evil would be entirely subjective: they would depend on what his appetites and aversions happened at any time to be. The transition from the condition of nature to that of membership in a society would make morality objective only for the reason that the goodness of peace is something on which, in Hobbes's view, all men agree; and what is here meant by peace is the assurance, which it is indeed the sole object and justification of the establishment of civil society to provide, that other men will not be permitted to stand in the way of one's achieving the ends that one naturally pursues. Thus, such 'moral virtues' as justice, gratitude, modesty, equity or mercy earn this title only through their being means to peace, in this special sense. The catch here, as in all theories based upon the fact or fiction of a social contract, is that one has to limit one's self-indulgence by behaving in such a way as to afford others the same assurance as one obtains from them. We shall see that a similar problem confronts the advocates of liberty. One is free to do as one pleases, so long as the exercise of one's freedom does not curtail the freedom of others. And how is this limit to be set?

A well-known difference between the political theories of Thomas

[1] *Leviathan*, ch. XV.

Hobbes and John Locke is that while they both employ the device of a social contract to deliver men from a real or imaginary condition of nature, Hobbes introduces a sovereign, who may but need not be a monarch, to enforce the observance of a contract to which he is not a party. Locke regards the contract as imposing obligations not only on the subjects of the sovereign in relation to one another but also on the sovereign himself. He ceases to be entitled to this obedience when he oversteps the bounds which the social contract sets to the powers of all governments, of whatever form. As Locke puts it:

> First: They are to govern by promulgated established laws, not to be varied in particular cases, but to have one rule for rich and poor, for the favourite at Court, and the countryman at plough. Secondly: These laws also ought to be designed for no other end ultimately but the good of the people. Thirdly: They must not raise taxes on the property of the people without the consent of the people given by themselves or their deputies. . . . Fourthly: Legislative neither must nor can transfer the power of making laws to anybody else, or place it anywhere but where the people have.[1]

Notoriously, Locke was concerned to vindicate the glorious Whig Revolution of 1688. The English were entitled to transfer their allegiance from James II to William and Mary, because James II had misused the powers assigned to him by the terms of a contract to which he was himself a party. Since Hobbes's sovereign remained in the state of nature with regard to his subjects, Hobbes exposed his theory to Locke's celebrated gibe:

> As if when men, quitting the state of Nature, entered into Society, they agreed that all of them but one should be under the restraint of laws; but that he should still retain all the liberty of the state of Nature, increased with power, and made licentious by impunity. This is to think that men are so foolish that they take care to avoid what mischiefs may be done them by polecats or foxes, but are content, nay, think it safety, to be devoured by lions.[2]

On the face of it, Hobbes's theory, contrary to Locke's, entails that rebellion is never justified, but this appearance could be deceptive. The

[1] John Locke, *An Essay Concerning the True Original Extent and End of Civil Government*, ch. XI para. 142.
[2] ibid., ch. VII para. 93.

compact which Hobbes's personae make with one another is to surrender their natural rights to an authority that will see to it that they conform to the moral precepts which, in his terminology, constitute a state of peace. If they continue to find themselves a prey to the inconveniences of the state of nature, whether this be due to the authority's own tyrannical practices, or its failure to protect them from the transgressions of their fellows, then they can reasonably hold the compact to have been nullified. The point was made by John Harington in his satirical epigram 'Treason doth never prosper. What's the reason? For if it prosper, none dare call it treason.' James II was just as vulnerable to a disciple of Hobbes as to a disciple of Locke. The difference was that the Hobbist needed the extra empirical premiss that James lacked the strength or resolution to maintain his authority. It is a lamentable feature of our own time, when we are witnessing a multiplication of tyrannical governments, that the corresponding empirical premiss has in their cases become increasingly hard to satisfy.

This is, however, a digression. The point to which I wish to draw attention is the difference between Hobbes's and Locke's conception of the state of nature. According to Locke, 'The state of Nature has a law of Nature to govern it, which obliges every one, and reason, which is that law, teaches all mankind who will but consult it, that being all equal and independent, no one ought to harm another in his life, health, liberty, or possessions.'[1] This does not sound so very different from Hobbes, but whereas we have seen that Hobbes's laws of nature are no more than utilitarian, Locke pretends to deduce his primary law from his assumption of man's equality and independence without attempting to show how the conclusion follows. I shall have a good deal to say later on about the dubiousness of this premiss.

Locke's moralizing of the state of nature goes so far that he not only follows Hobbes in attributing to his people a duty not to take their own lives and a right to do everything in their power to preserve them from others, but he accords them a right to avenge any injuries done to them physically and a right, indeed a duty, to punish any infractions of the laws of nature, whether or not they are detrimental to themselves. One is tempted to wonder what purpose remains for the institution of a civil society to serve except that of habituating men to resign the enforcement of the laws, including the adjudication of their grievances, to recognized authorities and the debatable advantage of subordinating their judgement to the voice of the majority, or what in some instances almost comically passes for it.

[1] *Essay Concerning the True Original Extent and End of Civil Government*, ch. II para. 6.

Another significant difference between Hobbes and Locke is to be found in their respective treatments of the question of property. As we have seen, Hobbes vaguely implies that there is such a thing as a natural right to property; but he makes little of this admission, and when it comes to the ends of civil society the preservation of property makes no showing in competition with the preservation of life. In contrast, Locke asserts, in one passage, that 'The great and chief end of men uniting into commonwealths and putting themselves under government, is the preservation of their property'.[1] In another he goes even further to the point of saying that the preservation of property is the sole end of government.

In these circumstances, it is strange and disconcerting to discover that Locke's account of the institution of property is very superficial. Nature, of course, yields everything in common. But a man has what appears to be a natural right to the sole possession of everything he is able to remove from the common store of property so long as he has 'mixed his labour with it'. Among the examples given are those of the gathering of acorns and apples, the drawing of water in a pitcher, the hunting of a deer or a hare, the catching of a fish. A slightly more sophisticated level is reached with the remark that 'the grass my horse has bit, the turfs my servant has cut, and the ore I have digged in any place, where I have a right to them in common with others, become my property without the assignation or consent of anybody'.[2] We are not told how Locke, in the state of nature, acquired the right to a servant, or a horse, or the capacity to dig ore, but the overall picture is that of an American frontiersman or participator in a gold rush. This is consistent with the further statement that 'As much land as a man tills, plants, improves, cultivates and comes into the product of, so much is his property',[3] though the phrase that immediately follows – 'He by his labour does, as it were, enclose it from the common' – is at least historically unfortunate.

Locke considers the objection that he is endorsing the principle, to which moral objection might be taken, of granting men a right to whatever they can grab. His answer is that they are not entitled to retain more than they can consume: it is wrong that the fruits of the earth should simply be allowed to go to waste. The solution is that the surplus should be exchanged; and in this way Locke slyly introduces the concept of money, without however expatiating on the enormous

---

[1] ibid., ch. IX para. 124.
[2] ibid., ch. V para. 26.
[3] ibid., ch. VI para. 31.

difference that it makes. He treats the subject rather as though it were just a matter of a hunter's, finding himself with more meat than he needs or can preserve, embellishing his cabin with a gold or silver ornament instead. Locke was indeed writing before the Industrial Revolution but not before the rise of capitalism, with the profound alterations, both for good and for evil, that it brought about in civilized society.

In view of the importance which he attaches to the security of property, it is strange that Locke has little to say about the topic of inheritance. For example, he does not enter into the question of primogeniture, in the current sense of this term. What he does assert, quite dogmatically, is that 'Every man is born with a double right', not only 'a right of freedom in his person' but 'secondly, a right before any other man, to inherit, with his brethren, his father's goods'.[1] This does not exclude all forms of primogeniture, since it is not stated that each of the brethren has a right to an equal share. It might appear unjust to deny it to any one of them, merely on the ground that he, or possibly she, since Locke's favouring of males in his terminology was most probably just a matter of convenience, had the misfortune to be younger than at least one of his or her siblings. On the other hand, if the family were numerous, the parcelling out of the property, especially if it took the form of land, could be economically disadvantageous, as in fact has frequently been proved to be the case in France. But how are we supposed to balance natural right against utility? It is to be remarked that if a man's offspring have a natural right to inherit his property, the man must consequently lack, at least to this extent, the natural right to dispose of it as he pleases. So are we to conclude that no man is ever justified in disinheriting his children? Not necessarily. Even if we were to accept the theory that the purpose of civil government was to safeguard natural rights, it would not follow that the theory accounted for every moral principle or that there could be no other moral ground for overriding one natural right than that it conflicted with another.

Locke's enlightened view that the transition from natural to civil right is mediated by consent gets him into trouble when he comes, towards the end of his essay, to deal with foreign conquest or that kind of 'domestic conquest' which he calls usurpation. Defying history, Locke is driven to say that 'The conqueror, if he have a just cause, has a despotical right over the persons of all that actually aided and concurred in the war against him, and a right to make up his damage

[1] *Essay Concerning the True Original Extent and End of Civil Government*, ch. XVI para. 190.

and cost out of their labour and estates, so he injure not the right of any other.'[1] But there it stops. The conqueror has no right over the persons or property of the descendants of those who fought against him; the usurper has no right at all. Since the Constitution of the United States owes so much to Locke, it is amusing to note that a whole-hearted adherence to his principles would lead to the conclusion that the greater part of its territory belongs by right to the American Indians. In the case of Great Britain we should need to discover persons who could trace their ancestry to forebears who owned land before the Norman or indeed even before the Roman conquest, and this would leave us with a very small number of lawful proprietors, perhaps even with none at all.

Of course it could be argued that the depredations of the conquerors and usurpers which predominantly account for the actual distribution of property are legitimized by the consent of those who suffer from them. But what does this consent amount to? Seldom anything more than an acquiescence in the existing state of affairs on the part of people who lack the energy, the imagination or the self-confidence to make any effort to change it. England and the United States pass for being democracies, mainly on the ground that they enjoy the fruits of representative government. But voting for or against a candidate, whom one may have played little or no part in choosing, every four years or so, does not give one much power, even if one votes with the majority. Perhaps it is in recognition of this fact that in the United States at least, less than two thirds of the electorate bother to vote at all. The English system is so ridiculous that the deplorable Conservative government maintains itself in power with less than one third of the electorate voting for its candidates. I am not implying that an authoritarian system works any better. On the contrary, I think that, with the possible exceptions of the theocracy of the Incas in Peru, and the rule of the Jesuits in Paraguay, it has always proved itself very much worse. What I do claim is that, once we advance beyond the stage where anarchism is practicable, as in isolated Spanish villages in the 1930s, and in some Polynesian islands, before they were corrupted by American missionaries, all societies display class structures; and the governing classes maintain their ascendancy by what Thorstein Veblen in his splendid book *The Theory of the Leisure Class* described as a combination of force and fraud.

As so often in philosophy, if one is looking for good sense one finds it

[1] ibid., ch. XVI para. 194.

in David Hume. The third book of his *A Treatise of Human Nature* is devoted to Morals and in the second chapter of its second part, where he addresses himself to the question of the origin of justice and property, he makes the obvious point that 'the first and original principle of human society . . . is that natural appetite betwixt the sexes, which unites them together and preserves their union, till a new tye takes place in their concern for their common offspring'. I leave it to anthropologists to describe the various ways in which families combined to form what we regard as primitive tribes. In the present context, it is sufficient to make the point that it was surely not simply a matter of rational calculation. If we are seeking a basis for political theory, we should avoid starting either with a picture of a set of individuals, at a fairly advanced stage of moral development, devising means to safeguard their property, or that of a set of independent savages, acquiring the wit to see that they risked losing more than they gained by the absence of any obstacle to their preying upon each other. Hume was not, indeed, the first to perceive that the presumption of a state of nature, conceived after the fashion either of Hobbes or of Locke, was more of a handicap than an asset in explaining the development of social institutions. Not to speak of Aristotle, who started from the premiss that man is a social animal, Hume's near contemporary Lord Shaftesbury, and in some degree his mentor in the domain of moral philosophy, agreed with Hume in crediting men with an instinct of benevolence as well as of self-love. The disposition to exercise benevolence may, in general, be weaker than the disposition to act in accordance with what one takes to be one's own interest, but it is no less natural, and the attempts occasionally made to explain away benevolence in terms of selfishness are easily shown to be fallacious. From this standpoint it is reasonable to infer, as Shaftesbury does in his *Characteristics of Men, Manners, Opinions, Times,* that society is natural to man and that he never either has existed or could exist out of it.

The distinction between society and government which is obliterated in Hobbes is maintained by other champions of the theory of the social contract, such as Locke and Thomas Paine. According to Paine, indeed, the two 'are not only different, but have different origins. Society is produced by our wants, and government by our wickedness; the former promotes our happiness positively by uniting our affections, the latter negatively by restraining our vices. The one encourages intercourse, the other creates distinctions. The first is a patron, the last a punisher' and as Paine went on to say, 'a necessary evil'.[1]

---

[1] *Common Sense,* opening paragraphs.

Nevertheless, even in Paine's case, the distinction is less important than he seems to consider it. For, whether consciously or not, he follows Locke in making the institution of society artificial, no less than that of government. Moreover Locke is explicitly and Paine, I believe, implicitly, conscious of the social contract as being buttressed by the moral obligation of keeping promises. They believe also in a natural right to property which government, more or less fairly, and more or less efficiently, protects. It is known that, in his different way, John Locke had as much influence as Tom Paine upon the drafting of the American Declaration of Independence.

All these assumptions were denied by Hume. He did not see much harm in the fiction of the state of nature, so long as it was seen to be a fiction, but he did have strong intellectual objections to the notion of there being rights or duties, which do not arise out of the formation of society. In particular, so far from believing that social contracts are sustained by the obligation to keep promises, he holds that the case proceeds in the opposite direction. There is no natural rule of morality which enjoins the performance of promises; the making and keeping of promises is the observance of an artificial convention, which is set up within an established society to promote the well-being of its members.

Hume's proof that we have no natural obligation to keep promises runs as follows.[1] If there were such an obligation it would have to depend upon 'some act of the mind' attendant upon the utterance of the formula which expressed the promise. But no such act of the mind is conceivable. Neither a resolution nor a desire can impose an obligation, and as for willing an obligation, that is an absurdity. For morality depends upon our sentiments, and the alteration of sentiment which the willing of a new obligation would require is not within our control.

The argument comes out more clearly when it is extended to cover the sense of duty, which was later to occupy a central place in Kant's grim moral theory. I quote the decisive passage.

No action can be required of us as our duty, unless there be implanted in human nature some actuating passion or motive, capable of producing the action. This motive cannot be the sense of duty. A sense of duty supposes an antecedent obligation: And where an action is not required by a natural passion, it cannot

[1] See Hume, *A Treatise of Human Nature*, book III, section V.

be required by any natural obligation; since it may be omitted without proving any defect or imperfection in the mind and temper, and consequently without any vice. Now 'tis evident we have no motive leading us to the performance of promises, distinct from a sense of duty. If we thought that promises had no moral obligation, we never should feel any inclination to observe them. This is not the case with the natural virtues. Tho' there was no obligation to relieve the miserable, our humanity would lead us to it; and when we omit that duty, the immorality of the omission arises from its being a proof, that we want the natural sentiments of humanity. A father knows it to be his duty to take care of his children: But he also has a natural inclination to it. And if no human creature had that inclination, no one could lie under any such obligation. But as there is naturally no inclination to observe promises, distinct from a sense of their obligation; it follows, that fidelity is no natural virtue, and that promises have no force, antecedent to human conventions.[1]

It may be objected that it is just not true that people keep promises only from a sense of duty. To revert to one of Hume's own examples, the motive from which a father keeps a promise which he has made to his child may above all be his wish that the child should not be disappointed. And in general there are very many instances in which one's affection for another person which was a causal factor in the making of a promise remains one's strongest motive for adhering to it. There may also be ulterior motives of various kinds, including, for example, the hope of commercial advantages.

The answer to this objection is that these motives do indeed operate, but that they do so within the institution of promising which does not become less of an artifice through the fact of its incorporating them. Because it is common ground between a father and his children that one has at least a *prima facie* obligation to keep one's promises, their disappointment at his failure to do so may slide into resentment: his own regret at denying them pleasure may be sharpened by a feeling of guilt. Even so, all that is natural, in Hume's sense of the term, is the father's affection for his children and their reliance on it. The resentment and the guilt are bred out of the 'artificial' vice of violating a useful social convention.

The question of property is included by Hume in his examination of

[1] *A Treatise of Human Nature*, book III, section V.

what he calls the 'cautious jealous virtue of justice'.[1] As one would expect, he treats the practice of justice as an artificial virtue. If men lived in circumstances of such abundance, that the satisfaction of one person's wants did not preclude that of another's, or in such a state of indigence that one could not afford to forgo anything upon which one could lay one's hand, or if men were wholly benevolent instead of being predominantly selfish, the principles of justice would serve no social function. In fact, as Hume puts it:

> The Common Situation of Society is a medium amidst all these extremes. We are naturally partial to ourselves, and to our friends; but are capable of learning the advantage resulting from a more equitable conduct. Few enjoyments are given us from the open and liberal hand of nature; but by art, labour and industry, we can extract them in great abundance. Hence the ideas of property become necessary in all civil society: Hence justice derives its usefulness to the public: And hence alone arises its merit and moral obligation.[2]

Obviously Hume's concept of justice is narrow. It encompasses no more than the impartial enforcement of civil and criminal laws, and not even all of those. But let us admit this restriction. The enforcement of the law ensures what Hume calls the stability of property. But what about its distribution? Does justice not come into question there? Hume implies that it does, but beyond listing the titles to property, such as occupation and inheritance, which were recognized in his society, his conclusion is indeed sensible but very short. 'Not only is it requisite, for the peace and interest of society, that men's possessions should be separated; but the rules, which we follow, in making the separation, are such as can best be contrived to serve farther the interests of society.'[3] I think that Hume was close enough to being a utilitarian for us to be justified in construing 'the interests of society' in terms of the diffusion of happiness.

Admitting, as he did, that all property in such durable objects as lands and houses must in some period have been founded on fraud and injustice, Hume expressed sympathy for the Levellers of Cromwell's time who argued, principally on religious grounds, in favour of an equal distribution of property. The best-known modern advocate of this view

---

[1] Hume, *An Enquiry Concerning the Principles of Morals*, section III, Part I, para. 145.
[2] ibid., para. 149.
[3] ibid., Part II, para. 154.

is George Bernard Shaw in his *The Intelligent Woman's Guide to Socialism and Capitalism.* His grounds were not religious but moral. Hume's objection to the proposal is that it is impracticable and that the consequences of any resolute attempt to put it into practice would be pernicious.

> Render possessions ever so equal, men's different degrees of art, care, and industry will immediately break that equality. Or if you check these virtues, you reduce society to the most extreme indigence; and instead of preventing want and beggary in a few, render it unavoidable to the whole community. The most rigorous inquisition too is requisite to watch every inequality on its first appearance: and the most severe jurisdiction, to punish and redress it. But besides, that so much authority must soon degenerate into tyranny, and be exerted with great partialities; who can possibly be possessed of it, in such a situation as is here supposed? Perfect equality of possessions, destroying all subordination, weakens extremely the authority of magistracy, and must reduce all power nearly to a level, as well as property.[1]

Except perhaps for the last sentence, this is good sense. The remark that the authority needed to repress the resurgence of inequality will lead to tyranny is borne out by the melancholy history of Soviet Russia. Not that the Soviets ever seriously aimed at economic equality. It might be said of Communism, what has been said of Christianity, that it has not failed, because it has not yet been tried. In fact, this would not be entirely true in either case. There have been groups of Christians who strictly adhered to their religious observances, and successfully practised Communism. They have invariably been small communities, living in rural districts not closely with their neighbours, and as a rule not maintaining their cohesion for very long. A counter-example is to be found in the Shakers who sustained eighteen communities mainly in the north-eastern sections of the United States, for upwards of a century. Their rule of celibacy, counteracted by their practice of recruiting orphans, preserved them from problems relating to inheritance.

I queried the last sentence of my quotation from Hume because it did not seem obvious to me that superiority in possessions was a necessary condition for the exercise of power. It could be that indigence was a bar

---

[1] *Enquiry Concerning the Principles of Morals*, Part II, para. 155.

to anything but the display, in certain cultures, of purely spiritual dominance, but there seems to be no good reason why a civil legislator or a judge should be any more wealthy than the average run of those who are subject to his authority. There has, indeed, been a tendency in the more prosperous Western countries during the past century for very rich men to exercise power behind the scenes, frequently by dishonest methods. This is one of the notoriously evil features of Capitalism, and one that threatens to increase. I am, however, not yet convinced that it is inevitable.

The ideals of the Levellers go far back into European history. For instance, the quotation 'When Adam delved and Eve span, who was then a gentleman' dates from Wat Tyler's rebellion in the fourteenth century. Their foremost exponent in the eighteenth century was, or was taken to be, Jean-Jacques Rousseau. I say 'was taken to be', because it is not at all clear, to me at least, what Rousseau's political theory was.

I suppose that everyone who has made even a cursory study of the subject can quote the opening sentence of Rousseau's *Contrat Social*: 'Man is born free, but everywhere he is in chains.' This sounds inspiring. In some fashion of its own it is a cry of protest. It helped to promote the French Revolution; but what exactly does it mean?

Let us concentrate on the first clause 'Man is born free'. Presumably this is not a statement of fact. In the normal way, an infant is free to satisfy his desires, mainly because they are so few in number. To be fed, to be kept warm, to by physically supported; but he has to be assisted to satisfy them, and he is not free from restraint. 'A burned child dreads the fire' is a much touted proverb but parents, unless they are sadists, will endeavour to prevent their infant from burning itself in the first place. As the child grows older he is increasingly impeded from doing whatever takes his fancy. His parents exercise more authority over him, he has to accommodate himself to the actions of other children, school-teachers come into the picture, his being too young to be accounted legally responsible does not put him in a position to defy the police. If he graduates to higher education, he will be subject, at least to some extent, to the discipline of his place of learning, when he finds employment he is unlikely to be his own master or at any rate not from the outset. However powerful he becomes, his freedom of action will be limited by social conventions, such as a code of manners – there are some things that are not done even by the most eccentric of English dukes. Not many married men, or women for that matter, are altogether dominant in their own households. Only an unbridled dictator can be wholly untroubled by the law.

But is not this subjection to the will of others the very thing that Rousseau is concerned to denounce? He is not saying that it does not occur, he is saying that it ought not to occur, or at any rate not in the forms in which it does. Part of the point, indeed, of saying that men are born free is to imply that all types of government are artificial. This is not, however, even in Rousseau's view, sufficient to condemn them, in spite of his succumbing to the myth of the noble and solitary savage. It is a common mistake to suppose that the second part of the opening sentence of *The Social Contract* is a demand that men's fetters should simply be struck off them. On the contrary, the argument of the book is that men should be in chains; only the chains are required to be of a peculiar sort: they have to be imposed by men upon themselves. For Rousseau, freedom in civil society, which he does not distinguish from a set of persons under government, consists in one's authorship of the laws to which one adheres. This idea infiltrated the moral philosophy of Immanuel Kant, who advanced the view that only in voluntary sub-mission to rigid moral laws did one escape from the causal determinism which reigned in the world of space and time. How Kant contrived, or thought that he contrived, to bestride the gap between our ideal volitions and our actual behaviour, which after all takes place in time, is something that I have never understood.

In Rousseau's case, the feat of excluding even the possibility of one's being socially constrained to conform to a rule which was not of one's own making and might indeed run counter to one's desires, is achieved by the device of the general will. It is through participating in the general will that one becomes a member of a legitimate society. Moreover, in some fashion which Rousseau never succeeds in making clear, the general will incorporates the wills of all the members of the society in question. Whatever it wills is decreed to be willed by each of them. It is for this reason that Rousseau is able to commit himself to the paradox that a thief in such a society who is sent to prison is being forced to be free.

But what is the general will? How does it function? If the actions which it causes are implicitly endorsed by every member of the group which it keeps in being, the process need not be conscious. Not only that, but even if it were conscious, this would not be enough. Rousseau makes a point of distinguishing the general will from the will of all. *A fortiori* we are not licensed to identify it with the will of the majority, though in certain circumstances its course of action may be decided by a majority vote. The only clue that we are given is that it necessarily wills the general good. Again, we seem to be approaching the notion of general happiness. But I doubt if Rousseau was a utilitarian.

Despite the lack of evidence, I think that I have some inkling of what Rousseau may have had in mind. I suggest that we are asked to envisage a society which has come and remains together for some common purpose; where its members co-operate in their several ways in an attempt to achieve this purpose and where they have a recognized method for deciding what is to be done. Majority voting might be one such method, but it need not be the only one. Discussion without any voting might lead to a consensus. A committee, or several committees, might be entrusted with the management of the society's affairs. Officers might be appointed, and even paid, to preside over these committees. A single person, like the Visitor of an Oxford or Cambridge college, might in certain circumstances have a decisive voice. Rousseau indeed makes provision for a legislator to expound the general will. It is not unkind to suspect that he was thinking of himself.

In fact the Fellows of an Oxford or Cambridge college provide a good example of a society answering to Rousseau's specifications. As things stand, the undergraduates should probably not be included, as having too inferior a status, but this is a situation that could be and to a small extent is being remedied. A better example is a gentlemen's club, where the common purpose is that of enjoying social amenities. Another, on a very small scale, is a rowing eight or indeed any association of sportsmen, where the game is played for pleasure.

It is a common feature of all these societies that while one is not entirely free to join them, since one has to be acceptable to the existing members and in some instances to possess the appropriate skills, one is not compelled to do so, and one is free to leave. Both these conditions are satisfied by the political parties which effectively function in some contemporary societies, but neither by any society as a whole. One does not choose the society into which one is born and it is not universally or straightforwardly true that one can leave it, unless one is prepared to go to the length of committing suicide. Some countries do not allow all their citizens to emigrate; no major country, at least, accepts immigrants unconditionally. Even if someone encounters no legal obstacle in changing his place of residence, he may not have the means to do so. One of the weaknesses of social contract theories is the assumption that by consenting to live in a society, one is bound by an implicit promise to abide by its laws. For this presupposes, what we have just found not to be true, that one is always presented with a genuine alternative.

Does the concept of the general will apply at all, or even approximately, to any modern State? I think that it may in time of war. There can then be a common purpose: a process of reaching agreement as to the way in which it is to be carried out; an acceptance of one's position in a hierarchy which sets limitations to the exercise of one's personal will. It is true that the society is likely to contain some who oppose the war, perhaps on conscientious grounds, perhaps because their sympathies lie rather with the enemy. I think it important that conscientious objection should be tolerated. In the second case, if those whose sympathies lie with the enemy are actually impeding the successful prosecution of the war, it is to be expected that they should at least be put under restraint. This might be thought to be a blemish on this example of the manifestation of the general will, but I claimed no more than that the concept might apply approximately. For example, I should not wish to say that a young conscript who was shot for cowardice was being forced to be free.

I have allowed myself to envisage a war of which I personally approved: one, like the Second World War, in which I had no hesitation in volunteering to fight for my country, but this is not to say that I was thereby displaying greater loyalty to Rousseau's principles than those who fought on the opposite side. Rousseau is thought of as a friend to democracy because his writings played a large part in fomenting the French Revolution, but among the men whom he chiefly influenced were Robespierre, who was hardly a quintessential democrat, and in this century Mussolini, who regarded himself as the embodiment of Italy's general will. Hitler might have made the same claim, with respect to himself and the Germans, with more justification, if the Jews and other outcasts are reckoned not to have been members of that society, a monstrous assumption but one that the vast majority of Germans and indeed Austrians were content to endorse. The point to be remembered is that the so-called common good at which the general will aims is what the members of a highly organized society collectively aspire to, probably under the direction of a leader with whom they identify themselves, and there is no reason why the aspirations of such a society and its very structure should not seem thoroughly evil to those who view it from outside.

Except in the circumstances of war, and then not always, the conditions set by Rousseau are not satisfied, in my opinion, by any of the Western democracies. Politicians speak of devising measures to promote the general welfare, but they tailor their advocacy to special groups, they yield to pressure in one form or another by holders of some vested interest, the societies which they aspire to govern are deeply divided in their ways of life and their political beliefs. What appears to be gaining ground at the present time, both in England and in the United States, is the principle of the devil take the hindmost, and the hindmost have become too numerous for their abandonment to count as the verdict of the general will.

If it was Tom Paine's pamphlet *Common Sense* that, more than anything else, induced representatives of the thirteen American colonies to move from the position which they almost unanimously held in 1775, that of having their grievances redressed while retaining allegiance to the British Crown, to their insistence on independence in 1776, the sentiments which are expressed in the Declaration of Independence go back beyond Paine. I wish to end this chapter by examining its famous preamble.

Let us begin with the proposition that all men are created equal. Not wishing to delve into theology, I waive the objection that if the use of the word 'created' was intended as I think it must have been, to imply the existence of a supernatural creator, there is no good reason to believe that men are created at all. What is of interest is the claim to original equality. On the face of it, it is manifestly false. Both physically and intellectually men and women enter the world with very different genetic endowments, not to speak of the inequalities arising from the different social environments into which they are born. These are such obvious facts that I cannot believe that so intelligent a man as Thomas Jefferson was oblivious to them. What then did his claim amount to? It was, I believe, an attack on aristocracy, in the sense that it denied there being any justification for distinctions of rank which depended solely on the accident of birth. On the positive side, it was a plea for equality of opportunity, for what Napoleon was to call '*la carrière ouverte aux talents*'. In contemporary jargon the Founding Fathers were meritocrats. The fact that a meritocratic system, coupled as it always has been, overtly or surreptitiously, with inherited privilege, itself fostered considerable differences in wealth and status did not worry them. It was left to more radical theorists, Tom Paine among them, to seek to diminish, if not to do away with, the social and financial advantages of inheritance. It was their idea also that the government had a duty to provide a tolerable standard of living for the members of society who were not yet, or no longer, or even had never been able to achieve it independently. This idea achieved some fruition in England after the Second World War in the organization of the so-called Welfare State. In the United States the spirit of charity has had to contend with the legacy of the Puritan belief that material poverty is a mark of God's disfavour.

We come next to the right to life. I had better confess at once that I do not understand what is meant by calling a right inalienable. I note only that it has not been taken to imply that the right, if it exists, can never be overridden. Except for out-and-out pacifists, of whom I am not one, men have always felt justified in killing their enemies in war. I happen not to be an advocate of capital punishment, but most people have been and many still are. The question of abortion admits of more arguments than I can devote to it here; I shall say only that I am not alone in believing that the decision should rest with the prospective mother. As for infanticide, it did not shock the Ancient Greeks, whose civilization we are brought up to admire, but we have gone rather to the opposite extreme, sometimes going to great trouble and expense to preserve a life that is altogether unlikely to be worth living. This is a question which defies attempts at generalization. Undoubtedly many handicapped children can be trained to lead lives of value to themselves and others. Undoubtedly, also, it is injurious, if not to the infant itself, at least to its parents, 'officiously to keep alive' a creature that has no prospect of leading anything more than a vegetable existence, or even one whose conscious life is likely to consist in continuous pain, without the compensation of intellectual achievement. Where the line is to be drawn is a matter for decision in each particular instance.

In the case of the aged, the question is easier because the value to themselves or others of the prolongation of their lives is easier to estimate. I see no good at all in obliging a person who is afflicted with a painful and incurable disease to continue to suffer. There is indeed the complication that their own wishes deserve to be respected, but the difficulty here is that they may have been reduced to a state where they are no longer capable of making a rational choice. I declare now that if I become senile, I hope that someone will do me the kindness of putting me to death. Correspondingly, if I became aware that I was entering the road to senility, I should have no qualms about taking my own life.

On the matter of liberty I have little to add to what I have already said, beyond making the point that it is a question not so much of right as of power. It is idle to tell a man that he has the inalienable right, whatever that may mean, to do what he wants if he lacks the resources to do so, or is physically prevented. Nevertheless the affirmation of the right to liberty is understood to uphold an important set of values:

freedom of speech, due process of law, freedom of worship, with certain restrictions such as the protection of converts from enslavement and the prohibition of human or even animal sacrifice, freedom to choose one's way of life, so far as it lies within one's power, absence of censorship, again with certain restrictions designed to protect children against sadistic pornography and consumers against blatant lies, freedom to unite for the purpose of obtaining fair conditions of employment. Such additions to the list as universal suffrage and the absence of discrimination, in theory if not always in practice, on the score of race, religion and sex, were latecomers to the scene. Until well into the twentieth century England, at least, was far from being a democracy, and the history of the slave trade is highly discreditable both to England and still more to the United States.

What is there to be said about the pursuit of happiness? The subject appears to have much in common with that of liberty, the pertinent question being not whether one has the right to pursue happiness, but how far the achievement of happiness lies within one's power. The parallel with liberty appears also in the proviso that the pursuit of one's own happiness should not unduly encroach upon the happiness of others, the difficulty lying once again in the interpretation of the word 'unduly'. Here too I think that it can often be decided in particular cases, without its being possible to lay down any general rules. As for the question whether one ought to pursue happiness, we have the authority of Aristotle that every human action has happiness for its end. I suspect, however, that Aristotle used the word 'eudaimonia', translated as 'happiness', so broadly that it covered any good whatsoever, with the result that his assertion would be no more than a tautology.

Avoiding this pitfall, let us ask whether it is psychologically possible that men should aim at failing to achieve what they most desire. If this is treated as an empirical question, I believe that there actually are such people, but that it is a fallacy to argue that they find their greatest satisfaction in being frustrated. However this may be, their number is surely small and their example not one to be followed, unless we take the step, which I am deliberately avoiding, of allowing the very performance of an action to count as a proof that it was, in the circumstances, what one most desired to do.

Whatever may be the case with happiness there is no doubt that there often have been and still are enemies of pleasure. I am content in their case to say no more than that my sentiments lie strongly in the opposite direction, with the chilly proviso that not all pleasures are

3

Common Sense and Its Effects

Thomas Paine at first intended to publish *Common Sense* in the form of a series of newspaper articles, but was persuaded by Dr Benjamin Rush, with whom he had made friends through their common opposition to slavery, that it would be more effective as a pamphlet. He entrusted it to the Philadelphia firm of printers, Robert Bell, on the understanding that the profits should be divided between them. Paine did not wish to make any money for himself but proposed to devote his share of the profits to buying mittens for Washington's troops. An edition of a thousand copies was printed and priced at two shillings a copy or eighteen shillings a dozen. It appeared, most probably, on 10 January 1776, and was immediately sold out. When Bell nevertheless denied that there were any profits, Paine broke with him and offered the work, augmented by an appendix and a rejoinder to Quaker criticism of the original text, to a rival Philadelphia firm of William and Thomas Bradford. They printed seven thousand copies, which they priced at a shilling apiece, and published on 14 February 1776. Bell claimed that he had been unjustly treated and published a second edition on his own, but the Bradford version prevailed. Both were anonymous, though the pamphlet, only on its first appearance, was described as 'written by an Englishman'.

The success of the pamphlet was extraordinary. Paine, who always denied that he made any money out of it, claimed that 120,000 copies were sold within three months. This may be an exaggeration, but it seems to be generally agreed that fifty-six editions had been printed and 150,000 copies sold by the end of 1776. It is also a matter of general agreement that the pamphlet played a decisive part in persuading the representatives of the colonists to commit themselves to independence.

How did Paine achieve it? More by rhetoric, of which he was a master, than by force of argument. His arguments are on two levels, not always kept distinct. In part they are designed to prove the superiority in general of representative over monarchical or aristocratic forms of government. Here the thrust of the reasoning is mainly negative. The emphasis is laid rather on the evils of any form of hereditary government, especially monarchy, than on the merits of representative government, though Paine does use the argument that it will prove convenient 'to leave the legislative part to be managed by a select number chosen from the whole body, who are supposed to have the same concerns at stake which those have who appointed them, and who will act in the same manner as the whole body would act were they present'.[1] Evidently this argument applies only to a small and harmonious electorate. Paine makes a faint attempt to cope with this difficulty by proposing that as the electorate increases, constituencies should be multiplied and elections held more frequently, but already there is a narrow limit to the practicability of these reforms, unless we shift to a much greater degree of decentralization than anything that Paine envisages.

The remainder of Paine's arguments advance the propositions that whatever may have been the case in the past, the Americans cannot now afford not to break with England, and that the chances of their doing so successfully are currently as great as they are ever likely to be. This line of attack is not incompatible with the first, since if the case for representative government were conclusively made out, it might be possible to show that England could never be in a position to endow the colonists with it in an acceptable form, but Paine shows some disposition to contrast them. For example, in an article written in 1778, one of the series collectively called *The Crisis*, he writes that when he first came to America, the colonists' 'idea of grievance operated without resentment, and their single object was reconciliation'. He himself 'had no thoughts of independence or of arms'. 'But when the country, into which I had just set my foot, was set on fire about my ears, it was time to stir. It was time for every man to stir. Those who had been long settled had something to defend, those who had just come had something to pursue; and the call and the concern was equal and universal.' And in *Common Sense* itself he goes even further.

No man was a warmer wisher for reconciliation than myself, before the fatal nineteenth of April 1775,[2] but the moment the event of that

---

[1] *Common Sense*, p. 67.
[2] Date of the 'massacre' of Lexington.

day was made known, I rejected the hardened, sullen tempered
Pharaoh of [George III] for ever; and disdain the wretch, that with
the pretended title of FATHER OF HIS PEOPLE can unfeelingly
hear of their slaughter, and composedly sleep with their blood upon
his soul.[1]

Even in the more general section of his polemic, Paine does not
clearly distinguish between the defects of monarchy and aristocracy, in
whatever form, and the demerits of the English 'Constitution', as it
actually functions. On the whole, it is the second to which he pays the
greater attention. Thus, having allowed the English Constitution some
merit as having been in its time an alleviation of tyranny, Paine attacks
it both for being too complex and for allowing far too large an element of
tyranny to survive. It is present in the influence of the king; it is present
in the influence of the peers. In both cases their holding hereditary
office is said to make them independent of the people. Consequently,
the freedom of England depends only on the virtue of the members of
the House of Commons whom Paine describes, not altogether accurately,
as 'the new republican materials'.

It is a little surprising that Paine failed to remark the distorted sense
and the very limited degree to which the members of the House of
Commons did, at that date, represent the English people.[2] The
exclusion of women and the relatively high property qualification
reduced the number of those eligible to vote at all to a very small
proportion, and the archaic distribution of constituencies not only
excluded voters who would otherwise have been qualified but ensured
that many 'representatives of the people' were no more than the
nominees of local magnates or landlords. It was not until 1832 that
Rotten Boroughs were done away with, at least ostensibly, in the First
Reform Bill, though this did not much augment the electorate, or do
away with electoral malpractices, or, at least in rural constituencies,
put an end to the dominance of the landlords, and it was not until
nearly a century later that the English people were granted anything
approaching universal suffrage. Paine himself wrote at least one article
in defence of the rights of women but he did not go so far as to suggest
that this should include the right to vote, and he seems at first to have
been in favour of some property qualification for male voters in the
United States, though it would not have been set so high as its English
counterpart.

[1] *Common Sense*, p.92.
[2] He does subsequently make this point in his *Rights of Man*.

Another point of which one might have expected Paine to make more than he does is the dependence of members of the House of Commons not only on their patrons, many of whom were in the House of Lords, but also on the Crown. He does not overlook the point entirely. Having deduced from the simile of a machine that whatever power in the constitution has the most weight will eventually govern, he continues:

> That the crown is this overbearing part in the English constitution needs not be mentioned, and that it derives its whole consequence merely from being the giver of places and pensions is self-evident, wherefore, though we have been wise enough to shut and lock a door against absolute monarchy, we at the same time have been foolish enough to put the crown in possession of the key.[1]

In fact the monarchy did not, even then, derive its whole consequence from being the giver of places and pensions. The blind adulation of the English royal family may indeed be a comparatively recent product of the frivolity of television and certain sections of the press, but Shakespeare's 'There's such divinity doth hedge a king' always had some basis in popular attitudes, even when the monarch was personally disliked. What is important is that this attitude is independent of the extent to which the monarch actually participates in politics. It was the existence of a 'King's party' in Parliament at the time of the American Revolution on which Tom Paine might have done better to lay stress.

One reason why he did not dwell on this point may have been that his reference to places and pensions occurs in his conclusion to a long argument in which he denies the virtue attributed to the English Constitution as a system of checks and balances, not so much on the ground that it merely masks the dominance of the monarch, as on the ground that the notion of the different powers acting as checks on one another is farcical. In fact Paine ignores the function of the House of Lords, whatever that might have been intended to be, and concentrates upon the King and the Commons. His argument proceeds as follows:

> To say that the commons is a check upon the king, presupposes two things.
>
> *First.* – That the king is not to be trusted without being looked after, or in other words, that a thirst for absolute power is the natural disease of monarchy.

[1] *Common Sense*, pp. 70–71.

Secondly. – That the commons, by being appointed for that purpose, are either wiser or more worthy of confidence than the crown.

But as the same constitution which gives the commons a power to check the king by withholding the supplies, gives afterwards the king a power to check the commons, by empowering him to reject their other bills; it again supposes that the king is wiser than those whom it has already supposed to be wiser than him. A mere absurdity.[1]

This is in fact an argument against any form of bicameral or multicameral system and I do not think that it is cogent. For example, it seems to be desirable in any type of government that the judiciary act independently of the executive. This is not to imply that judges are in general wiser than those who put the laws into force but only that they are capable of fulfilling the important function of ensuring that the members of the executive do not overstep their constitutional powers. I do think it undesirable that the judges be chosen by the executive, though it is only if the judges also tend to be venal, which has for the most part appeared not to be the case, that I should call it an absurdity. Even so, the fact that the judges may be selected at least partly in virtue of their political opinions, and the fact that their tenure of office may outlast that of those who chose them, create dangers which have made themselves manifest in the recent history of the United States.

In criticizing Paine's argument, I do not wish to imply that the executive should not be subject to legislative control. On the contrary, I think that the growing tendency of the British Cabinet, or still worse, of a section within it, of the President of the United States and his entourage, and of the President of France, to take actions of moment without previously obtaining the authority of their parliaments is thoroughly objectionable. Of course, when a policy has been approved, a minister must be left free to carry it out in detail, aided or impeded by his civil servants. This differs from his running amok with orders in council; and it differs a great deal more from committing a country, more or less deviously, to military action and presenting its parliament with a *fait accompli*.

In this context, when I expressed a preference for a bicameral system, I had in mind a division of the legislature. I shall not digress

[1] ibid., p. 69.

into the question how the members of these bodies should be chosen, beyond saying that I should very much prefer some form of proportional representation, possibly that of the transferable vote which was used in the elections to University Seats before the war, to the present method of electing members to the British House of Commons. I think that, in its limited way, the British House of Lords performs a useful function, and would do so even more if it were limited to Life Peers. Perhaps it is too much to hope that membership of the House will ever altogether cease to be open to purchase.

The difference between the political power of Queen Elizabeth II and that of George III, before he became incapable of exercising it, is so great that it would take us too far afield to discuss the merits and demerits of the survival of monarchy at the present time, in Great Britain or elsewhere. Paine's arguments were indeed directed primarily against the institution of monarchy in general rather than the particular misuse of the office ascribable to George III, but what he had in view in *Common Sense* was always absolute monarchy, or something approaching it, and what is also important, monarchy in which the rule of succession was hereditary. He left out of account the sorts of elective monarchy that existed in Denmark and in Poland, or for considerable periods in the Roman Empire, not that the Roman Empire, where the principal effect was to convey power to the legions, is a happy advertisement for the system.

Curiously, in view of the want of respect he was later to show for the Old Testament, the first argument that Paine brings against the institution of kingship is scriptural. After remarking that it took the Jews nearly three thousand years since the Mosaic date of the Creation to ask God for a king, he devotes an inordinate amount of space to pointing out first that Gideon declined the office and secondly that when the Jews renewed their request through the prophet Samuel, the Lord, after failing to dissuade his people by a discourse on the evils of kingship with which he supplied Samuel, succeeded in convincing them by a display of thunder and rain. It is probable that Paine was writing with an eye to his Puritan readership, though he may at that date not have been wholly insincere. In any case one of the numerous pamphleteers who commented, for the most part adversely, upon *Common Sense* was able to find scriptural passages in which the Lord expressed his approval of kingship.

In his attempt to enlist scriptural authority for his repudiation of kingship, Paine may also have been striking a glancing blow at the doctrine of the divine right of kings. The main weakness which he sees in this doctrine is not, however, so much the lack of any evidence for it, as the fact that even if some person had been divinely appointed to reign over a nation, it would not follow that the same was true of any one of his descendants. Moreover, the same objection would hold good in a case where some person was chosen by a group of people to rule them. Here Paine was, consciously or unconsciously, in agreement with Locke who also held that no political contract could bind the descendants of those who made it, though we have seen that he diminishes the force of this principle by his doctrine of tacit consent. Paine also made much of the point that, however good a king might be, there was no guarantee that the same virtue would be found in his successor, a fact which also tells against entrusting power to hereditary peerage, or indeed, though Paine does not here take the argument so far, against hereditary privilege of any kind. In *Rights of Man*, which he was to publish in 1792, he argues that the concept of hereditary rule is 'as absurd as an hereditary mathematician, or an hereditary wise man; and as ridiculous as an hereditary poet-laureate'.[1]

Clearly this argument would retain its force even if the first in line of a series of hereditary rulers had displayed qualities which were especially suited to the part. But Paine denies that this can safely be assumed. His example of the descent of English kings from William the Conqueror is a good instance of his swashbuckling style. 'England,' he writes, 'since the conquest, hath known some few good monarchs, but groaned beneath a much larger number of bad ones, yet no man in his senses can say that their claim under William the Conqueror is a very honorable one. A French bastard landing with an armed banditti, and establishing himself king of England against the consent of the natives, is in plain terms a very paltry rascally original.'[2]

Having remarked that 'the most plausible plea, which hath ever been offered in favour of hereditary succession, is, that it preserves a nation from civil wars', he denounces this claim as 'the most barefaced falsity ever imposed upon mankind'.[3] Once again he uses England as a counter-example, asserting that 'Thirty kings and two minors have reigned in that distracted kingdom since the conquest, in which time there have been (including the Revolution) no less than eight civil wars and nineteen rebellions.'[4] These figures seem high to me, but Paine does not explain how he arrives at them.

[1] Paine, *Rights of Man*, Penguin Classics, p. 83.
[2] *Common Sense*, pp. 77–8.
[3] ibid., p. 79.
[4] ibid.

His final verdict on monarchy is again reduced to its exemplification in the powers of George III. The phrasing is characteristically polemical.

> In England a k[ing] hath little more to do than to make war and give away places; which in plain terms, is to impoverish the nation and set it together by the ears. A pretty business indeed for a man to be allowed eight hundred thousand sterling a year for, and worshipped into the bargain! Of more worth is one honest man to society, and in the sight of God, than all the crowned ruffians that ever lived.[1]

Being committed to Republicanism Paine felt obliged to sketch the outline of a Constitution for the 'United States', a term he was apparently the first to use, not in *Common Sense* but in one of his *Crisis* articles. Its main features were that there should be only a single Assembly, that the representation of each of the thirteen colonies should be equal, amounting to at least thirty persons from each colony, that the Congress should meet annually, with a President chosen each year from a different colony successively so that all had their turn. He put this set of suggestions forward as one among others which were to be considered at a Continental Congress, convened in order to frame a Continental Charter. The members of this Congress were to be a committee consisting of twenty-six members of the existing Congress, that is, two from each colony, in addition to two representatives of each of the colonial assemblies, and five qualified citizens chosen in each colony by those who took the trouble to attend an election held in its capital city at an appointed date.

To the question where the King of America features in his scheme, Paine replies that in his America 'THE LAW IS KING'. He envisages a ceremony in which the Charter is crowned, and the crown is then demolished 'and scattered among the people whose right it is'.[2]

There is no evidence that Paine's suggestions were seriously considered either by the drafters of the Articles of Confederation, which were submitted to the States for ratification on 1 January 1777 and finally ratified by Maryland, the most recalcitrant of them, in 1781, or, what is more important, by the framers of the Constitution which superseded the Confederation, in a movement which was initiated by Virginia in 1785 and completed by Rhode Island in 1790, Delaware, New Jersey and Pennsylvania having taken the lead in 1787, North

---

[1] *Common Sense*, p. 81.
[2] ibid., p. 98.

Carolina delaying until 1789, and the other eight States committing themselves together in 1788. It was too much to expect that the larger States should acquiesce in an equality of membership in the House of Representatives, but the adoption of a bicameral legislature enabled the principle of there being two delegates from each State, irrespective of its population, to obtain in the Senate. The chief departure from Paine's suggestions consisted in the tenure of offices, especially that of the President, who was to be elected for a period of four years, possibly increased by his re-election or by his having already come into office through the death of his predecessor, a progress normally due to his previous election as Vice-President. It is only quite recently, in reaction against Franklin Roosevelt's achievement in winning four successive Presidential elections, that the Presidents have become limited to a maximum of ten years in this office.

Paine's strongest arguments in favour of America's achieving her independence of England were that her 'parent country' was not England but Europe, not one third of her inhabitants being of English descent, that she would no longer be drawn automatically into English wars, particularly with France and Spain, and that she could trade freely with any country that she pleased. He is at his least convincing and also least interesting when he adduces figures to show that the comparative fiscal military and naval capabilities of England and America are such that the current moment is the most propitious for an American victory. He even falls into the inconsistency of claiming on one page that it is to America's advantage that she has no debts and on the next page recommending that she contract a national debt, adding that no nation should be without one. The trouble is that he was here arguing a weak case. I believe that even after refusing to make the reasonable concessions which would have enabled the American Tories, who favoured staying loyal to the Crown, to carry the day, the British government still had the resources to overcome its rebellious subjects. If they proved insufficient, it was mainly because of the incompetent generalship and diplomacy displayed in a cause which never commanded the wholehearted support of the Whig opposition in Parliament.

Paine concludes the appendix to his pamphlet with a plea for unity among the thirteen colonies and reconciliation between the Whigs and Tories in America. It is because it will put an end to the chief cause of dissension between them that he declares that 'Independance is the only Bond that can tye and keep us together.'[1]

[1] ibid., p. 121.

The rhetorical note on which the pamphlet might well have ended is struck rather earlier, before Paine embarks on his questionable statistics:

> O ye that love mankind! Ye that dare oppose, not only the tyranny, but the tyrant, stand forth! Every spot of the old world is over-run with oppression. Freedom hath been hunted round the globe. Asia, and Africa, have long expelled her. – Europe regards her like a stranger, and England hath given her warning to depart. O! receive the fugitive, and prepare in time an asylum for mankind.[1]

The success of *Common Sense* may have ensured that the colonists would settle for nothing less than independence, but it did not give military strength to their cause. On the contrary, General Washington's army was on the defensive throughout nearly the whole of 1776. Very soon after the Declaration of Independence on 4 July, it was forced to give up New York and retreat across the Hudson to New Jersey. By that time Paine himself had enlisted, being attached to the Pennsylvania division of a body of militia drawn also from New Jersey and Maryland. He acted successively as secretary to one general and aide-de-camp, with the rank of Brigade-Major, to another, General Nathanael Greene. It was General Greene who first introduced Paine to Washington, under whom he served intermittently for the following two years, including a period in which he was paid to send regular reports to the President of the Pennsylvania Assembly.

The winter of 1776 found Washington's troops in such a miserable condition that even their commander expressed private doubts about their prospects. Reduced in number to five thousand, they suffered from a general shortage of supplies, especially clothing to protect them from the bitter weather. In these circumstances Paine published a series of pamphlets and articles collectively entitled *The Crisis*. A periodical with the same name, running to ninety-two numbers, including one entitled *Crisis Extraordinary*, a title which Paine was also to plagiarize, had appeared in London throughout the years 1775 and 1776. It supported the American cause, favouring independence after the American Declaration. Copies of it circulated in America, but they never had anything approaching the effect of Paine's *Common Sense*, and his usurpation of its title has led to its being largely overlooked.

Though in the end Paine had no qualms about this usurpation, he

---

[1] *Common Sense*, p. 100.

began by making a slight effort to avoid it. The first five pamphlets, which inaugurate *The Crisis* in his collected works, were published under the title *The American Crisis*. Afterwards he dropped the prefix, though some of the essays that might well have been included in the series were labelled 'Supernumerary' or 'Extraordinary'. Paine himself officially limited their number to thirteen, probably because of its accordance with the number of colonies, and issued them at irregular intervals from 23 December 1776 to 19 April 1783, the eighth anniversary of the battles of Lexington and Concord.

After the first five pamphlets, the essays took the form of newspaper articles which were reproduced in periodicals throughout the country. The collection owes its enduring fame almost entirely to the opening and closing sentences of its first number, the opening sentences being especially favoured in anthologies of American prose. They run as follows:

> These are the times that try men's souls. The summer soldier and the sunshine patriot will, in this crisis, shrink from the service of their country; but he that stands it *now*, deserves the love and thanks of man and woman. Tyranny, like hell, is not easily conquered; yet we have this consolation with us, that the harder the conflict, the more glorious the triumph. What we obtain too cheap, we esteem too lightly; it is dearness only that gives everything its value. Heaven knows how to put a proper price upon its goods; and it would be strange indeed if so celestial an article as FREEDOM should not be highly rated.[1]

The conclusion of the pamphlet is less celebrated but also eloquent:

> By perseverance and fortitude we have the prospect of a glorious issue; by cowardice and submission, the sad choice of a variety of evils – a ravaged country – a depopulated city – habitations without safety, and slavery without hope – our homes turned into barracks and bawdy-houses for Hessians, and a future race to provide for, whose fathers we shall doubt of. Look on this picture and weep over it! and if there yet remains one thoughtless wretch who believes it not, let him suffer it unlamented.[2]

The mention of Hessians refers to the fact that a considerable portion of the British army consisted of German mercenaries. Since he

---

[1] See *The Writings of Thomas Paine*, ed. M. C. Conway, vol. I, p. 170.
[2] ibid., pp. 178–9.

presumably did not intend to put the virtue of American womanhood in question Paine must have been taking it for granted that these men fitted Burke's description of 'a rapacious and licentious soldiery' and would consequently be addicted to rape.

Apart from the fact that the final number of *The Crisis* begins by echoing the first with the words ' "The times that tried men's souls" are over – and the greatest and completest revolution the world ever knew, gloriously and happily accomplished',[1] the essays that compose it do not contain very much of political or even literary interest. The main reason for this is that Paine was primarily an advocate, and that it must very soon have become clear to him that he had won his case. I should say that this was probable when General Burgoyne surrendered at Saratoga in October 1777, though the English army overran Georgia and South Carolina in 1780, and there may have been doubters or ardent Tories who thought that the issue was undecided until the defeat of Lord Cornwallis's army at Yorktown on 19 October 1781.

Presumably as a reward for writing *Common Sense*, Paine obtained official recognition in April 1777 by being appointed secretary to the Congressional Committee for Foreign Affairs. He held the position until January 1779 when he was forced to resign, in consequence of his having published an attack on Silas Deane, an American who had been sent as an emissary to Paris to obtain arms from the French. Deane joined forces with Pierre Beaumarchais, the enterprising author of *The Barber of Seville* and *The Marriage of Figaro*, and they set up a private company for the transhipment of the arms, in payment for which they had obtained a million francs from Louis XVI. There then arose a dispute concerning Deane's entitlement to a monetary commission, in the course of which Arthur Lee, the American representative in London, accused Deane of dishonesty. Paine rallied vehemently to Lee, but the fact that France was supplying the Americans with arms, during one of the rare periods when she was at peace with England, was meant to be a secret and it was his revelation of the secret that cost Paine his appointment. He received 4,000 dollars for his services, though the money was withheld from him until 1783.

Having no other source of income Paine acted as secretary to a private citizen before being appointed clerk of the Pennsylvania Assembly in November 1779. When his arrears of salary, amounting by then to 1,699 dollars, were paid to him on 7 June, Paine at once subscribed five hundred dollars of it for the relief of Washington's

---

[1] *Writings of Thomas Paine*, vol. I, p. 370.

currently hard-pressed army. His example was followed and by the end of the year a sum of three hundred thousand pounds had been raised by private subscription, making possible the establishment of a bank which was incorporated by Congress and supplied the army through-out the campaign.

This bank was the precursor of the Bank of North America which a committee of the Pennsylvania Assembly attempted to deprive of its charter in 1785. Paine came to its defence in a pamphlet entitled *Dissertations on Government: The Affairs of the Bank: and Paper Money*, which is thought to have been largely responsible for its preservation. The main motive of those who were seeking to destroy it was to increase the circulation of paper money, a tendency to which Paine was violently opposed. One of his arguments, which appears to be sound, is that the ease with which paper money is produced, compared with the relative difficulty of increasing the supply of gold and silver – a greater difficulty at that time than it is now, though not so much greater as to invalidate the comparison – acts as a stimulus to inflation, though there are grounds for suspecting that Paine thought of gold and silver as 'real' money in a way that paper could never be, ignoring the fact that anything whatever of which there is a sufficient quantity available can serve as a means of exchange, so long as those who employ it agree on its legitimacy.

The distrust of paper money was not just a quirk of Paine's. It was widespread well into the nineteenth century and fostered by the collapse of 'bubble schemes'. The concept of it is amusingly satirized by Thomas Love Peacock in *Calidore*, his Fragment of a Romance, most probably written in 1816. The character Calidore, a transplant from the court of King Arthur, goes to the Bank of England to exchange his gold Arthurs for contemporary English currency. He is presented with several slips of paper signed by one John Figginbotham and promising to pay the bearer £1,000. When he asks for these promises to be redeemed, it is explained to him that all he can hope to receive is more paper. 'Assuredly,' he says, 'this Figginbotham must be a great magician, and profoundly skilled in magic and demonology; for this is almost more than Merlin could do, to make the eternal repetition of the same promise pass for its eternal performance, and exercise unlimited control over the lives and fortunes of a whole nation, merely by putting his name upon pieces of paper.'

Though I am old enough to remember talk of 'Bradburys', it is worth remarking that English banknotes of any denomination are not now known by the name of the Bank of England's chief cashier. Even so I suspect that a superstitious belief in the greater genuineness of the gold standard is not yet extinct. The fact remains that the science of economics, such as it is, has cast aside the prejudices of Peacock and Paine.

On 1 March 1780, the Pennsylvania Assembly passed an Act for the abolition of slavery within the State, entailing the emancipation of the six thousand slaves which it then contained. Pennsylvania was the first of the thirteen States to take this course. Notoriously its example was not followed by the Southern States, Virginia, Georgia and the Carolinas, nor by every one of the other States that were later admitted to the Union up to the time of the Civil War. On internal evidence, it is generally supposed that the preamble of this Pennsylvanian Act was composed by Tom Paine. It runs as follows:

When we contemplate our abhorrence of that condition, to which the arms and tyranny of Great Britain were exerted to reduce us, when we look back on the variety of dangers to which we have been exposed, and how miraculously our wants in many instances have been supplied, and our deliverances wrought, when even hope and human fortitude have become unequal to the conflict, we are unavoidably led to a serious and grateful sense of the manifold blessings, which we have undeservedly received from the hand of that Being, from whom every good and perfect gift cometh. Impressed with these ideas, we conceive that it is our duty, and we rejoice that it is in our power, to extend a portion of that freedom to others, which hath been extended to us, and release them from the state of thralldom, to which we ourselves were tyrannically doomed, and from which we have now every prospect of being delivered. It is not for us to enquire why, in the creation of mankind, the inhabitants of the several parts of the earth were distinguished by a difference in feature or complexion. It is sufficient to know that all are the work of the Almighty Hand. We find in the distribution of the human species, that the most fertile as well as the most barren parts of the earth are inhabited by men of complexions different from ours and from each other; from whence we may reasonably as well as religiously infer, that He, who placed them in their various situations, hath extended equally his care and protection to all, and that it becometh not us to counteract his mercies. We esteem it a peculiar blessing granted to us, that we are enabled this day to add one more step to universal civilization, by removing as much as possible, the sorrows of those who have lived in undeserved bondage, and from which, by the assumed authority of the Kings of Great Britain, no effectual legal relief could be obtained. Weaned, by a long course of experience, from those narrow prejudices and partialities we had imbibed, we find our hearts enlarged with kindness and benevolence towards men of all conditions and nations; and we conceive ourselves at this particular period particularly called upon by the blessings which we have received, to manifest the sincerity of our profession, and to give a substantial proof of our gratitude.

And whereas the condition of those persons, who have heretofore been denominated Negro and Mulatto slaves, has been attended with circumstances, which not only deprived them of the common blessings that they were by nature entitled to, but has cast them into the deepest afflictions, by an unnatural separation and sale of husband and wife from each other and from their children, an injury, the greatness of which can only be conceived by supposing that we were in the same unhappy case. In justice, therefore, to persons so unhappily circumstanced, and who, having no prospect before them whereon they may rest their sorrows and their hopes, have no reasonable inducement to render their service to society, which they otherwise might, and also in grateful commemoration of our own happy deliverance from that state of unconditional submission to which we were doomed by the tyranny of Britain.

Be it enacted . . . etc.[1]

Whether because of his composition of this preamble or for his services to the cause of American independence, most probably the latter in view of the date, the University of Pennsylvania awarded Paine the honorary degree of Master of Arts on 4 July 1780. This is the only academic honour that he is known to have received.

After publishing a pamphlet entitled *Public Good*, in which he successfully disputed the claim of the State of Virginia, based on a patent granted by James I in the year 1609 to the South Virginia Company, to incorporate all the territory lying between it and the Pacific Ocean, Paine accompanied John Laurens at his own expense on a mission to try to obtain more money from Louis XVI. Having acquired two and a half million livres they returned to America on a French frigate in June 1781.

Paine's secretaryship to the Pennsylvania Assembly had come to an

[1] *Writings of Thomas Paine*, vol. II, pp. 29–30.

end, and as he made no profit out of his pamphlets he found himself in serious want of money. He overcame his pride so far as to appeal to General Washington for help, faintly reproaching the American authorities for their failure to remunerate him for his services, and declaring his design to settle in France or Holland. After consulting Robert Morris, his Superintendent of Finance, and Robert Morris's assistant, Gouverneur Morris, Washington decided, in a letter which all three men signed, to recommend to Congress that Paine should be awarded a salary of eight hundred dollars a year, paid by the Secretary of Foreign Affairs out of secret funds. It was thought that the secrecy would preserve the force of Paine's propaganda and remove any suspicion that he was expressing anything other than his own views. The response of Congress was to refer the question to a committee which recommended that Paine be appointed historiographer to the continent, but nothing came of it.

In September 1782 Paine published a reply to a history of the American Revolution, written by the Abbé Raynal and translated into English. The Abbé's main arguments were that no principle was at stake except the right of the mother country 'to lay, directly or indirectly, a slight tax upon the colonies' and that it was only because they had just made an alliance with France that the colonists rejected a British offer, communicated to them in April 1778, of everything for which they were asking, short of independence. Paine's rejoinder was that it was not just a question of a slight tax on tea but of complete subservience to the whim of the British government and that while the treaty with France may have been signed in Paris before the British proposals were made the proposals were rejected before knowledge of the treaty had reached America. On this second point Paine is inaccurate. In April 1778 the American Congress had declared its willingness to negotiate provided Great Britain had already withdrawn its armed forces or expressly acknowledged the independence of the States. When on 3 June 1778 the English Commissioners, who had been despatched to America, formally apprised Congress of the resolution to negotiate which had been adopted by Parliament in February, Congress merely referred them to the refusal which it had given in April, but it now said that the States would treat only as an independent nation. Since it also spoke of its having 'sound regard' to its treaties, and proof of the treaty with France had reached Yorktown on 2 May, the treaty may after all have helped to stiffen the American attitude, though I think that it would be a mistake to say that it turned the scale.

Perhaps the most interesting part of the letter is its correction of the Abbé's perfunctory reference to the military operations conducted by General Washington at Trenton in 1776 and Princeton in January 1777 and Paine's consequent detailed description of events in which he himself had taken part. He also pays an elaborate compliment to the good motives of the French in entering into an alliance with the United States. It may have been chiefly for this reason that the French government made him a present of three hundred dollars.

In spite of this bonus, Paine continued to be in financial straits. He had bought a small house at Bordentown in New Jersey, in order to be near his friend Colonel Joseph Kirkbride, who was also of Quaker origin, but this left him with little money to spare. He wrote in June 1783 to the President of Congress, Elias Boudinot, suggesting that something more was due to him for his services to the country but received no satisfaction and took no part in the ceremonies which were held at Princeton to celebrate the declaration of peace with England in September.

George Washington then again took up his case, writing to all the State Assemblies to remind them of what they owed to Paine and suggesting that they grant him some reward. Unfortunately Paine had chosen at that time, when the various States were inclined to reassert their sovereignties at the conclusion of the war, to maintain in his letters and pamphlets that there should be no sovereignty but that of the United States, with the result that only two States responded favourably to Washington's appeal. They, however, did so generously. In 1784 New York presented him with an estate of two hundred and seventy-seven acres and a handsome house at New Rochelle, and at the end of the year Pennsylvania voted him five hundred pounds.

Freed from financial anxiety, and having no immediate motive for continuing to write about politics, Paine was able to pursue his scientific interests. He was assisted by John Hall, a skilled mechanic, who emigrated from Leicester in 1785, carrying letters to Paine, and soon came to lodge with Colonel Kirkbride in Bordentown. Paine was concentrating his efforts on the construction of an iron bridge with only a single arch. An iron bridge, the first of its kind, with which Paine had nothing to do, had already been erected over the River Severn in 1779, but whereas it had a span of only 100 feet, Paine aimed at building a bridge which would have a span of 400 or even 500 feet. Apparently he had no hopes of getting it constructed in the United States, but thought that there were good prospects in England or in France. Another motive for visiting England was to see his parents. There is no evidence

of his fearing that his American activities would make trouble for him
even with the British government.

In fact, he went first to Paris in May 1787 to display a model of his
bridge to the French Academy of Sciences. It was admired, but no
move was made to have the bridge constructed in France. Paine stayed
in France until September, then made his way to Thetford only to
discover that his father had died of smallpox in November 1786. He
settled nine shillings a week on his mother, by which she was not in a
condition to profit for very long, dying in May 1790 in her ninety-fourth
year. Before returning to Paris in December 1787, for no obvious reason
beyond that of cementing his friendship with Thomas Jefferson, who
was serving there as the American Ambassador, he remained at
Thetford, putting the finishing touches to a pamphlet entitled *Prospects
on the Rubicon* in which he warns the British government against
alienating Holland or renewing the war with France. His objections are
basically moral:

> When we consider, for the feelings of Nature cannot be dismissed, the
> calamities of war and the miseries it inflicts upon the human species,
> the thousands and tens of thousands of every age and sex who are
> rendered wretched by the event, surely there is something in the
> heart of man that calls upon him to think! Surely there is some tender
> chord tuned by the hand of its Creator, that struggles to emit in the
> hearing of the soul a note of sorrowing sympathy. Let it then be
> heard, and let man learn to feel that the true greatness of a nation is
> founded on the principles of humanity; and that to avoid a war when
> our own existence is not endangered, and wherein the happiness of
> man must be wantonly sacrificed, is a higher principle of true honour
> than madly to engage in it.[1]

But Paine's arguments are also practical:

> Independent of all civil and moral considerations, there is no
> possible event that a war could produce benefits to England or
> France, on the present occasion, that could in the most distant
> proportion recompense to either the expense she must be at. War
> involves in its progress such a train of unforeseen and unsupposed
> circumstances, such a combination of foreign matters, that no
> human wisdom can calculate the end. It has but one thing certain

[1] *Writings of Thomas Paine*, vol. II, pp. 194–5.

and that is increase of TAXES. The policy of European courts is now so cast, and their interests so interwoven with each other, that however easy it may be to begin a war, the weight and influence of interfering nations compel even the conqueror to unprofitable conditions of peace.[1]

This has not turned out to be true in general. Victory in the two Great Wars of this century has indeed proved very costly to England, but the defeat of Napoleon, though it initiated a period of civil disturbance, did not impoverish the victors, nor have the Great Wars of this century brought material detriment to the United States. What chiefly led Paine astray was his antipathy to paper currency. It was summarized in his saying that 'the delusion of paper riches is working as rapidly in England as it did in America'.

Having delivered his warning to Pitt, Paine concentrated his energy upon the promotion of his bridge. He took out patents for it in England, Scotland and Ireland, persuaded an American merchant Peter White-side, who was living in London, to invest £620 in the enterprise, and, most importantly, discovered a firm of ironmakers, Walker Brothers, located at Rotherham in Yorkshire, who had the means and the skill to execute the work.

In view of what was to follow, it is fascinating to learn that on his tour of Yorkshire, in 1788, in search of a firm like Walker Brothers, Paine was accompanied by Edmund Burke. Not only that but Burke invited Paine to spend a week at his estate in Buckinghamshire. There was indeed no reason at that date why the two men should not have found each other congenial. Both men had advanced by their talents from humble origins. Both enjoyed and were skilful in debate. Burke's views had never been so radical as Paine's but we have noted that like other Whigs he had supported the cause of the American colonists and spoken eloquently on their behalf. There is no evidence of their continuing to meet after the Revolution broke out in France.

Surprisingly, Paine published nothing about the fall of the Bastille. His letters to Jefferson in Paris, written at fairly long intervals between September 1788 and 1789, are much more concerned with his bridge than with politics, though he does furnish Jefferson with an occasional item of political gossip, or criticism of the British government. For instance he writes on 12 March some time after the manifestation of George III's insanity which was to lead to the appointment of the Prince Regent:

> With respect to political matters here, the truth is, the people are fools. They have no discernment into principles and consequences.

[1] ibid., p. 195.

Had Mr. Pitt proposed a National Convention, at the time of the King's insanity, he had done right; but instead of this he has absorbed the right of the Nation into a right of Parliament, – one house of which (the Peers) is hereditary in its own right, and over which the people have no control (not so much as they have over their King); and the other elective by only a small part of the Nation. Therefore he has lessened instead of increased the rights of the people; but as they have not sense enough to see it, they have been huzzaing him. There can be no fixed principles of government, or anything like a Constitution, in a country where the Government can alter itself, or one part of it supply the other.[1]

Paine's only reference to the English response to the progress of the French Revolution occurs in a letter dated 18 September 1789:

The people of this country speak very differently on the affairs of France. The mass of them, so far as I can collect, say that France is a much freer Country than England. The Peers, the Bishops, etc., say the National Assembly has gone too far. There are yet in this country, very considerable remains of the feudal System which people did not see till the revolution in France placed it before their eyes. While the multitude here could be terrified with the cry and apprehension of Arbitrary power, wooden shoes, popery and such like stuff, they thought themselves by comparison an extraordinary free people; but this bugbear now loses its force, and they appear to me to be turning their eyes towards the Aristocrats of their own Nation. This is a new mode of conquering, and I think it will have its effect.[2]

It did have its effect but there was no conquering. The Reform Bill of 1832 did not bring power to the common people of England. Neither, it may be said, did the French Revolution bring power, even in the short run, to the common people of France. There was, however, at least this difference: that the English aristocracy retained a large measure of power, for over another century, whereas the French aristocracy never regained it.

Jefferson remained in Paris until the late autumn of 1789, when he returned to the United States. In 1792 he was to be replaced by Gouverneur Morris, a secret enemy of Paine's, under a profession of

---

[1] *Writings of Thomas Paine*, vol. II, pp. 233–4.
[2] See M. C. Conway, *The Life of Thomas Paine*, vol. I, p. 267.

friendship. Paine visited the city towards the close of 1789 and was presented by the Marquis de Lafayette with the key of the Bastille, which he was requested to send to President Washington. Paine did so with an accompanying letter and the gift was gratefully acknowledged.

Meanwhile Walker Brothers had made progress with the construction of Paine's bridge. Though their product had a span of only 110 feet, a great deal short of Paine's original ambition, he was anxious to put it on show and returned to England for the purpose. By May 1790, he had found a site for it at Lisson Grove near Paddington, and exposed it to the public at a charge of a shilling a head. It proved a great attraction and remained on show for a year, in spite of the bankruptcy of Peter Whiteside. Paine repaid Whiteside's creditors the £620 which he had invested in the bridge, though since Whiteside had made the investment for his own profit, Paine might have argued that he was not strictly liable for the debt.

Paine took no further part himself in the furtherance of what he called 'pontifical invention'. In 1796, however, an iron bridge, answering to Paine's specifications, was built over the River Weir near Sunderland. It had a span of 240 feet. There is no reason to believe that Paine derived any profit from it.

The reason for Paine's detachment from his bridge was not that he had lost interest in engineering but that he had been reclaimed by politics. Whether or not the French Revolution had already propelled him in that direction, the decisive stimulus was the publication in November 1790 of Edmund Burke's *Reflections on the Revolution in France*.

4

The Onslaught of Burke

Edmund Burke was born in Dublin in January 1729 and baptized into the Church of England. His mother and many of his relations were Catholics and there is some reason to believe that his father Richard Burke became an Anglican only because he would not otherwise have been permitted to practise as an attorney. Even so, Edmund Burke received a Protestant education, being sent to a school kept by a Quaker in 1741 and to Trinity College, Dublin, in 1744, where he stayed for four years and left with a BA degree. In 1750 he went to London to read for the Bar, but was never called to it.

It is not known how he spent his early years in London. In 1756, he published two books, one of them a contribution to aesthetics which retains a place in the history of the subject. At some time during the winter of 1756–7 he married Jane Nugent. There is a tradition that they underwent a Catholic ceremony in Paris, but there seems to be no evidence to support it, beyond the fact that Jane's father was a Catholic. They had two sons, one who died in childhood and another, Richard, born in 1758, who followed his father into politics but died young in 1794, to the great grief of his father who outlived him by three years.

Burke started to earn a regular income in 1758–9 by undertaking the production of the *Annual Register*, a practice which he continued for thirty years. From 1759 to 1765 he acted as secretary to William Gerald Hamilton, during which time Hamilton himself became chief secretary to the Lord Lieutenant of Ireland, and after breaking with Hamilton, Burke found a patron in the newly appointed Prime Minister, the second Marquis of Rockingham, for whom he acted as private secretary. His friendship with Rockingham, who assisted him financially, lasted until Rockingham's death in 1782.

Burke was first elected to Parliament in 1765 as a nominee of Lord Verney's for the borough of Wendover. He naturally supported the Rockingham Whig administration and followed it into opposition in 1766. He could not afford and never succeeded in affording the Buckinghamshire estate, at Beaconsfield, which he bought in 1768, though he was helped by his appointment in 1771 as London agent to the State of New York at a salary of £500. This was the year in which he published *Thoughts on the Cause of the Present Discontents*, perhaps the best known of his political pamphlets.

In the parliamentary election of 1774 Burke was both elected a member for Bristol and nominated by Lord Rockingham to the borough of Malton. He chose to represent Bristol, after enunciating the principle that a parliamentary representative should not subordinate his judgement to the opinions of his constituents. I think that this is an excellent principle, so far as it relates to such questions as capital or corporal punishment, or the toleration of homosexuality, or abortion. On the other hand, I think that a member should at least offer himself for re-election if he thoroughly repudiates the purely political programme on the strength of which he was elected. This is not to say that a back-bencher is committed to supporting his party on every particular issue.

For all its merits, Burke's principle may have led him to take rather a loose view of representative government. He never showed any qualms about sitting for a rotten borough. When the electors of Bristol rejected him in 1780, he was content to accept Rockingham's offer and remained a member for Malton until his retirement from Parliament in 1794. This may seem inconsistent with his endorsing the colonists' slogan of 'No taxation without representation' when he allied himself with Charles James Fox in 1774, in opposition to Lord North's American policy, but I have been convinced by Conor Cruise O'Brien, to whose introduction to the Penguin Classics edition of Burke's *Reflections on the Revolution in France* I am very much indebted, that Burke was chiefly moved by what he saw as the similarity between the situation of the American colonists and that of the Irish Catholics. He had no such motive for sympathizing with French Republicans.

Karl Marx was later to accuse Burke of being bribed first by the colonists to support their cause and then by the English oligarchy to attack the French Revolution. So far as I know, there is no evidence for the first charge and I doubt the second, in spite of his joining Pitt's government in 1792 and Paine's allegation that he was enabled by Pitt to take out a pension of £1,500 a year in someone else's name. He was awarded a civil list pension of £125 a year in 1795, but I believe that his hostility to the French Revolution was genuine, and that his disagreement with the Whigs over this question widened a breach which had already been caused by his feeling that they had not treated him fairly. He was made Paymaster of the Forces by Rockingham in 1782 and held the same office under the Duke of Portland in 1783, the year following Rockingham's death, but in neither case was he included in the Cabinet. Nor, in spite of their long association, did Fox intend to appoint Burke to any higher office when he expected to form a government in 1788.

By that time Burke was busy conducting the impeachment of Warren Hastings on the charge of his tyrannical misconduct as Governor of Bengal. The case dragged on till 1795, when Hastings was acquitted, in spite of Burke's eloquence, which cannot be gainsaid, whatever view one takes of his political judgement.

Burke was a prominent and early member of the Literary Club, founded by Sir Joshua Reynolds in 1764, and made famous by Boswell in his *Life of Samuel Johnson*. Dr Johnson's tribute to Burke's powers of conversation is well known:

Boswell   Mr Burke has a constant stream of conversation.
Johnson   Yes, Sir, if a man were to go by chance at the same time with Burke under a shed to shun a shower, he would say – 'This is an extraordinary man'. If Burke should go into a stable to see his horse drest, the ostler would say – 'We have had an extraordinary man here'.

A little later, however, he allowed Burke's conversation to be very superior so long as he 'does not descend to be merry', an opinion not shared by Boswell, who admired Burke's 'pleasantry', though he did not venture to say so at the time. An earlier tribute of Johnson's, also quoted in Boswell's *Life*, is less equivocal. 'Burke is the only man whose conversation corresponds with the general fame which he has in the world. Take up whatever topick you please, he is ready to meet you.'

Burke made his first public attack on the French Revolution in a speech which he delivered in the House of Commons on 8 February 1790. It was his contribution to a debate on the Army Estimates and the burden of his speech was that the French 'distemper' must not be allowed to spread to England. He said that he felt so strongly opposed not only to the end of democracy, on the French pattern, but to the means by which it was then being introduced, that if any of his friends showed the least tendency to imitate these means, he would abandon them and join his worst enemies.

These remarks were directed primarily against Fox, who had recently announced in Parliament that he 'exulted' in the French Revolution 'from feelings and from principle'. Even Pitt referred to it in favourable terms. Pitt was soon to make it clear that, whether or not the Revolution suited the French, he did not regard it as an article of export. On the other hand Fox supported the French Revolution in all its vicissitudes and even transferred his sympathy to Napoleon. This was true of many English Radicals, including radical writers like Byron and Shelley. They contrasted the principles of Liberty, Equality and Fraternity which Napoleon had spread throughout Europe, admittedly by force of arms, but arms used to weaken the tyrannical governments of Austria and Prussia, with the odious, arbitrary, repressive policies of Pitt and his successors.

> I met Murder on the way –
> He had a mask like Castlereagh.[1]

Burke's estrangement from Fox and Fox's Whig associates did not greatly endear him to the Tories. In their drunken fashion, they applauded his oratory, but they never took him to their hearts even after they included him in their councils. Politically, until the end of his life, he remained a rather isolated figure. His reputation as a profound political theorist, as one who had already supplied the answer to John Stuart Mill's characterization of the Conservatives as 'the stupid party', is almost entirely a twentieth-century development. It is mainly based on his *Reflections on the Revolution in France*. Let us see whether this work deserves the construction which has been put upon it.

Rather awkwardly, *Reflections on the Revolution in France* is cast in the form of a reply to a letter written to Burke from Paris in November 1789 by a young Frenchman called Chames-Jean-François de Pont. Burke had already sent a relatively brief answer before the close of 1789 and his *Reflections* express the conclusions at which he had arrived in the light of further information and more concentrated thought. He began work on the book early in 1790 and published it in November of that year. It runs to nearly two hundred pages in the Penguin Classics edition but since it masquerades as a letter, it is not divided into chapters. The result is not easily digestible, like an old-fashioned

---

[1] Shelley, *The Mask of Anarchy* (1819).

Christmas pudding, with a few sixpences buried in it for the benefit of
the children. The task of the critic is to find the sixpennyworths of
theory and extract them from the pudding. The pudding is rhetoric, of
which Burke was a master.

The motive for Burke's diatribe, ostensibly, and probably also in fact,
was a meeting of a group called the Revolution Society, founded in 1788 to
commemorate the Glorious Whig Revolution of which that year was the
centenary. The proceedings included a sermon by a well-known dissent-
ing Minister, Dr Richard Price, which the Society published, together
with a congratulatory address to the French National Assembly. Burke
was committed to approving of the deposition of the English King James
II in favour of William and Mary, and therefore to discounting any show
of similarity between the two 'revolutions'. In particular, he had to argue
that neither was justified merely by the fact that they resulted in an
increase of popular liberty. 'I should,' he writes

> suspend my congratulations on the new liberty of France, until I was
> informed how it had been combined with government; with public
> force; with the discipline and obedience of armies; with the collection
> of an effective and well-distributed revenue; with morality and
> religion; with the solidity of property; with peace and order: with
> civil and social manners. All these (in their way) are good things too;
> and, without them, liberty is not a benefit whilst it lasts, and is not
> likely to continue long.[1]

A considerable part of Burke's discourse is devoted to showing that
in the case of France these further conditions have not been satisfied.

In the course of his sermon Dr Price asserted that through the
Revolution of 1688 the people of England had acquired three fundamental rights, namely '1. "To choose our own governors." 2. "To
cashier them for misconduct." 3. "To frame a government for
ourselves."' Burke flatly denies that any such rights have been
acquired. Not only that but he denies just as strongly that any belief in
their enjoyment of such a bill of rights is held by 'the body of the people
of England'. 'They utterly disclaim it. They will resist the practical
assertion of it with their lives and fortunes. They are bound to do so by
the laws of their country, made at the time of that very Revolution,
which is appealed to in favour of the fictitious rights claimed by the
society which abuses its name.'[2]

---

[1] Burke, *Reflections on the Revolution in France*, Penguin Classics, pp. 90–91.
[2] ibid., p. 99.

It seems to me that this is an idle dispute. In the first place, who are our governors? Probably, in the context, our monarchs. Do we choose them? Not since 1688. Or possibly not since 1714, since George I could be said to have been chosen, though he had an hereditary claim. This does not apply to all countries. Lord Rothermere was offered the throne of Hungary after the First World War, though he had the good sense to refuse it. In any case, it is unfair to take the argument into the twentieth century, especially the latter part of it when there are very few monarchs left, and they govern to a very limited extent. But what about dictators? Was Mussolini chosen by the people of Italy? Hardly. He marched on Rome and met with no serious resistance. Was Hitler chosen by the Germans? A more difficult question. His party never won a majority at a general election, but there was a period when most Germans at least appear to have supported him, many of them with great enthusiasm. As a general rule, dictators are not chosen by any but a very small body of persons: they usurp power.

Two rulers who are neither monarchs nor dictators but something between the two can most fairly be said to be popular choices. They are the President of the United States and, under its new constitution, the President of France. They are not unanimously chosen, but it is not to be supposed that even Dr Price intended that his 'governors' should be. Neither is it pertinent, however interesting, that the proportion of registered voters who actually cast their votes in Presidential elections in the United States does not normally exceed fifty per cent. Their right is not abolished by the fact that they do not bother to exercise it.

Do we have the right to cashier our governors, and now let this include not only monarchs, but dictators and presidents? Did Mr Baldwin have the right to prevent King Edward from marrying Mrs Simpson and so engineer his abdication? Did the American Senate have the right to force President Nixon to resign his office by threatening to impeach him on account of his part in the Watergate scandal? I suppose that the answer is yes in both cases. The American Senate kept within the bounds of the American Constitution. By now it is taken for granted that an English monarch has no legitimate authority if he or she is denied the services of a ministry in the House of Commons. But what of the body of the people? They hardly come into it. Perhaps neither Mr Baldwin nor the American senators could have acted as they did if King Edward or Mr Nixon manifestly commanded great popular support. But they did not. There may just have been a balance of sympathy for Edward. 'Hark the herald angels sing, Mrs

Simpson's pinched our king,' sang the children in the streets. And that was that.

Let us not now go further into the question of representative democracy. The recent history of England shows how small a percentage of electoral support is needed to keep a government in power. This does not prevent it from being a legitimate government, according to our electoral system. The system may seem irrational and just missed being altered in 1931. At present the body of the people has not only the right but even, indirectly, the power to change it. As yet, it has shown no strong disposition to do so.

Does the body of the people ever effect a revolution? I cannot think of a straightforward example. Not the French Revolution, which was far from commanding universal support throughout the French provinces, though *a* body of people, the Parisians, did contribute very largely to it. Not either of the two Russian revolutions in 1917, in which the peasants had no say, though Lenin and Trotsky took advantage of the widespread desire for Russia's withdrawal from the war. Not the Cuban Revolution, which Castro initiated with a handful of followers, though again he profited by the fact that he was overthrowing an unpopular dictatorship. Perhaps the American Revolution is as close an example as any, if slaves are not counted as people, though, as we have seen, it was slow in coming to a head and dominated by what amounted to an oligarchy.

What does quite often happen is that a monarch or a dictator or a group of usurpers surrender their position when they discover, not necessarily that they are disliked by the body of the people, but that they can no longer rely on the loyalty or strength of their supporters. This became a frequent occurrence in the Roman Empire, when the Emperor's surrender of power might take the form of his suicide or assassination. A good modern example would be that of the Greek Colonels, who were in fact unable to withstand the pressure of popular hostility, though it has to be added that they might have stood their ground if they had not also alienated foreign opinion. I hope that the same will be true of the present governments of South Africa and of General Pinochet in Chile.

If I were a citizen of Chile and had the opportunity of organizing a successful coup against General Pinochet, should I ask myself whether I had the right to do so? The question would not occur to me. What would occupy me would be the question whether I had the power. Hobbes may have gone too far with his famous saying 'Covenants, without the Sword, are but Words, and of no strength to secure a man

at all.'[1] Many men keep their covenants out of a sense of moral
obligation. Even so, at least at the national level, there is always a
background of authority. The fundamental question in politics, as
Lenin put it, remains 'Who – Whom?'

This is not an attempt to divorce politics from morality. For instance,
one of the merits of the United States is the moral surveillance to which
its rulers are subjected, making it difficult and perilous for them to
overstep the bounds of constitutional propriety. A less welcome
product of the same tendency is the belief, I think unquestioningly held,
by members of the administration and an increasing number of its
citizens that the United States has not only the right but the duty to
check the advance of what it chooses to regard as Communism,
wherever it appears in the world, without being very scrupulous either
about the means or the results. How far economic interests foster this
belief and profit by it is a question into which I am not equipped to
enter.

I fear that I have strayed a long way from Burke. But perhaps not
quite so far as it may seem, since he paid great attention to the concept
of legitimacy. What may seem strange is the very great importance that
he attached to the factor of heredity. The Glorious Revolution of 1688 is
made less revolutionary by Mary's being a daughter of James II. The
Hanoverian intrusion is legitimized by the fact that George I was
descended from the Stuarts through the Princess Sophia. 'No experience has taught us,' says Burke, 'that in any other course or method
than that of an *hereditary crown*, our liberties can be regularly perpetu-
ated and preserved sacred as our *hereditary right*.'[2] Again,

> In the famous law of the 3rd of Charles I, called the *Petition of Right*,
> the parliament says to the king, 'your subjects have *inherited* this
> freedom,' claiming their franchises not on abstract principles 'as the
> rights of men,' but as the rights of Englishmen, and as patrimony
> derived from their forefathers.[3]

And more generally:

> You will observe, that from Magna Charta to the Declaration of
> Right, it has been the uniform policy of our constitution to claim and
> assert our liberties, as an *entailed inheritance* derived to us from our

[1] *Leviathan*, ch. XVII.
[2] *Reflections on the Revolution*, p. 109.
[3] ibid., p. 118.

forefathers, and to be transmitted to our posterity; as an estate specially belonging to the people of this kingdom without any reference whatever to any other more general or prior right. By this means our constitution preserves an unity in so great a diversity of its parts. We have an inheritable crown; an inheritable peerage; and an house of commons and a people inheriting privileges, franchises, and liberties, from a long line of ancestors.[1]

Burke's emphasis on heredity goes together with his reverence for property, since it is the common practice that property is transmitted by inheritance. He admits that the possession of ability as well as property should figure in the representation of a State but goes on to argue that property should predominate 'out of all proportion', on the extraordinary ground that property needs to be protected from ability which is 'a vigorous and active principle' whereas 'property is sluggish, inert, and timid'. This is followed by his saying that 'the characteristic essence of property . . . is to be *unequal*.'[2] No doubt it is, but one reason why it is is that those who chiefly busy themselves with the acquisition and retention of property, so far from being sluggish, inert, and timid are energetic, active and sometimes bold to the point of lacking scruple. Above all they are tenacious. In fact Burke's contrasting of ability with property is a false antithesis. It may be that some owners of large property at the time that he was writing had become inert, because their interests were not seriously threatened, but if they had become inert the mere fact that they owned property should not have qualified them for office. I rather fear that Burke thought that it should, especially if the property had been passed down to them through several generations.

But how can Burke have come to hold such a belief? He was a very intelligent man and it must have been obvious to him that no right can be founded on heredity alone. There must have been some title to it in the first place, otherwise there would be nothing to inherit. In the case of government, what did he suppose this title to be?

The two sensible answers that he gives are that 'Government is a contrivance of human wisdom to provide for human *wants*,'[3] and that 'all just governments owe their birth' to and 'justify their continuance' on 'principles of cogent expediency'.[4] I said that these answers were

---

[1] *Reflections on the Revolution*, p. 119.
[2] ibid., p. 140.
[3] ibid., p. 151.
[4] ibid., p. 276.

sensible but they are also very vague. Human wants vary in different societies and at different stages of a society's development. What is expedient in one set of circumstances will not be in another. Burke, indeed, would have been the last to deny these platitudes. His appeal to Conservatives chiefly consists in the precept, which they extract from his writings, that one should proceed cautiously, preserving and reforming, in the light of what exists, and how it will be variously affected, rather than risk causing havoc by the indiscriminate application of however seductive a moral principle. Nevertheless, Burke's reference to 'principles of cogent expediency' surely does commit him to a rather more positive theory of some degree of generality.

I believe that there is one passage of the *Reflections* in which this theory is set out. It is a very long passage and, typically, not divided into paragraphs. The passion with which it cleaves to what emerges almost as a religious doctrine has induced me to overcome my hesitation over quoting it in full:

> Society is indeed a contract. Subordinate contracts for objects of mere occasional interest may be dissolved at pleasure – but the state ought not to be considered as nothing better than a partnership agreement in a trade of pepper and coffee, callico or tobacco, or some other such low concern, to be taken up for a little temporary interest, and to be dissolved by the fancy of the parties. It is to be looked on with other reverence; because it is not a partnership in things subservient only to the gross animal existence of a temporary and perishable nature. It is a partnership in all science; a partnership in all art; a partnership in every virtue, and in all perfection. As the ends of such a partnership cannot be obtained in many generations, it becomes a partnership not only between those who are living, but between those who are living, those who are dead, and those who are to be born. Each contract of each particular state is but a clause in the great primaeval contract of eternal society, linking the lower with the higher natures, connecting the visible and invisible world, according to a fixed compact sanctioned by the inviolable oath which holds all physical and all moral natures, each in their appointed place. This law is not subject to the will of those, who by an obligation above them, and infinitely superior, are bound to submit their will to that law. The municipal corporations of that universal kingdom are not morally at liberty at their pleasure, and on their speculations of a contingent improvement, wholly to separate and tear asunder the

bands of their subordinate community, and to dissolve it into an unsocial, uncivil, unconnected chaos of elementary principles. It is the first and supreme necessity only, a necessity that is not chosen but chooses, a necessity paramount to deliberation, that admits no discussion, and demands no evidence, which alone can justify a resort to anarchy. This necessity is no exception to the rule; because this necessity itself is a part too of that moral and physical disposition of things to which man must be obedient by consent or force; but if that which is only submission to necessity should be made the object of choice, the law is broken, nature is disobeyed, and the rebellious are outlawed, cast forth, and exiled, from this world of reason, and order, and peace, and virtue, and fruitful penitence, into the antagonist world of madness, discord, vice, confusion, and unavailing sorrow.[1]

This is a fine piece of prose, if one cares for rhetoric, but what does it all mean? What is the great primaeval contract of eternal society and who are the parties to it? What is the inviolable oath which holds all physical natures in their appointed places? What is the first and supreme necessity which alone can justify a resort to anarchy: a necessity of which it is first said that it is not chosen, and then, inconsistently, that it can be chosen but only with the direst consequences?

I have no answer to the last question, beyond the conjecture that the necessity might consist in the utter breakdown of civilization, as a result perhaps of something like a widespread plague. This would fail to explain, however, why it should be called 'first and supreme' or why anyone should want to choose it. A reply to the second point might be that what is chosen is not the necessity but the anarchy, unforeseen by the chooser, to which it leads: a reply to the first that the necessity, if it came about, would have been pre-ordained.

This last conjecture is admittedly far-fetched. I think, however, that it does supply us with a clue to the way in which our other questions should be answered. Remembering that Burke was very religious, I suggest that the parties to the great primaeval contract and the inviolable oath were meant to be God and Man. What Burke is maintaining is that an upheaval like the French Revolution runs counter to the natural order, itself divinely appointed. An obvious comment is that this would not be possible, since there is no such thing as an unnatural event, any more than there could be a violation of an

---

[1] *Reflections on the Revolution*, pp. 194–5.

inviolable oath. Anything that happens, however bizarre, is part of the course of nature. It is, however, quite common in moral and political philosophy to find the word 'natural' used normatively, to imply not that the event in question never does occur but that it should not be permitted to, and clearly this is the sense in which Burke is using it here. I presume that he also allows it to be possible for men to misuse the freedom which God has granted them so far as to pervert the social, if not the physical, order which he has organized, though they are bound to suffer in consequence.

But why should the social order be hierarchical? Again I can find no satisfactory answer, though there is plenty of evidence in the *Reflections* that Burke thought it had to be. Two passages, in particular, seem to me decisive. They have the greater weight in so far as they do not sustain the implications of Burke's intemperate reference, so often quoted against him, to 'the swinish multitude'.

The first of these passages occurs at a point where Burke is defending the 'useless' life of monks. 'They are,' he says,

> as usefully employed as if they worked from dawn to dark, in the innumerable servile, degrading, unseemly, unmanly, and often most unwholesome and pestiferous occupations, to which by the social economy so many wretches are inevitably doomed. If it were not generally pernicious to disturb the natural course of things, and to impede, in any degree, the great wheel of circulation which is turned by the strangely directed labour of these unhappy people, I should be infinitely more inclined forcibly to rescue them from their miserable industry, than violently to disturb the tranquil repose of monastic quietude.[1]

Why then does he not attempt to rescue these victims of society? Why does he tolerate the conditions that force them to be 'swinish'? The answer he gives is 'the necessity of submitting to the yoke of luxury, and the despotism of fancy, who in their own imperious way will distribute the surplus product of the soil'.[2] But what could conceivably be the ground of the necessity? The answer appears in a previous paragraph. 'In every prosperous community something more is produced than goes to the immediate support of the producer. This surplus forms the income of the landed capitalist. It will be spent by a proprietor who does not labour. But this idleness is itself the spring of labour; this repose the spur to industry.'[3]

[1] ibid., p. 271.
[2] ibid.
[3] ibid., p. 270.

What a surprising foretaste of Karl Marx! Only for Marx the appropriation of 'surplus value' was an evil to be abolished. In fairness to Burke, it should be added that he does recommend that 'the capital taken in rent from the land, should be returned again to the industry from whence it came; and that its expenditure should be with the least possible detriment to the morals of those who expend it, and to those of the people to whom it is returned.'[1]

What is more, he even refers to this as 'the concern of the state'. At the same time he does not pretend that it actually happens or suggest any way in which the state might effectively display its concern. It would rather seem that he takes 'the yoke of luxury and the despotism of fancy' to be ingredients in the natural order.

My second passage comes towards the end of the book:

> To keep a balance between the power of acquisition on the part of the subject, and the demands he is to answer on the part of the state, is a fundamental part of the skill of a true politician. The means of acquisition are prior in time and in arrangement. Good order is the foundation of all good things. To be enabled to acquire, the people, without being servile, must be tractable and obedient. The magistrate must have his reverence, the laws their authority. The body of the people must not find the principles of natural subordination by art rooted out of their minds. They must respect that property of which they cannot partake. They must labour to obtain what by labour can be obtained; and when they find, as they commonly do, the success disproportioned to the endeavour, they must be taught their consolation in the final proportions of eternal justice. Of this consolation, whoever deprives them, deadens their industry, and strikes at the root of all acquisition as of all conservation. He that does this is the cruel oppressor, the merciless enemy of the poor and wretched; at the same time that by his wicked speculations he exposes the fruits of successful industry, and the accumulations of fortune, to the plunder of the negligent, the disappointed, and the unprosperous.[2]

What, I wonder, are 'the final proportions of eternal justice' that are to console the wretches, whom Burke pities, for their misfortunes? I thought at first that he was locating them in an after-life, but how in that case could Burke's villains deprive them of them? Perhaps by

[1] *Reflections on the Revolution*, pp. 194–5.
[2] ibid., p. 372.

undermining their religious beliefs, but why should the loss of religious belief on the part of the unfortunate lead to the outrages which he then proceeds to list? I think that there is a way of making the argument coherent. We are to suppose that the recompense in the world to come for those who have not prospered on earth is not offered unconditionally: it will be a consolation only for those whose success has not been proportionate to their endeavours; those whom Shaw's Alfred Dolittle called 'the undeserving poor' will be given no benefits. But now suppose that 'wicked' men persuade even the deserving poor that their religious beliefs are false. They have nothing to look forward to beyond what they can achieve in this world. Will they not consider it unjust that they languish in poverty however hard they work? And will not the result be that, if they are given the opportunity, they will strip the 'accumulator' of his fortune, especially if he has done nothing to earn it?

I think that I have succeeded in putting the best construction on Burke's argument, in so far as I have made it coherent: this is not to say that I have made it convincing. If one is going to talk about 'eternal justice' why should it not operate in this world? And if the answer be that it does operate in this world why should it entail such huge measures of inequality? 'The rich man in his castle, the poor man at his gate, God made them high and lowly, and ordered their estate.' Does it really come down to that? Can Burke's political philosophy be captured in a quatrain of Cecil Frances Alexander's children's hymn? We have perhaps to add the rider that it is possible but at the best foolhardy to tamper with what God has ordered.

It would, however, be unfair to Burke to expose the thinness of his political philosophy, when stripped of its layer of rhetoric, and fail to acknowledge his political acumen. In criticizing his *Reflections on the Revolution in France* we need to bear in mind the year in which it was written, 1790, a year of comparative tranquillity in Paris, three years before the outbreak of the Reign of Terror. Burke devotes several eloquent pages to the plight of Marie-Antoinette on 6 October 1789, when she was compelled with her husband to forsake Versailles for Paris, taunted all along the way by a mob of women and of men disguised as women in a procession headed by two of her murdered guards with their heads on spikes. What would he have found to say if he had been writing after she and Louis had been guillotined in 1793, with their son the Dauphin left to die in prison? He did not predict their execution but he did predict that Louis XVI who still retained his office after he had been brought back to Paris was already in a position where he could exercise so little power that he might just as well have been deposed.

A fact which Burke did foresee is that once the three Orders of the States General of France, the Nobility, the Clergy and the Third Estate, ceased to act separately, each having an equal voice in the decisions that were taken, but were merged into a single National Assembly, the Third Estate, though its six hundred representatives were not more numerous than the sum of the other two, would dominate the proceedings. One reason for this was that the representatives of the nobility and the clergy were not united in their views. This was especially true of the clergy, a large proportion of whom were country curates who were not only unfitted for their responsibility as legislators by having no experience of public affairs beyond the narrow concerns of their small parishes, but were also jealous of their ecclesiastical superiors, many of whom enjoyed an immensely higher standard of living than they could ever aspire to. The members of the nobility were more strongly disposed to act in concert, but there were those among them whose loyalty to their own order succumbed to the temptation of improving their position within it by coming forward as champions of the people. In this instance, Burke failed to do justice to noblemen like the Comte de Mirabeau who acted not primarily out of self-interest but rather in accordance with his belief that the established order in France had palpable defects which he was in a favourable position to attempt to remedy.

Though he did not predict that the Third Estate would tear itself to pieces, but rather assumed that it would continue to act homogeneously, Burke expressed a shrewd criticism of the selection of its representatives. Noting that a great proportion of them were lawyers, he went on to remark that for the most part they were not 'distinguished magistrates' or 'leading advocates' or 'renowned professors of universities' but 'obscure provincial advocates' and their like whose practices lay 'in the petty war of village vexation'.[1] Such men could outmanoeuvre the farmers, traders and even doctors of medicine who were their colleagues in the Third Estate but they had neither the experience nor the intellectual equipment to serve the best interests of the nation.

I think that this criticism was not altogether wide of the mark. It would, indeed, be absurd to contend that such a man as Robespierre was lacking in ability, but his attitude was legalistic and it was his inflexibility, shared by his enemies and his associates, that brought discord to the National Assembly, and supplied the guillotine with its victims, including himself.

[1] *Reflections on the Revolution*, pp. 129–30.

Where it seems to me that Burke went astray was in underrating the sincerity if not of all the representatives of the Third Estate, at least of the leaders of its several factions. A group of petty attorneys would have resorted to compromise; they would have been content with the pickings that their elevation made available to them. Whatever their origins, such men as Danton, Robespierre and Desmoulins believed in their mission to reform the constitution of France. They died for their principles.

The most striking proof of Burke's political prescience was his foretelling the emergence not of Napoleon personally, of whom he would not have heard in 1790, but of someone who would play Napoleon's part. 'Some popular general,' he wrote:

> who understands the art of conciliating the soldiery, and who possesses the true spirit of command, shall draw the eyes of all men upon himself. Armies will obey him on his personal account. There is no other way of securing military obedience in this state of things. But the moment in which that event shall happen, the person who really commands the army is your master; the master (that is little) of your king, the master of your assembly, the master of your whole republic.[1]

Have we at last found the explanation, other than the absence of plausible competitors, for the homage paid to Burke as a standard-bearer of Conservatism? What is required is the flair for predicting the immediate course of events. One need not then probe very far into political philosophy. The danger here, however, is that of saddling Burke with Hegel. For all his reverence for ancient institutions, Burke did not equate the real with the rational; he did not believe that whatever is is right. We should remember also, first that the theory that democracy leads to dictatorship goes as far back as Plato and Aristotle; secondly that Burke was primarily a Whig who never was entrusted by his party with any high political office.

[1] ibid., p. 342.

5

Rights of Man: Part One

Thomas Paine's most famous book *Rights of Man* was published in two parts. Each of them is short, the first, dedicated to George Washington, running to 112 pages in the Penguin Classics edition, and the second, dedicated to M. de Lafayette, to 127 pages in the same edition, including a short appendix. As in the case of *Common Sense* the brevity of these works, priced at three shillings or less, stimulated rather than retarded their sale. The population of Great Britain was then about ten million. M. D. Conway, still the best and most thorough of Paine's biographers, though his Life of Paine was published as long ago as 1892, estimated that the two parts of *Rights of Man* had sold 200,000 copies in Britain by 1793. Eric Foner, in his introduction to the Penguin Classics edition, puts the number at 250,000. We shall see, however, that for all its popularity, the book came nowhere near to matching *Common Sense* in its political effect.

The first part of *Rights of Man* was published in a small edition by Joseph Johnson in February 1791. Though he remained a friend of Paine's and was associated with the sale of the second part a year later, Johnson took fright and allowed the publication to be taken over in March 1791 by J. S. Jordan, who also published the second part in February 1792.

The interval between November 1790 when Burke's *Reflections* was published and February 1791 is so short and the topic of the French Revolution so congenial to Paine that I think it quite likely that he had already gone so far as to make some notes upon it, before Burke's book appeared. Nevertheless the first part of *Rights of Man*, while it contains other matter of more positive interest, is mainly presented as a rejoinder to Burke, and is so described in Paine's preface to it.

Having begun his book with some personal abuse of Burke and condemnation of his style of writing, Paine passes to the defence of Dr Price and the proceedings of the Revolution Society. In fact, he has hardly anything to say about the rights proclaimed by the Society and roughly dismissed by Burke, beyond making the point that the rights in question were not ascribed to this or that person but to the nation as a whole. This is not, however, a distinction that he takes the trouble to elucidate. Instead, he sets out to destroy Burke's objections to any attempt to connect the French Revolution with the English 'revolution' of 1688. The members of the Parliament which sanctioned the deposition of James II in favour of William III and Mary were anxious that this should not set a precedent; they did not wish to undermine the principles of hereditary succession to the English throne. Accordingly they issued the following declaration:

> The lords spiritual and temporal, and commons, do, in the name of all the people aforesaid, most humbly and faithfully submit themselves, their heirs and posterities for ever; and do faithfully promise, that they will stand to, maintain, and defend their said majesties, and also the limitation of the crown, herein specified and contained, to the utmost of their powers.

Burke quotes this declaration with approval but draws no further inference from it than that it denies to all future generations of British subjects the constitutional right to depose their monarchs if their fancy so takes them. He does not maintain that there are no circumstances in which such action could be justified. He requires only that in a matter of this sort 'occasional will' should be subjected 'to permanent reason, and to the steady maxims of faith, justice, and fixed fundamental policy'.[1] In reply, Paine denies the right and the power of 'a parliament, or any description of men, or any generation of men, in any country . . . to bind all posterity for ever'.[2] He admits that laws remain in force beyond the lifetime of those who first enact them but that is only because the living still consent to them. He concludes his argument rhetorically: 'That which may be thought right and found convenient in one age, may be thought wrong and found inconvenient in another. In such cases, Who is to decide, the living, or the dead?'[3]

[1] *Reflections on the Revolution*, p. 104.
[2] *Rights of Man*, pp. 41–2.
[3] ibid., p. 45.

I do not see this as a serious dispute. Burke's was an argument *ad hominem*. He was concerned to show that Dr Price and his friends were misrepresenting the political intentions of those who brought about the English revolution of 1688, if they treated them as a precedent for the overthrow of the French monarchy more than a hundred years later. Even Burke would not have argued that the declaration of rights, imposed on William III by the Whigs, should have prevented their Liberal descendants from curbing the power of the House of Lords by forcing through the Parliament Act of 1911. Nor would he have denied that something describable as consent, on the part of those who comply with it, is necessary for a law to remain effectively in operation. It is, indeed, obvious that consent does not here imply approval. At the same time lack of approval does not imply a rejection of right. A thief who steals property need not agree with Proudhon that property is theft. Whether a law is held to be legitimate, not only by those who respect it but also by those who violate it, depends chiefly, though not entirely, upon its provenance. In certain forms of society, a law may fail to be sustained because it offends the moral sense of a necessary section of those who are needed to enforce it. An example would be the refusal of English juries in the early nineteenth century to convict persons who were proved to have committed minor offences for which the penalties inflicted were excessively severe. The roots of the English legal system remained intact. For them to have been demolished, there would have to have been a wholesale rejection of the pretensions of those who in one way or another, had acquired the authority to mould and administer the law. In short, we come upon another instance of the dependence of rights upon power.

In spite of his devoting the greater part of a book to rebutting Burke's strictures on the French Revolution, Paine manages to accuse him of regarding it too lightly. For instance, he complains that Burke makes only three casual references to the capture of the Bastille. He is particularly shocked by Burke's apparent indifference to the plight of those who were imprisoned in it. I quote the passage because it is one of the most conspicuous examples of Paine's forensic style:

> Not one glance of compassion, not one commiserating reflection, that I can find throughout his book, has he bestowed on those who lingered out the most wretched of lives, a life without hope, in the most miserable of prisons. It is painful to behold a man employing his talents to corrupt himself. Nature has been kinder to Mr Burke than he is to her. He is not affected by the reality of distress touching

his heart, but by the showy resemblance of it striking his imagination. He pities the plumage, but forgets the dying bird. Accustomed to kiss the aristocratical hand that hath purloined him from himself, he degenerates into a composition of art, and the genuine soul of nature forsakes him. His hero or his heroine must be a tragedy-victim expiring in show, and not the real prisoner of misery, sliding into death in the silence of a dungeon.[1]

For all his pity for the prisoners in the Bastille, Paine felt that its capture needed some further justification. He therefore represented the assault as a popular response to the exposure of a plot organized by the King's younger brother, the Count d'Artois, to employ troops to arrest the members of the National Assembly. Writing as he was before the outbreak of the Reign of Terror, he was able to give the National Assembly credit for the fact that it had nobody executed for taking part in this plot. He had to admit that four persons, including the Governor of the Bastille and the Mayor of Paris, succumbed to the fury of the populace. As for their heads being carried around upon spikes, he offers no defence beyond a *tu quoque*. The heads of English criminals were so exhibited at Temple Bar. I must make it clear that this is not presented by Paine as an excuse. On the contrary, it affords him an opportunity of making a general attack upon 'sanguinary punishments which corrupt mankind'.[2]

Paine's rejoinder to Burke takes a similar form with respect to the events of 5 and 6 October 1789. He claims that the mob were provoked into marching on Versailles by learning that the King's bodyguard, responding to a signal, 'tore the national cockade from their hats, trampled it under foot, and replaced it with a counter cockade prepared for the purpose'.[3] He implies that their intention was to convey the King from Versailles to Metz where they would 'set up a standard'. He does not say whether this was known to the mob, though his version of the incident would seem to require that something of that sort was at least suspected by them. What then happened, as Paine relates it, was that M. de Lafayette at the head of twenty thousand of the Paris militia followed the mob, with the intention not of joining forces with them but preventing any outbreak of violence. He was so far successful that no blood was shed during the night of 5–6 October, once the King had been persuaded to sign the Assembly's declaration of the Rights of Man.

[1] *Rights of Man*, p. 51.
[2] ibid., p. 58.
[3] ibid., p. 61.

Such violence as did occur on the morning of 6 October was initiated, according to Paine, by one of the King's bodyguard who appeared at a window of the palace and, instead of withdrawing when the people who had slept in the courtyard started jeering at him, opened fire upon them. This caused them to invade the palace and insist that the King and Queen return to Paris. Paine refers in passing to 'the loss of two or three lives'[1] but so far from confirming Burke's allegation that the Queen was endangered in the Palace and she and the King insulted throughout their journey, he asserts that the King accepted the original demand for his return to Paris as 'the shout of peace' and that thereafter there was no further trouble.

As we shall see later on, Paine felt none of the personal hostility to Louis XVI that he had expressed towards George III. His attack is directed against the institution of monarchy, conceived either as absolute or at least as endowed with a considerable share of power. He would not have had the same ground for objecting to a monarch who fulfilled an almost purely ceremonial function, though it would run counter to his republican principles. He might have treated such a form of monarchy with the same contempt as he displays for titles, which the French at that time abolished though they subsequently restored them. 'Titles,' he says, 'are but nick-names, and every nick-name is a title. The thing is perfectly harmless in itself; but it marks a sort of foppery in the human character, which degrades it.'[2] For my own part, I am content to let this pass.

Paine is not seriously concerned with what could be taken, or could once have been taken, as an outward sign of aristocracy. Here again, it is the institution of aristocracy that he seeks to abolish and the reason why he seeks to abolish it is that he associates it with what he regards as two major evils: primogeniture and hereditary power.

Paine's objection to primogeniture is that the automatic transference of property to the eldest son, irrespective of the hardship which this may inflict upon his siblings, is a manifestation of 'tyranny and injustice'. He goes on to draw the rather dubious inference that anybody who has profited by such injustice is thereby unfitted to legislate for a nation.

With regard to the idea of hereditary legislation, I have already quoted his comments on its absurdity in the course of my examination of his *Common Sense*.[3]

[1] *Rights of Man*, p. 63.
[2] ibid., p. 80.
[3] see above p. 41.

The three further charges that Paine brings against the maintenance of an aristocracy appear less substantial. They are, respectively, that 'a body of men holding themselves accountable to nobody, ought not to be trusted by anybody',[1] that 'it is continuing the uncivilized principle of governments founded in conquest',[2] with the corollary that aristocrats have servants whom they 'govern by personal right',[3] and that aristocrats tend to degenerate, like Jews, as the result of their intermarrying.

The trouble with the first two of these arguments is that their picture of the aristocracy is feudal. No doubt there are still some English peers who resent the fact that their measures can be rejected by the House of Commons but this does not add to their political influence. Probably all the governments of which Paine knew, including America, were founded in conquest, but this would not be an objection to finding room for an aristocracy, if its existence were defensible on other grounds. Nor is there any evidence that Paine objected to the employment of domestic, as opposed to feudal, servants, so long as they chose their occupation freely and were not exploited. As for the degeneracy of either the aristocracy or the Jews towards the end of the eighteenth century, I do not know that they were any worse than their forebears. Later on the aristocracy, in England at least, was to gain strength by its readiness to incorporate new blood.

I am not saying that any of this invalidates Paine's principal objections to hereditary offices. On the contrary, I think that they are cogent. I have already remarked that as an out-and-out Republican Paine would have taken exception even to the mild form of monarchy that we still possess in England but if our snobbery is ineradicable, as it appears to be, I suppose that it might as well play upon the royal family as upon television personalities or pop-stars. So far as this goes, it does not seem to me to matter that our monarchy should be hereditary.

Whatever arguments there may be for or against hereditary offices, they can surely not be claimed as natural rights. But is there anything that can? I have already suggested that natural rights are fictions. At best, the invocation of them is a disguise for some moral judgement, which may very well be acceptable.

As we have seen, this is not Paine's view, though his position would not be weakened if it were. It might even be strengthened since he would then be required to give some tenable account of the provenance

[1] ibid., p. 83.
[2] ibid.
[3] ibid.

of civil rights, instead of making 'natural rights' do all the work. The following is a clear statement of his theory:

> Natural rights are those which appertain to man in right of his existence. Of this kind are all the intellectual rights, or rights of the mind, and also all those rights of acting as an individual for his own comfort and happiness, which are not injurious to the natural rights of others. – Civil rights are those which appertain to man in right of his being a member of society. Every civil right has for its foundation, some natural right pre-existing in the individual, but to the enjoyment of which his individual power is not, in all cases, sufficiently competent. Of this kind are all those which relate to security and protection.[1]

The question whether one has a right to one's own opinions is not so simple as it would at first appear. One is tempted to say that a man is free to think what he pleases, so long as the expression of his thoughts or the actions to which they lead him do not cause excessive injury to others. But should not the disposition to have such thoughts be in any way controlled? A child does not come into the world with a set of ready-made opinions. In a liberal society, he will be encouraged to think for himself, but his method of thinking and the conclusions which he reaches will be causally dependent, to a considerable extent, upon his upbringing and education. One may in fact strongly disapprove of both, but can one reasonably expect of those who train the child that they make no effort to induce him to believe what they think true or act in the ways that they think right? Unfortunately, the number of fanatics more than keeps pace with those who are ready to admit that they are fallible. It is not even universally the case, though undoubtedly it should be, that men are not caused to suffer through the mere suspicion of their entertaining thoughts, which they do not venture to express.

What if they do express them? The right of free speech is on a par with what Paine and Jefferson deem the natural right to the pursuit of happiness. In both cases, there is the proviso that some account must be taken of the effect upon others. In both cases also the answer is platitudinous. In view of the ruthlessness which many men and women display in their pursuit of happiness, there is a strong case for subjecting it to greater restrictions than apply to freedom of speech. This is not, however, to say that so far as freedom of speech goes there

[1] *Rights of Man*, p. 68.

should be no restrictions at all. I should indeed be happy to discover a cogent argument in favour of complete tolerance, but I am not able to do so. As to where the limits should be set, I have nothing more helpful to say than that it is only in very exceptional circumstances that they should be narrowed.

Paine's assertion that every civil right grows out of a natural right is rather surprising, since he has not included the acquisition and retention of property in his own list of natural rights though we shall see that he acquiesces in its inclusion in the French Declaration of them. Perhaps he meant it to be comprised in 'all those rights of acting as an individual for his own comfort and happiness, which are not injurious to the natural rights of others,' but this description is so vague and its range so extensive that there is no saying what civil rights might be represented as growing out of the 'natural right' to which it refers. There is also the problem that they would not be the same in all forms of society or at every stage of a society's development. This problem does, indeed, become less serious for Paine through his denial of the legitimacy of any government that does not satisfy his strict conditions for being genuinely representative; but even among the governments that do come up to his standards, the unavoidable differences in the societies which they govern will make for diversity in the measures which they would be best advised to take in promoting the happiness of their electors.

Without bothering, or perhaps being equipped, to delve into anthropology, Paine distinguishes successive stages in the emergence of government out of society. In his own words:

> They may be all comprehended under three heads. First, Superstition. Secondly, Power. Thirdly, The common interest of society, and the common rights of man.
>
> The first was a government of priestcraft, the second of conquerors, and the third of reason.[1]

At this point Paine appears to be caught in a contradiction. On the one hand, we have found him holding that society precedes any form of government; on the other, he now goes on to say that only governments of reason 'arise out' of society. There seem to me to be two ways in which the contradiction could be shown to be merely apparent. We might construe the expression 'arise out of' as implying only a

[1] ibid., p. 69.

legitimate process. Alternatively, we might assume that Paine regarded the social contract not as responsible for the formation of society out of 'the state of nature' but as the necessary condition for the emergence of any rational form of government. I favour the second option, both because the first seems rather the more strained, and also, irrationally, because the second diminishes Paine's commitment to a fiction.

Lest my choice should seem altogether biased, I shall argue that it has some slight textual support. Without mentioning Locke, Paine rejects Locke's theory of the social contract as being a contract between a sovereign, whether it be a single person or an assembly, and the persons who voluntarily put themselves under the sovereign's rule. The ground on which Paine rejects this theory is that

> it is putting the effect before the cause; for as man must have existed before governments existed, there necessarily was a time when governments did not exist, and consequently there could originally exist no governors to form such a compact with. The fact therefore must be, that the *individuals themselves*, each in his own personal and sovereign right, *entered into a compact with each other* to produce a government: and this is the only mode in which governments have a right to arise, and the only principle on which they have a right to exist.[1]

Paine's argument is fallacious, since Locke's theory is consistent with the parties' to the contract choosing a sovereign from among themselves, rather than agreeing to acknowledge a sovereign who already existed as such. Neither is it conclusive on the question at issue, since it does not explicitly reject Locke's view of the individuals who participate in the social contract as only thereby emerging from the state of nature. There are, however, three points that seem to me to tell in my favour. One is that Paine would have no good reason for distinguishing, as he firmly does, between society and government if he agreed with Hobbes and Locke that the same act brought them both into existence. Another is his referring to his version of the social contract in the conclusion of the passage which I have just quoted as the only mode and principle on which governments have a right to exist, as opposed to saying that it is the only way in which they do originate. The third is his asserting in the following paragraph that 'governments must have arisen, either *out* of the people, or *over* the people'.[2] In the

[1] *Rights of Man*, p. 70.
[2] ibid., p. 71.

second case, there need be no social contract. Yet it would not follow from this that the unfortunate people who were governed by priests and conquerors did not count as a society.

A fact which might be adduced against me is Paine's saying that 'a government is only the creature of a constitution',[1] which is antecedent to it; for plainly this need not be true of governments other than those of reason. It is, however, soon made clear that Paine has only governments of this third sort in mind, since he goes on to tease Burke by finding it doubtful whether there is an English Constitution, surely without intending to imply that there was no English government.

Paine then proceeds to list a series of items in the new Constitution of France to each of which he challenges Burke to find a satisfactory English equivalent.

The first is that whereas in England the qualifications for being a parliamentary elector were arbitrary and capricious, as indeed they very largely were in 1791, in France every man who pays a small tax is qualified. What is still surprising here is that Paine consents to there being any financial qualification at all. In fact he was soon to declare himself in favour of universal male suffrage. Unlike Mary Wollstonecraft, who also published a rebuttal of Burke's *Reflections*, Paine never went so far as to advocate votes for women.

The next item in which the French clearly had the advantage was the establishment of a ratio between the number of electors in a given constituency and the number of its parliamentary representatives. The extreme disproportion that obtained in England in this matter was mitigated, though not wholly removed, by the passage of the Reform Bill of 1832.

A more dubious item was the rule that the National Assembly should be elected every two years. While this is clearly preferable to a state of affairs in which the duration of a parliament is subject to no fixed rules at all, the shortness of its life would surely lead, among other disadvantages, to a surfeit of electioneering.

The next mark of superiority that Paine discovers in the French Constitution is a conjunction of its abolition of the game laws, leaving the farmer free to take any game that he finds on his land, and the rule 'That there shall be no monopolies of any kind – that all trade shall be free, and every man free to follow any occupation by which he can procure an honest livelihood, and in any place, town or city throughout the nation.'[2] About the game laws there need be no argument but I

[1] ibid.
[2] ibid., p. 74.

confess that it is not clear to me what Paine regarded as coming under the heading of monopolies. The only example he gives, apart from a further reference to electoral anomalies, is that of a 'chartered town'. Possibly he was referring to privileges which were relics of the mediaeval guilds. Later on he was to pronounce himself in favour of the trade unions, but he may not have envisaged the growth of their commitment to restrictive practices.

I can see no objection to the statement, quoted with approval by Paine, that 'the right of war and peace is in the nation', except that it is redundant. Obviously except in the case of civil war, which is not here in question, the decision to go to war or to make peace is always going to be taken by the government, so that the attribution of it to the nation is no more than a way of repeating the claim that the government, which conforms to the French Constitution, properly represents the nation.

There remains one item in Paine's summary of the French Constitution that seems to me controversial. It is that 'to preserve the national representation from being corrupt, no member of the National Assembly shall be an officer of the government, a place-man, or a pensioner'.[1] While I am willing to let the cases of place-men and pensioners, that is to say, persons paid for their covert services to the government, go by default, I am not convinced that the separation between the legislature and the executive should be so wide as this article of the Constitution makes it. Such a separation still exists in the United States, and the recent examples of the way in which it operates are not encouraging. In fact the difficulties which the members of the legislature encounter in finding out what the Chief Executive and his lieutenants are actually doing are not much of a safeguard against corruption. Even if there is less to be gained by bribing legislators, the greater opportunity afforded for bribing members of the executive, whose identity may not even be known, is likely to cause greater mischief and to bring the nation into greater disrepute.

After an historical excursion into the cause of the summoning of the Third Estate, leading to a description of the manner in which the National Assembly came to power, Paine turns to consider the Assembly's *Declaration of the Rights of Man and of Citizens.* The number of articles in the Declaration is seventeen but Paine remarks that fourteen of them do no more than elucidate or follow from the first three which comprehend the whole Declaration in general terms. As usual, the preamble to the Declaration acknowledges the rights which it enunciates

[1] *Rights of Man*, p. 76.

as 'natural, imprescriptible, and inalienable'. In this instance, they are also said to be sacred.

The three articles on which Paine takes the rest to depend run as follows:

I   Men are born, and always continue, free, and equal in respect of their rights. Civil distinctions, therefore, can be founded only on public utility.

II   The end of all political associations, is, the preservation of the natural and imprescriptible rights of man; and these rights are liberty, property, security, and resistance of oppression.

III   The nation is essentially the source of all sovereignty; nor can any INDIVIDUAL, or ANY BODY OF MEN, be entitled to any authority which is not expressly derived from it.[1]

In discussing these assertions I have little to add to what I have already written on the subject of the American Declaration of Independence. The only new problems that arise out of the first of them are those of divining what Paine understood by 'civil distinctions' and 'public utility'. In default of any elucidations to be found in the remainder of the French Declaration, I venture to take 'civil distinctions' as comprising not only differences in the amount and type of authority that is entrusted to different citizens, but also in the amount and type of property to which they are severally held to be legally entitled. Paine's Republicanism bore only on the forms of government; he was not an economic leveller. We shall see, in a moment, that he was very greatly concerned with the welfare of the poorer members of society, but he never thought it possible, or perhaps even desirable, to do away with all disparities in wealth.

So far as I know there is no evidence that Paine ever met Jeremy Bentham or that he had read Bentham's *An Introduction to the Principles of Morals and Legislation*, though it would have been possible for him to have done so, since Bentham's book was published in 1780. Nevertheless I think it reasonable to equate his concept of 'public utility' with Bentham's principle of utility, which is a summarization of his dictum: 'The right and proper end of government in every political community is the greatest happiness of all the individuals of which it is composed,

[1] ibid., p. 110.

say, in other words, the greatest happiness of the greatest number.'
There are well-known objections to this formula, including the
objection that it is impossible for anyone to estimate all the consequences of any given action. This is usually met by confining the
application of Bentham's principle to those consequences of his actions
that an agent can reasonably be expected to foresee.

Even when it is restricted in this way it may be objected that the
principle cannot be applied with anything approaching mathematical
exactitude. Nevertheless I do think it possible to attach at least a high
probability to the judgement that the general observance in some
society of a given set of rules will spread more happiness throughout the
society than the neglect of those rules or the substitution for them of
some other set; and this seems to me all that Bentham and Paine
require.

Bolder than Jefferson, the authors of the French Declaration, as we
have just seen, include property among man's natural rights, asserting
in their final article that no one ought to be deprived of his property
'except in cases of evident public necessity, legally ascertained, and on
condition of a previous just indemnity'.[1] Unfortunately, they do not
explain with what amount or kind of property man is naturally
endowed, or what he is permitted to do with it. For instance, it seems to
me quite probable that they would have allowed a natural right of
barter, but would not have extended it to usury. Yet they make no
attempt to justify or even trouble to draw any such distinction. The fact
is, as I have already argued, that one's right to possess and dispose of
property is a civil right, and what a political theorist calls a natural
right to property is no more than the distribution of property which is
endorsed by the political system of which he morally approves.

The question how the concept of liberty is to be interpreted is the
only one that is thoroughly elucidated in the declarations that follow
the first three. Political Liberty is said to consist in 'the power of doing
whatever does not injure another'. The trouble with this definition is
not only that there is no authoritative way of delimiting the bounds of
injury, but that people injure one another in ways that have nothing to
do with politics. This would apply, for example, to many family
quarrels and other social contexts in which one person hurts another's
feelings, or even does him physical injury in the course of some sporting
event, possibly without infringing the rules of the game. Not even the
most authoritarian regime could extend its mastery over all such

[1] *Rights of Man*, p. 112.

occurrences. Besides, the purpose of the definition was to extend the range of political liberty, not diminish it. Not but what the fifteenth declaration strikes an alarming note. 'Every community has a right to demand of all its agents, an account of their conduct.' Even bearing in mind that the word 'agents' here refers only to the minority of citizens who are entrusted by their fellows with some public office, one might think this an excessive encroachment of the State upon personal liberty. This objection might, however, be removed if one took the word 'conduct', as the authors of the declaration most probably intended, to refer only to the agents' performance of their official duties. Even so, admittedly with hindsight, one can perceive the seeds of the Reign of Terror being sown.

That 'the law ought to prohibit only actions hurtful to society'[1] is a principle that suffers, once again, from the difficulty of determining what is or is not 'hurtful to society'. There is, however, the point, to which I have already alluded, that it is easier to make a rough estimate of what is hurtful to a given society in general, than to measure the harm likely to be suffered by its members individually. There is also the difficulty, with which I have not yet dealt, that actions which are not directly hurtful to society, may be so indirectly. One is inclined to say that a man ought to be allowed, at least in private, to drink when and what and how much he pleases, and also to take whatever drugs he can obtain, if they give him satisfaction. On the other hand, there is abundant evidence that addiction to alcohol and certain sorts of drugs is not only a source of harm to the addict's family and friends but frequently conducive to crime, and surely it is the duty of any government to prevent crime if it can.

Let me say at once that we need to be wary of this last assertion. I admit that so far as political liberty is concerned, the position of the average citizen in this country compares favourably with that of the average member of an Eastern European or Latin American State. All the same I hold it to be true of England at the present time that the power of the police 'has increased, is increasing and ought to be diminished'. Consequently, I am opposed to any measure that gives the police the authority, which they are already prone to assume, to harass any citizen, of whatever colour, on the mere suspicion that he is likely to commit a criminal offence. I am equally chary of allowing them the right to search people's houses, except under strict legal conditions, and am unmoved by the rubbish that politicians talk about national

[1] ibid., p. 111.

security. Nevertheless the police must clearly be allotted some more useful function than those of controlling motor traffic, directing tourists to Madame Tussaud's and escorting elderly persons across the streets.

What does this amount to concretely? To say that the police should not engage in harassment is not to say that they should connive at the harassment of Asians by white hooligans, which there is evidence that they do. I believe also that they should be allowed to judge when an assembly, such as a protest march, is likely to provoke a riot, and then be given the authority to control it, and in extreme cases obtain legal sanction to prohibit it. I think that there is also a case for their being allowed to frustrate criminal conspiracy, though the evidence that it is going forward needs to be very strong.

As regards alcohol and drugs, I take the conventional view that the sale of alcohol should not be a criminal offence, whereas the sale of more noxious drugs, such as heroin, should be. To some extent this judgement may reflect my personal taste. Even in the case of drugs, I do not think that mere possession should be accounted criminal, unless it can be shown to be for the purpose of sale.

A great deal of this may sound platitudinous, but it does not follow that the questions at issue are easy to decide. Neither is there any easy answer to the question whether and in what ways the law should be used to protect a person from himself, even when his actions are not plainly injurious to others. Here the example of cigarette smoking is currently in point. Once more I take the conventional view that the sale of cigarettes should not be prohibited, but that the means adopted by their manufacturers to promote sales should not be unimpeded.

The other articles concerning law in the French Declaration appear to me obviously acceptable. I entirely agree that 'no man should be accused, arrested, or held in confinement, except in cases determined by the law, and according to the forms which it has prescribed'; that 'the law ought to impose no other penalties but such as are absolutely and evidently necessary: and no one ought to be punished, but in virtue of a law promulgated before the offence, and legally applied'; and finally that 'every man being presumed innocent till he has been convicted, whenever his detention becomes indispensable, all rigour to him, more than is necessary to secure his person, ought to be provided against by the law'.

Here too, however, there are problems. For instance, it is not clear that the second of the principles that I have just quoted is consistent with the Nuremberg trial of war criminals. I find this disturbing, though an attempt might be made to justify the Nuremberg proceedings on the ground that International Law was not at that time sufficiently developed for such principles to be applicable to it. If this sounds rather specious, one might assert more boldly that while Hobbes's version of the state of nature does not explain the origin of all forms of society, it did apply over a long period of time to the relationship between nations; and that the imposing of a legal pattern at Nuremberg on the vengeance taken upon men who had been proved to have been engaged in very evil deeds was an attempt on the part of the victorious nations to show that the state of nature in which they had mutually dwelt was a thing of the past; an attempt which I am sorry to say has not yet proved to be altogether successful.

The other problems to which I referred were that it is not at all obvious when a penalty is 'absolutely and evidently necessary' and that while there are cases in which the probability of a man's guilt and his contriving to avoid being brought to trial are such as to justify his detention before he has been convicted, it is difficult to determine where to draw the line or even enforce a consistent policy. I do not intend to embark upon a further discussion concerning the current deficiencies of this country's penal system. I claim only that they are not likely to be remedied by making a political slogan out of the need for the restoration of law and order.

Though there is no mention of a natural right to free speech in any of the three articles in which Paine takes all the others to be rooted, it is mentioned in two of the subsequent articles.[1] Thus article X runs:

No man ought to be molested on account of his opinions, not even on account of his *religious* opinions, provided his avowal of them does not disturb the public order established by the law.

And article XI:

The unrestrained communication of thoughts and opinions being one of the most precious rights of man, every citizen may speak, write, and publish freely, provided he is responsible for the abuse of this liberty in cases determined by the law.

I have already commented on the difficulty of deciding how far freedom of speech is diminished by such provisos and have nothing further to say which would help to resolve it.

[1] *Rights of Man*, pp. 111–12.

The third of Paine's three main articles can more easily pass without further comment. It reduces to a reaffirmation of the belief, which he shares with the authors of the French Declaration, that only a representative form of government is legitimate.

Following his exposition of the French *Declaration of the Rights of Man and of Citizens*, Paine reverts to his attack on Burke, which occupies the greater part of what he appropriately entitles a 'Miscellaneous Chapter'. He now accuses Burke of crediting the British government with hereditary wisdom and ridicules his political empiricism by saying, unfairly, that it means that the government is governed by no principle whatever, coming, however, closer to the facts when he goes on to equate it with arbitrary power. He reaffirms his contempt for William the Conqueror, describing him as 'the plunderer of the English nation' and on this occasion not merely as a bastard but as 'the son of a prostitute'.[1] In appearing to regard this as a disqualification for kingship he has allowed himself to overlook his objections to the notice taken of heredity.

That this is not a serious lapse is proved by the fact that the passage occurs in the course of a renewed onslaught on the theory and practice of hereditary succession in any form of government. This onslaught, constantly reinforced by forays against Burke, is conducted with relish at considerable length but it adds no further arguments to those that Paine has previously advanced.

Eventually, Paine professes to change the subject by concluding his chapter with 'a concise review of the state of parties and politics in England'. He does not, however, change it very much as the salient points in his concise review are that England does not possess a Constitution, that the popularity unprecedentedly enjoyed by the Hanoverian court in the period following the American Revolution was due to the nation's antipathy to the Coalition Parliament, that in the dispute between Fox and Pitt over the appointment of the Prince Regent, Pitt only appeared to take the parliamentary ground, but in fact took the hereditary ground in an even worse way than Fox, absorbing the rights of the nation into the unrepresentative House of Commons and making the nation itself into a cypher, and finally that England was bound to follow the lead of France in undertaking a constitutional reformation, if only because of the financial troubles which its government was already suffering as a result of its substitution of paper money for honest gold and silver coinage. In his distrust of

[1] *Rights of Man*, p. 118.

the employment of paper money, Paine is for once in agreement with Burke, but he will not allow that it presents the same danger to France, on the grounds that France, with a smaller debt than England, still has a greater quantity of gold and silver in circulation, that it has a much larger population to support the payment of taxes and that it possesses 'an extent of rich and fertile country above four times larger than England'. It is to be remembered that he was writing near the start of the Industrial Revolution before its development had enabled English manufacturers and merchants to enjoy the greater prosperity.

In the fairly short chapter with which Paine brings the first part of his book to its conclusion he equates the difference between government by election and representation and government by hereditary succession with that between reason and ignorance. Having begun by saying that these are the two modes of government that prevail in the world, he proceeds to criticize what he calls mixed governments, of which the government of England is presumably his chief example. His objections to a mixed government are not stated with his usual clarity or supported by his usual profusion of argument. I will, however, quote the paragraph in which they are summarized for what it is worth:

> When there is a part in a Government [in England, the Monarch] which can do no wrong, it implies that it does nothing; and is only the machine of another power, by whose advice and direction it acts. What is supposed to be the King in mixed Governments, is the Cabinet; and as the Cabinet is always a part of the Parliament, and the members justifying in one character what they advise and act in another, a mixed Government becomes a continual enigma; entailing upon a country, by the quantity of corruption necessary to solder the parts, the expense of supporting all the forms of Government at once, and finally resolving itself into a Government by committee; in which the advisers, the actors, the approvers, the justifiers, the persons responsible, and the persons not responsible, are the same persons.[1]

I have to say that it is not clear to me why a mixed government should be intrinsically more expensive than a representative government, though it might become so owing to the expense of maintaining a royal family and an aristocracy. Nor do I see why a single Assembly should be more liable to corruption than a government in which the

[1] ibid., p. 141.

executive is separated from the legislature. In fact, while the limitations on the English parliamentary electorate did foster corruption, American politicians, operating under a system which was closer to satisfying Paine's criteria, were notoriously more corrupt throughout the nineteenth century than members of the British House of Commons.

The only argument that Paine puts forward on this question is that in 'a well-constituted republic' where the representatives who govern it all have 'one and the same natural source', 'the parts are not foreigners to each other, like democracy, aristocracy, and monarchy' and will therefore be more disposed to reach political agreement without the influence of intrigue or bribery. He could indeed hardly have been expected to foresee how soon the leaders of the French Assembly would be destroying one another, though it might have occurred to him that emergence from the same natural source was not incompatible with murderous differences of principle.

Having fastened on monarchical governments the dubious charge that they favoured wars because they entailed an increase of taxes which added to their revenues, Paine attributes to Henri IV of France, no later than 1610, the proposal to create what amounted to a League of Nations, with delegates appointed to settle all disputes by arbitration. Paine not only hoped but came near to predicting that this proposal would be soon revived. In the light of the history of the past two centuries, his final paragraph makes sad reading:

From what we now see, nothing of reform in the political world ought to be held improbable. It is an age of Revolutions, in which everything may be looked for. The intrigue of Courts, by which the system of war is kept up, may provoke a confederation of Nations to abolish it: and an European Congress, to patronize the progress of free Government, and promote the civilization of Nations with each other, is an event nearer in probability, than once were the Revolutions and Alliance of France and America.[1]

[1] *Rights of Man*, pp. 146–7.

6

Rights of Man: Part Two

The second part of Paine's *Rights of Man* is, in my view, the most impressive of all his writings. The timing of its dedication to Lafayette was fortunate, since Lafayette, fearing to return to France after the defeat of the expedition against Prussia which he commanded in the spring of 1792, took refuge with the Austrians, who at once imprisoned him, possibly because he would not then disavow his republican principles. Since he was also opposed to the fanaticism of such men as Robespierre, it was unfortunate for him that he remained beyond the reach of their jurisdiction. He eventually came back to France in 1799.

So far was Paine from foreseeing Lafayette's defeat that he implied, in his dedication, that the Germans, following the example of France, might well embark on a revolution of their own. In the improbable event that a campaign were needed, he offered, but in fact made no practical attempt, to join Lafayette, in the hope that the campaign would 'terminate in the extinction of German despotism, and in establishing the freedom of all Germany'.[1] If there was a serious fault in Paine's political judgement, it lay in his consistently underestimating both the determination of monarchs and aristocrats to retain their privileges and the strength of the habit of obedience which secured them the loyalty even of those whom they oppressed. I think that he had been misled by the comparative ease[2] with which America had gained its independence, overlooking the fact that the loss of these colonies had not turned out to be a major disaster for England, and I think also that in the case of the French Revolution he mistook for a pure triumph of reason what was at least partly a stage in the transference of power to

[1] *Rights of Man*, pp. 151–2.
[2] Though he himself described the conflict as 'severe'. See below p. 110.

middle-class interests from a degenerate aristocracy. This is not to deny that the average Frenchman was better off after the final departure of the Bourbons than he had been under the old regime, but only to reiterate the point that even in representative governments, both liberty and rationality remain at risk.

In the preface to the second part of *Rights of Man*, Paine briefly rebukes Burke for failing even to try to answer the charges which Paine had brought against him in the first part. Burke had gone so far as to assert in his *Appeal from the New to the Old Whigs* (1791) that Paine's writings might be thought to deserve no other refutation than that of *criminal* justice, and Paine's reply was that in that case the jury should be 'a convention of the whole nation fairly elected'.[1] He had no doubt that the verdict of such a jury would be in his favour.

After an introduction which ends with the optimistic remark that 'Government founded on a *moral theory, on a system of universal peace, on the indefeasible hereditary Rights of Man*, is now revolving from west to east, by a stronger impulse than the government of the sword revolved from east to west',[2] Paine further emphasizes the distinction which we already found him drawing in *Common Sense*, between government and society, and while he agrees with the apostles of the social contract in so far as he locates the need for society in the fact that nature has made man's natural wants exceed his individual powers, with the result that 'no one man is capable, without the aid of society, of supplying his own wants',[3] he refuses to follow such theorists as Hobbes and Locke in representing society as the creature of government. Rather, he takes the view of Shaftesbury and Hume that nature 'has implanted in [man] a system of social affections, which, though not necessary to his existence, are essential to his happiness'.[4] He also agrees with them, at least implicitly, in discovering in these social affections the source of morality. This has the curious consequence that while he does not at all conceive of men as the out-and-out egoists that Hobbes takes them to be in the state of nature, he employs the term 'laws of nature' in the same moral sense that we have shown that Hobbes gave it in its application to society. He is thus enabled to say that 'All the great laws of society are laws of nature.'[5] Ideally, then, in his view, 'government is nothing more than a national association acting on the principles of society'.[6]

[1] *Rights of Man*, p. 157.
[2] ibid., pp. 161–2.
[3] ibid., p. 163.
[4] ibid.
[5] ibid., p. 165.
[6] ibid., p. 167.

This is not to imply that the ideal origin of government was its actual origin. Indeed, Paine almost immediately implies that it was not. 'Can we possibly suppose,' he asks,

> that if governments had originated in a right principle, and had not an interest in pursuing a wrong one, that the world could have been in the wretched and quarrelsome condition we have seen it? What inducement has the farmer, while following the plough, to lay aside his peaceful pursuit, and go to war with the farmer of another country? or what inducement has the manufacturer? What is dominion to them, or to any class of men in a nation? Does it add an acre to any man's estate, or raise its value? Are not conquest and defeat each of the same price, and taxes the never-failing consequence? – Though this reasoning may be good to a nation, it is not so to a government. War is the Faro table of governments, and nations the dupes of the games.[1]

It is strange that it did not occur to Paine, writing even at that date, that it might be in the interest of manufacturers to promote wars, in order to obtain raw materials more cheaply, or acquire, even to the point of monopolizing, new markets for their goods. After all, the granting of a monopoly to the East India Company which was at least a pretext for the Boston Tea Party may have been a source of wealth to some aristocratic shareholders but the Company was not the personal property of George III. We have already remarked that Paine's conception of monarchy tended to be feudal, and he persisted in locating the cause of wars exclusively in the pride and avarice of monarchs and of the aristocrats who mingled with them.

This leads him to renew his attack on hereditary systems of government. The pages that follow contain some of his most pungent writing, but in effect they do no more than reiterate points which he has already made: that hereditary government has no basis in natural right, and is consequently tyrannical by nature; that even if a king should turn out to be good and wise, there is no guarantee that the same will be true of his successor; that it may put power, at least nominally, into the hands of an idiot or a dotard, that it often gives rise to civil as well as foreign wars, and in short that it is in every way inferior to the representative system which 'takes society and civilization for its basis; nature, reason, and experience, for its guide'.[2]

[1] ibid., p. 169
[2] ibid., p. 175.

Very often Paine writes as if there were only two systems of government, the hereditary and the representative. In one passage, as we have seen, he mentions three, the governments of priestcraft, conquerors, and reason; apparently placing them in historical order and identifying reason with representation and conquerors with monarchs. Sometimes he remembers that some monarchies have been elective, and in the second part of *Rights of Man*, he sharply dissents from the opinion of his friend, the Abbé Sieyès, that while both forms of monarchy are bad, the elective is worse.[1] Shortly afterwards, continuing to ignore the government of priestcraft, he nevertheless increases the total number of forms of government to four, 'the democratical, the aristocratical, the monarchical, and what is now called the representative'.[2] He explains that he does not include republicanism among them, for what is indeed the good reason, that republicanism is not a particular form of government but being 'wholly characteristical of the purport, matter, or object for which government ought to be instituted, and on which it is to be employed',[3] that is, the public good, it signifies the rejection of monarchy. He goes on to question the right of Poland, 'an hereditary aristocracy, with what is called an elective monarchy', and of Holland, 'which is chiefly aristocratical, with an hereditary stadtholdership', to style themselves republics, thereby leaving himself free to conclude that 'the government of America, which is wholly on the system of representation, is the only real republic in character and in practice, that now exists'.[4] One must bear in mind that both parts of *Rights of Man* were written before the deposition of Louis XVI.

It could be argued that Paine's four types of government strictly amounted once again to three, since the representative type is depicted by him as an extension of the democratical. He does not invariably claim that the democratic type was historically prior to all the others, and would indeed have been mistaken if he did. Historical priority must surely be granted to associations, the government of which, while one may not choose to call it monarchic, was at least patriarchal or possibly matriarchal. There is, however, one passage in which he allows himself to assert that departures from democracy, other than its development into representative government, were not only a moral and political but also an historical decline.

[1] *Rights of Man*, p. 173.
[2] ibid., p. 178.
[3] ibid.
[4] ibid.

The passage occurs after Paine has said of the ancient Athenians that 'We see more to admire, and less to condemn, in that great, extraordinary people, than in any thing which history affords.'[1] As all too often happens, when the civilization of fifth- and fourth-century Athens is singled out for special praise, Paine overlooks the very large part played by slavery in its economy.

After commending the Athenians, Paine continues:

Representation was a thing unknown in the ancient democracies. In those the mass of people met and enacted laws (grammatically speaking) in the first person. Simple democracy was no other than the common-hall of the ancients. It signifies the *form*, as well as the public principle of the government. As these democracies increased in population, and the territory extended, the simple democratical form became unwieldy and impracticable; and as the system of representation was not known, the consequence was, they either degenerated convulsively into monarchies, or became absorbed into such as then existed. Had the system of representation been then understood, as it now is, there is no reason to believe that those forms of government, now called monarchical or aristocratical, would ever have taken place.[2]

I believe that I am right here in detecting a note of regret. If only it were feasible, democracy, a state of affairs in which every citizen, or at least every male citizen, had the right to a voice in every political decision, would be the best of all forms of government. This was, more obviously, the opinion of Rousseau, who wished all political societies to be small enough to allow for democratic government in this sense. But then Rousseau deplored the growth of population and the luxury which resulted from the ensuing increase of trade, agreeing on this point only with the far from democratic Plato, but no longer carrying Paine with him. My understanding of Paine is that he welcomed material prosperity so long as it did not lead to excessive disparities of wealth or power. The superiority of representative government consisted in its preserving as much of primitive democracy as was consistent with the provision of what he regarded as a 'genteel sufficiency' for every member of the nation under review.

When we consider the actual record of parliamentary government in this country during the twentieth century, when owing to the grant of

[1] ibid., p. 177.
[2] ibid.

votes to women the proportion of adult electors has been higher than Paine himself foresaw, we can hardly fail to be thankful, if we have any sympathy for him, that he was denied the power of precognition: witness the following paragraph:

> In the representative system, the reason for everything must publicly appear. Every man is a proprietor in government, and considers it a necessary part of his business to understand. It concerns his interest, because it affects his property. He examines the cost, and compares it with the advantages; and above all, he does not adopt the slavish custom of following what in other governments are called LEADERS.[1]

Was it naïve of Paine not to have foreseen the development of party politics? I do not think so, seeing that he wrote at a time when it had not yet come to birth in the United States, and when it existed in England only in an unstable condition, before the main body of the people's representatives came to be paid for doing little more than play the game of 'follow my leader'. If Paine is to be convicted of naïveté, the fault lay rather in his assuming that every elector would have sufficient property to be concerned with the way that it was being affected by the government's actions. One might object that this assumption has been vindicated by the resurgence of Conservatism in the form in which Mrs Thatcher has cast it, but against this it should again be remarked that her party has been maintained in power at the best by little more than two fifths of the votes cast in the elections which it has won. It is also possible to argue that, however much Paine may have wanted to abolish any form of property qualification for those entitled to vote, he could not have been expected to foresee that this would actually come about.

Having restated his defence of representative government, Paine returned to the topic of constitutions. He was one who did not mind reiterating points which he considered important, and he did attach great importance to the matter of constitutions, if only because he believed that 'government without a constitution, is power without a right'.[2] Believing the Constitution of the United States to be the only existing model that deserved the name, he proceeds to take his readers step by step through the process of its formation, relating how Pennsylvania constructed its Assembly with its own Constitution,

---

[1] *Rights of Man*, p. 184.
[2] ibid., p. 185.

followed in their respective fashions by the other States, how the States agreed to allow Congress, which had previously had only the authority to issue recommendations, to draw up an Act of confederation, how this Act was deemed to confer too much power on the several States and too little on the federal government, how this defect was remedied at a continental convention held at Philadelphia in May 1787, and how the convention promulgated a Constitution, which needed to be ratified by each State, a process which took two years, with the final result that George Washington, who had been elected to preside over the convention, was again elected in 1789 to become the first President of the United States.

Paine then turned his attention to England, which in his view lacked a Constitution. He reproached Dr Johnson for failing to understand the difference between constitutions and governments and therefore being content with a government which controlled, instead of being controlled by, the nation. He then deplored the history of England from William the Conqueror to William III, saying of Magna Carta that it 'was no more than compelling the government to renounce a part of its assumptions'[1] and of William III's Bill of Rights that it was 'but a bargain, which the parts of the government made with each other to divide powers, profits, and privileges'.[2] According to Paine, the consequence of this bargain and 'the corruption introduced at the Hanover succession, by the agency of Walpole'[3] had been the putting into operation of 'the most productive machine of taxation that was ever invented'.[4]

With an eye on Burke, whom he had finally but this time very briefly denounced for rejecting the view that governments are founded on the Rights of Man, and after making the feeble joke that since Burke could hardly have supposed that government was founded on no rights at all, he must have held it to be founded on the rights of beasts, Paine characterizes the government of England as government by precedent, with the animadversion that 'Government by precedent, without any regard to the principle of the precedent, is one of the vilest systems that can be set up.'[5] Paine was too honest not to allude to the improvements 'in agriculture, useful arts, manufactures, and commerce'[6] that were currently being made in England, but he argued that so far from being

[1] ibid., p. 192.
[2] ibid., p. 193.
[3] ibid.
[4] ibid., p. 194.
[5] ibid., p. 196.
[6] ibid., p. 197.

due to the policies of the English government, they took place in opposition to them.

Concluding that no further proof is needed to show that if governments are to serve the interest of a nation, they need the backing of a Constitution, Paine proceeds to consider what that Constitution should be. As one would expect, his proposals are mainly in accordance with the American Constitution, but not entirely so. There are at least two important points of difference.

The first of them concerns the division of government. Under the influence of Montesquieu and Locke, the Americans had provided for a threefold separation of power, the legislature, the executive and the judiciary. Paine finds himself able to perceive no more than two divisions of power, 'namely, that of legislating or enacting laws, and that of executing or administering them'.[1] This limitation of his vision results from his identifying the executive power with the judicial. He argues that it is the judicial power which causes laws to be executed and that to which every individual appeals when he considers that he has been unjustly treated.

Here it seems clear to me that Paine is wrong, and that not merely on a point of terminology. For one thing, he overlooks the need for a civil service, perhaps not to advise the legislators, since his assumption that the interests of the legislators could not fail to coincide with those of the persons whom they represented would have led him to the dubious conclusion that they had no need of any such advice, but at least to undertake the practical task of administering the measures which the legislators have enacted. More importantly, Paine also fails to perceive the need for an independent judiciary to keep watch on the legislature itself. He takes it for granted both that the elements of a well ordered Constitution will be so clearly defined that there can never be any honest doubt about their interpretation and that the representatives of the nation will never assent to laws that contravene the Constitution. Unfortunately, both these assumptions are false.

The fact that these assumptions are false supplies the justification for the institution of the Supreme Court in the United States. Its members having originally consisted of a Chief Justice and five Associate Justices at its inauguration in 1789, the number of Associate Justices was increased, after several variations, to eight in 1869, at which point it has remained. Since all of them, including the Chief Justice, are appointed by the President, provided that his choice is

[1] *Rights of Man*, p. 198.

endorsed by the Senate, their independence is threatened by the executive, especially when the political temper of the majority of the Senators agrees with that of the President, which is, perhaps fortunately, by no means always the case. In theory the President appoints the judges whom he believes to be the best-qualified in terms of their ability, irrespective of their political opinions, but in practice he has not always avoided the attempt to make appointments which appear to be primarily political. As late as the 1930s this was considered shocking and an electoral issue was made of what was described as Franklin Roosevelt's endeavour to 'pack' the Supreme Court.

The difficulty which Roosevelt faced was that the judges appointed to the Supreme Court by his conservative predecessors were preventing the enactment of portions of his 'New Deal', on constitutional grounds. He proposed to overcome this nuisance by increasing the number of the Associate Justices, and appointing persons of a more liberal outlook to these new posts. The revulsion against such an opportunistic constitutional change was so strong that Roosevelt allowed his proposal to drop.[1] Since he remained in the Presidency for over twelve years, the operation of natural causes enabled him, by making suitable substitutions, to alter the balance of the Supreme Court in his favour. Even so, his appointments were less blatantly political than those of President Reagan, whose behaviour in this respect has aroused some resentment, little surprise, and, recently, opposition.

It should, however, be added that such appointments do not always have what looked like being their intended effect. I believe that Chief Justice Earl Warren, appointed by President Eisenhower, proved unexpectedly liberal, whereas Associate Justice Felix Frankfurter, a friend and adviser of Franklin Roosevelt with a distinguished liberal record, delivered opinions which allied him with his more conservative colleagues. The reason for this, however, in his case was not so much, if at all, that he had changed his political opinions, as that he believed that the Judiciary should not encroach upon the Legislature except when the reform was plainly in accordance with public opinion. Others have maintained that it was the duty of the Justices to interpret the original Constitution and the Articles which have since been added to it, in accordance with what might most reasonably be presumed to have been the intentions of those who framed them, rather than venture on 'constructive' interpretations which, being in accordance with the moral sentiments of at least a majority of the members of the Court,

---

[1] I owe thanks to Professor Ronald Dworkin for this information.

would have the effect of redressing injustices which were not explicitly at variance with the Constitution. If these injustices were so flagrant as to offend the consciences of the members of Congress, it was their duty to enact the legislation that would bring them to an end. In certain cases this might mean making a further amendment to the Constitution. So far, twenty-six Articles have been added to the original seven, ten of them as early as 1791.

How far the Supreme Court should indulge in what amounts to legislation is a much debated question into which I cannot enter here. The practice of Judicial Review, as it is called, has been in operation ever since Chief Justice John Marshall in 1803 emphasised the judicial supremacy of the court over James Madison, at that time Secretary of State. The problem is how far it should extend. On the one hand, we have the opinion of President Woodrow Wilson that the Supreme Court resembles a constitutional convention in continuous session; on the other, the view which, on one ground or another, reduces the subservience of the Legislature to the Supreme Court. For the most part, it is the liberal members of the Court who take what I have called the constructive view of its powers, the conservatives who are more narrowly legalistic. On political grounds, my sympathies lie with the liberals. On either view, I think that the Supreme Court compares favourably with the English courts of appeal, whose power to redress miscarriages of justice appears to me excessively restricted.

The second main point on which Paine's proposals differed from the actual Constitution of the United States lay in his advocacy of a single legislative 'house'. He has three arguments against the addition of a second house, none of them at all powerful. The first is that there is an inconsistency in one house's coming to a final vote on any matter, while the fact that the other house has still to come to its decision entails that the matter is not settled. The simple answer to this is that if the measure requires the assent of both houses, then the vote of the first house is not final, in the sense that it decides the issue. It may be given the opportunity to vote again or it may not. In neither case is there any inconsistency.

Paine's second argument is even more feeble. It is that if each house votes as a separate body it may happen that the minority governs the majority, which is again inconsistent. The first answer to this is that whatever other objections there be to this outcome, inconsistency is not among them. Secondly there is no reason *a priori* why the members of the second chamber should not outnumber those of the first. For all I know, if you count all the backwoodsmen there are more members of the British House of Lords than there are of the House of Commons. What does it matter? But let us take the example which Paine presumably had in mind, that of the United States Senate whose members have always been outnumbered by those of the House of Representatives. From the mere fact of there being the two houses it does not follow that, in cases of disagreement, the Senate is bound to prevail. And even if there were cases in which it did prevail, why should it not be right? After all, the members of the Supreme Court, whose decisions have been overridden by constitutional amendments on only four occasions between 1793 and 1970, are fewer still.

Paine's third argument is that it is inconsistent that two houses should arbitrarily check or control each other 'because it cannot be proved, on the principles of just representation, that either should be wiser or better than the other'.[1] Here the first remark to be made is that the use of the word 'arbitrarily' is merely forensic. There is no reason why the checking should not be carefully carried out or that there should not be a system of control. I think that the system at which we have arrived in England, where the House of Lords can delay measures and propose amendments but the final decision is taken by a majority in the House of Commons, is reasonably satisfactory, or rather, that it would be if the members of the House of Commons were more fairly chosen. This is not to say that it could not be improved. For instance, with regard to the House of Lords, even if hereditary peerages were abolished, and in spite of the general superiority of its debates to those that take place in the House of Commons, I should not wish to claim that every life peer who is currently appointed is either good or wise.

The only objection that Paine considers to there being a single house is that it may arrive at its decisions too hastily. To obviate this, he proposes that it be divided by lot into two or three parts, presumably equal in number, that each section debate every proposed Bill successively, so that they are informed of one another's opinions, and that they then reassemble for a final debate and this time take a vote. Except for the equality in number, which Paine does not actually specify, this seems to me not to differ in any essential way from there being separate houses. The drawing of lots is of no consequence, especially if the United States is setting the standard of comparison, as only those who have already been elected as representatives will be eligible to draw them.

Paine's final suggestion is that one third of the representation of each

[1] Paine, *Rights of Man*, p. 200.

'county' should retire every year, and 'the number be replaced by new elections'.[1] It seems to be implied, though not explicitly stated, that a retiring member is not eligible for re-election. There is also to be a general election every three years. This is not fundamentally different from the system of rotation that still prevails in the United States, though, as I said earlier, the shortness of tenure which Paine advocates implies what I at least should regard as a surfeit of electioneering.

I come now to what, apart from an appendix in which he virtually accuses Pitt of delaying the publication of the book in order to purloin one or two of its proposals for reducing taxation, is the final and most remarkable chapter of the second volume of Paine's *Rights of Man*. Its full title is 'Ways and Means of improving the condition of Europe, interspersed with Miscellaneous Observations'. Much of it is difficult reading, since it is crammed with financial statistics, in appraising which we have to bear in mind that the purchasing power of £1 in 1791 was equivalent to that of £40 today. It is worth mentioning that this vast discrepancy has developed only in the last fifty years. As late as 1939, according to the same method of calculation, the equivalent figure was no larger than £1.39.[2] What makes Paine's chapter remarkable is its advocacy of what we know as the Welfare State, not in every way anticipating but in some ways outdoing the reforms which were carried out in Britain by the Liberal government of 1906 and the Labour government of 1945.

Almost at the start of the chapter Paine makes a strong commitment to utilitarianism: 'Whatever the form or constitution of government may be, it ought to have no other object than the *general* happiness.'[3] It does not appear to have occurred to him, here or elsewhere, that there could be conflict between utilitarianism and a theory of natural rights. In this chapter, as we shall see, the notion of right is employed rather to direct the utilitarianism, since it is the unfairness with which the English government of the time treated the poorest members of the nation that Paine was mainly concerned to remedy.

The first way in which the general happiness not only of the people of England, but of those of other nations, could and should, in Paine's view, be increased is by the promotion of commerce. In spite of the record of the East India Company, he does not take the Leninist view that, by fostering imperialism, capitalism leads to war. On the contrary he argues that 'the expense of maintaining dominion more than

---

[1] *Rights of Man*, p. 201.
[2] I owe this information to Professor Amartya Sen, to whom I express my thanks.
[3] *Rights of Man*, p. 210.

absorbs the profits of any trade'.[1] I am not at all sure that Paine is wrong upon this point, especially as he admits that the profits arising out of foreign dominion may benefit some individuals, while the enterprise is a loss to the nation as a whole. Unfortunately, politicians are not always rational and the motives for imperialism, let alone war, are seldom purely economic. Where Paine was surely right is in his assertion that 'the uncivilised state of European governments is injurious to commerce'[2] for the simple reason that 'when the ability in any nation to buy is destroyed, it equally involves the seller'.[3] This was essentially the point on which Keynes based his denunciation of the Treaty of Versailles. And in fact, after both the Great Wars of this century, the losers had to be assisted to recover their prosperity; in the present condition of England it may now seem to us, who lack a larger vision, all too effectively.

After his eulogy of commerce Paine turns to the question of English taxation. He remarks that before the arrival of the Hanoverians taxes on land slightly exceeded taxes on consumption, but that the balance has since been greatly altered, to the disadvantage of the poor industrial and agricultural workers. He gives the telling example of the tax on beer, which was not paid by the aristocracy who brewed their own. He claims that with its proportion of the taxes on malt and hops it alone exceeds the whole of the land-tax.

Paine seldom misses an opportunity to denounce the landed aristocracy, especially if it also enables him to ridicule Burke. 'Why then,' he asks,

> does Mr Burke talk of his house of peers, as the pillar of the landed interest? Were that pillar to sink into the earth, the same landed property would continue, and the same ploughing, sowing, and reaping would go on. The aristocracy are not the farmers who work the land, and raise the produce, but are the mere consumers of the rent; and when compared with the active world are the drones, a seraglio of males, who neither collect the honey nor form the hive, but exist only for lazy enjoyment.[4]

While I have nothing against lazy enjoyment as such, I find this a powerful argument. It becomes ever stronger when one considers the

---

[1] ibid., p. 216.
[2] ibid., p. 213.
[3] ibid.
[4] ibid., p. 227.

incomes that landed proprietors have drawn from their ownership of mineral rights and every form of urban development upon their territory. They have, indeed, lost their political power, though it is debatable whether they used it worse than the Conservatives who have replaced them. Death duties have diminished much of their wealth but the richest remain very rich indeed. The argument that we need an aristocracy, or at any rate men of outstanding wealth, for the patronage of arts and letters was valid in the Renaissance and continued to be plausible as late as the eighteenth century, but with the proliferation of public libraries and museums on the one hand, and on the other the growing taste of the wealthy for conspicuous consumption and the slaughtering of animals, its force is much diminished, in spite of the philistinism of our present government. In fairness, I think I ought to add that this is not to deny that there are cultural grounds for the survival and indeed the further development of a meritocratic system of education.

Paine, as we know, was not an aristocrat either by birth or by adoption. It might, therefore, be suspected that in seeking to deprive them of their privileges, he was not disinterested. He makes a point of denying this in one of his most frequently quoted phrases:

Independence is my happiness, and I view things as they are, without regard to place or person; my country is the world, and my religion is to do good.[1]

Having proclaimed his own genuine lack of pecuniary interest, Paine plunges into the details of English taxation. He asserts that whereas the amounts of taxes steadily declined from the £400,000 levied annually by William the Conqueror to £100,000 in 1466, it had subsequently risen to £500,000 in 1566, £1,800,000 in 1666 and £17,000,000 in 1791. The only explanation that he gives for this startling increase, especially in the preceding century and a quarter, is 'extravagance, corruption, and intrigue', besides the engagement in foreign wars.

Of the £17,000,000 currently raised in taxes, Paine estimates that nine millions go to pay the interest on the national debt, leaving eight millions to defray the current expenses of each year. It is by raiding these eight millions, or rather the seven millions that remain after he has rather surprisingly allowed for the annual expenditure of a million on the army and navy, that he achieves his economies.

[1] *Rights of Man*, p. 228.

Paine's first argument is that no more than five hundred thousand pounds will be needed to defray the expenses of government. His House of Representatives will consist of three hundred members who for attending six months in a year, on average, will be paid a total of £75,000. The remainder of the money will go to 1,773 officials, with a salary range of £10,000 to £75 a year, the £10,000 going to just three of them and seven hundred of them getting the £75. The remaining salaries are strung out in between, but only seventy-three persons in all are allocated £1,000 a year or more. The comparative modesty of most of the salaries is justified by the expectation that there will not be very much work for either the representatives or the officials to do. Paine rather inconsistently remarks that, as things are, the Chiefs in several offices do little more than occasionally sign their names, the work being done by under-clerks. Presumably in his new order rates of pay will exhibit a fairer correspondence to labour and responsibility. Revenue officers do not figure in his estimates because they are to be paid out of the revenues which they collect. This would appear to be a dangerous proposal, even with Paine's proviso that their pay should be considerably increased, but no doubt he envisaged that some watch would be kept upon them.

It would be tedious to enumerate all the statistics which Paine provides in great detail. It should be sufficient to say that he budgets for a population of seven million, of whom one fifth will be so poor as to be in need of support, that he assumes that out of these poor persons one hundred and forty thousand will have attained the age of fifty or sixty, at which age they are to receive pensions, the sixty-year-olds at a higher rate, and that there will be 630,000 children under fourteen years of age, they being not the only ones who will need financial assistance for their education. The principal means by which he would raise the money for the proposals which follow would be, in his own words:

to abolish the poor rates entirely, and in lieu thereof, to make a remission of taxes to the poor of double the amount of the present poor-rates, viz. four millions annually out of the surplus taxes. By this measure, the poor will be benefited two millions, and the housekeepers two millions. This alone would be equal to a reduction of one hundred and twenty millions of the national debt, and consequently equal to the whole expense of the American war.[1]

[1] ibid., p. 240.

In addition to doing away with the poor-rates, Paine also proposes only to abolish the tax on houses and windows, which 'falls heavy on the middling class of people',[1] and the commutation tax. Even, therefore, allowing for the economies that he thinks that he can effect, he is aware that he will need much more money to carry out all his intended reforms. His solution is to introduce what we now call a graduated income tax, proceeding from 3d per pound on incomes up to £500 a year, 6d per pound on incomes from £500 to £1,000, rising by increments of 3d up to the second and third thousand, sixpence to the fourth and fifth, and thereafter by a shilling per pound on each additional thousand up to the limit of £23,000, on the last £1,000 of which the plutocrat will be paying 100 per cent. Thus, according to Paine's calculations, the most that anyone will be able to keep out of his annual income, however great it may be, will be £12,370, that is, nearly half a million pounds in today's purchasing power. It may be remarked that this is more than would be allotted to the best-paid civil servants. At the other end of the scale a man earning £50 a year would pay only twelve shillings and sixpence in tax and a man with an income of £1,000 a year would retain £979 of it. If one keeps bearing in mind that these figures have to be multiplied by forty to reach today's equivalents, Paine's tax can hardly be considered punitive, even for the possessors of great wealth.

We come at last to his proposals for reform. I list them in his own words.

Provision for two hundred and fifty-two thousand poor families.

Education for one million and thirty thousand children.

Comfortable provision for one hundred and forty thousand aged persons.

Donation of twenty shillings each for fifty thousand births.

Donation of twenty shillings each for twenty thousand marriages.

Allowance of twenty thousand pounds for the funeral expenses of persons travelling for work, and dying at a distance from their friends.

Employment, at all times, for the casual poor in the cities of London and Westminster.[2]

[1] *Rights of Man*, p. 250.
[2] ibid., pp. 247–8.

The last measure was to be effected by appropriating, or erecting, two large buildings in each of which there would be 'as many kinds of employment as could be contrived' for six thousand persons. Any person who presented himself would be allowed into them, without any questions being asked. On condition that he worked, he would receive 'wholesome food, and a warm lodging, at least as good as a barrack'. He could come as often and stay as long as he chose and would receive, on going away, some portion of what his work had been worth. There is no suggestion that persons who do not care to work should be forced to enter these places, but no other provision is made for them, beyond what accrues to the members of all poor families. No provision appears to be made, either, for poor bachelors and spinsters who have ceased to be children and not yet attained the age of fifty, but this is most probably a textual oversight.

Paine's notion of a comfortable provision appears a little austere since he reckons to pay old age pensions of only £6 a year to persons in their fifties and £10 to those who have reached or passed the age of sixty. Presumably an assumption that many of those in their fifties will still be working accounts for the difference, which we have seen that he was later to abolish in *Agrarian Justice* where he proposed that everyone, on attaining the age of fifty, should receive an annual pension of £10. Perhaps, rather than question the adequacy of these sums, we should admire Paine for his thinking at that date that it was a matter of right and not just charity that elderly persons should receive any pension at all.

At this point, we should recall that in *Agrarian Justice*, published in 1797, Paine proposed that a single payment of £15 be made to every person on his or her reaching the age of twenty-one.

Foreseeing an alliance between England and France, Paine believed that fleets and armies would 'in great measure, become useless'.[1] Nevertheless, as we have seen, he makes financial provision for a military establishment. Since this will be rather smaller than the existing establishment, and since Paine also typically considers that soldiers are underpaid, he adds the following proposals to his programme:

Allowance of three shillings a week for life to fifteen thousand disbanded soldiers and a proportionable allowance to the officers of the disbanded corps.

Increase of pay to the remaining soldiers of £19,500 annually.

The same allowance to the disbanded navy, and the same increase of pay, as to the army.[2]

[1] ibid., p. 249.
[2] ibid., p. 258.

A surprising omission from this programme, especially in view of Paine's consistent hostility to the landed aristocracy, is that of death duties. The explanation lay in his belief that his schemes of progressive taxation on income would have the effect of destroying primogeniture, without the pressure of death duties. He argued that a man with an estate yielding £23,000 a year, faced with the alternative of bequeathing the estate to a single person, who would be paying an annual tax of £10,360 on the income from it, and dividing the estate into five parts of £4,000 each and one of £3,000, in which case the small amount of tax paid by each inheritor would entail that the tax on the whole income of the estate amounted to no more than 5 per cent, would be bound to opt for the second alternative, especially as it would also give him the satisfaction of providing for his younger offspring. In terms of finance and even of benevolence, this is a good argument, but Paine again underestimates the complexity of people's motives. A wealthy landowner may take pride in his splendid estate, apart from the wealth and influence which he derives from it, and may think it his duty to hand it on intact, whatever his personal feelings about his heir. Not all parents care for all their children equally, some do not care for them at all. There is also the difference in the children's abilities and characters to be considered. Some may stand in greater need than others of parental help. It may have been considerations of this sort that later induced Paine in his *Agrarian Justice* to advocate the imposition of death duties amounting, in general, to 10 per cent of every estate.

Two obvious reforms to which Paine refers in passing, without introducing them into his calculations, are the abolition of the laws governing workmen's wages, leaving them free to make their own bargains, and at least a reduction of the vast disparity in the incomes paid to the superior and the inferior clergy. At this point, Paine shows no hostility even to the Christian religion in any of its diverse forms. 'Every religion,' he writes, 'is good that teaches man to be good; and I know of none that instructs him to be bad.'[1]

In spite of its large contribution to the nation's annual expenditure, Paine has very little to say about the national debt. He does not propose that the interest on it be reduced, but only that it should be subjected to a mild progressive tax. His suggestion is that the stockholders pay a halfpenny in the pound in the first year, a penny in the second and so increasingly, according to a ratio and up to a limit which he does not mention, stipulating only that it always be less than any other tax upon property.

[1] *Rights of Man*, p. 260.

This brings me to the end of Paine's blueprint for what I have felt justified in calling his Welfare State. Its main difference from the package introduced in 1945 is the absence of a scheme of National Health Service. I suggest that the reason for this is that Paine's principal aim was to abolish poverty. He may, therefore, have assumed that once this was achieved, there would be no need to make special provision for health. His measures would ensure that those who needed medical attention would be able to pay for it.

It is widely assumed that the concept of the Welfare State has been discredited. I do not share this view. Without entering into the variegated reasons for the decline of the British Labour Party, and their intertwining with the shift in the character of our economy, I believe that a second Industrial Revolution can be brought about without the callousness and the consequent degree of human suffering that marked the first. This is a point on which we can take a lesson from Japan, though I hope that we can achieve approximately the same result, without assuming the intense collective spirit which is not the most attractive feature of the Japanese way of life. The fundamental issue is whether in pursuit of wealth and power we are ready to let the weakest go to the wall. My contention is that this is not a defensible option, whether we are utilitarians, or take our stand on a moral conception of human rights or, as in my own case, oscillate between the two. It is not consistent with any political theory that associates politics with morality, unless it be the morality of Thrasymachus. If you take the view, attributed to him by Plato, that what passes for morality is nothing but the interests of the stronger, then so long as the rich grow richer, you will not trouble yourself about the poor. We hear much, at the present time, of the failure of Britain to keep pace with other Western countries in economic growth. It is supposed to justify the retention of a government which fosters and relies on an appeal to greed. But the standard of living of the average Englishman is higher than it has ever been in the past, and far higher than that of the vast majority of the world's population. Why should it matter to us that the citizens of a few other countries live, on an average, even more luxuriously? The question that we should be asking is whether we are not purchasing the standard of living that perhaps a majority of us do actually enjoy at too high a cost to the large numbers, even of our own countrymen, who are less fortunate than ourselves.

We started with Paine as a champion of what I continue to regard as the dubious concept of natural rights. Later he proclaimed himself a utilitarian. In the chapter that we have been examining he gives priority to the succouring of the poorest members of society. Though Paine himself does not draw this conclusion, it can be seen that such a policy might go counter to utilitarianism in cases where a highly unequal distribution of benefits caused an amount of satisfaction to those who profited by it which exceeded the misery caused to those who suffered from it. In such circumstances, at least so long as the contest was at all close, I should opt for Paine's latest policy on moral grounds. In itself it is not sufficient to sustain a comprehensive theory of justice but I think that it supplies a condition which any acceptable theory of justice should be required to satisfy.

To defend the conception of the Welfare State, as I have tried to do, is not quite to vindicate Thomas Paine, since he believed that its existence was imminent. Moreover his vision of it was more utopian than anything that ever has, or, I am afraid, is ever likely to, come into effect. I quote two paragraphs which illustrate these points.

> When it shall be said in any country in the world, my poor are happy; neither ignorance nor distress is to be found among them; my jails are empty of prisoners, my streets of beggars; the aged are not in want, the taxes are not oppressive; the rational world is my friend, because I am the friend of its happiness: when these things can be said, then may that country boast its constitution and its government.
>
> Within the space of a few years we have seen two Revolutions, those of America and France. In the former, the contest was long, and the conflict severe; in the latter, the nation acted with such a consolidated impulse, that having no foreign enemy to contend with, the revolution was complete in power the moment it appeared. From both those instances it is evident, that the greatest forces that can be brought into the field of revolutions, are reason and common interests. Where these can have the opportunity of acting, opposition dies with fear, or crumbles away by conviction. It is a great standing which they have now universally obtained; and we may hereafter hope to see revolutions, or changes in governments, produced with the same quiet operation by which any measure, determinable by reason and discussion, is accomplished.[1]

How did Paine come to be so far astray? I think that the most serious charge which can be brought against him on this count is that although he was writing at a time when the Industrial Revolution had already

[1] *Rights of Man*, pp. 264–5.

started, he did not understand the nature of capitalism. Above all, he seems not to have seen that it was essentially competitive, in such a way that the need to outstrip one's rivals in the acquisition of profits would become a motive for paying as little as possible to those whom one employed. If he was aware of this danger, he overrated both the power and the readiness of the exploited to defend themselves. He overrated their power because he did not allow for the possibility that a government, composed of their nominal representatives who were supposed to protect their rights, would be dominated by their oppressors. It would be unfair to criticize him for failing to foresee the extraordinary increase in the British population throughout the nineteenth century, but his theory of representative government, like Rousseau's, is better adapted to a Swiss canton than to a country of the size that Britain was soon to become. He overrated their readiness to militate for their rights because he underrated the strength of their habit of subordination. The monarchy and the aristocracy seemed to him such absurdities that he simply overlooked the fact that they enjoyed a very considerable ungrudging respect. He found it easy enough to prove that they did not deserve it, but that was largely beside the point. Only a small minority of those for whom he was writing judged the matter in those terms. The others were divided, not exclusively, into those, like the members of the police and the armed forces, to whom, with very few exceptions, it did not occur to question the authority of their masters, those who truly admired the persons whom God or fate had placed in a superior position, and took a vicarious pleasure in their pursuits, those who did not care much one way or the other, so long as they had the means to enjoy what they regarded as a tolerable, or even, as in the case of artists of one sort or another, a valuable way of life, those who took to crime, and finally those who regarded themselves as doomed to wretchedness. We should not forget that the alleviation of the hardships of this last group was due not only to Socialists but to nineteenth-century Conservatives. It has been left to the Conservatives of our own day to restore their *status quo*.

I conclude this review of Paine's *Rights of Man* with what we may regard as his deepest illusion: his belief that in consequence of the American and French Revolutions the world was poised to enter upon a course of lasting peace. In the last eight pages of his book, he sketches a scenario which begins with an alliance between England, France and Holland, the principal naval powers, the terms of which will be that no new ships shall be built by any power in Europe, including themselves, and that their own fleets shall be reduced to one tenth of their current strength. These allies will then join the United States of America in proposing to Spain that she grant independence to all her South American colonies, thereby 'opening those countries of immense extent and wealth to the general commerce of the world'.[1] It is taken for granted that Spain would calmly accept this proposal, or at least would not be in a position to resist it. Paine remarks in passing that South America would furnish 'a ready money market for manufactures, which the eastern world does not'.[2] I suppose that for him 'the eastern world' consisted primarily of India. I doubt if he had much knowledge of China or Japan.

The scenario is not developed in further detail. It is simply assumed that once 'the insulted German and the enslaved Spaniard, the Russ and the Pole'[3] perceive the benefits that have accrued to America, France and England, from the institution of representative government, they will almost automatically follow suit, if only from the motive of enlightened self-interest. Paine has nothing to say about Africa except that when despotism and corrupt government have been expelled from Europe and America, Algerine piracy, which thrives on 'the malicious policy of old governments', 'may be commanded to cease'.[4]

Is this not a ludicrous tale? Was it not already refuted in Paine's lifetime by the outbreak of the Napoleonic Wars? Paine himself did not think so. He regarded Napoleon's early campaigns as instruments of liberation, as putting the common people of Austria, Prussia and the Italian States in a position to form their own representative governments. Dying as he did in 1809, he did not have to face the disaster of Napoleon's Russian campaign, Napoleon's defeat at Waterloo, and the temporary restoration of the old order in France. All along, Britain was the chief stumbling block, but this was something that Paine was always reluctant to accept. We shall see that as late as 1804, admittedly before the battle of Trafalgar had removed the threat of a French invasion, Paine believed that a revolution in Britain could be organized. In addition to his other political oversights, we are bound to notice his failure to appreciate the force of nationalism to which, especially in Germany, the brotherhood proclaimed, if not always practised, by Napoleon's armies acted not as a deterrent but as a stimulus. When it limits itself to patriotism, the spirit of nationalism should probably be seen as a virtue. Aggressive nationalism is a great political evil and it is constantly on the increase.

[1] *Rights of Man*, p. 267.
[2] ibid.
[3] ibid., p. 268.
[4] ibid., p. 270.

The admirers of Thomas Paine, of whom I continue to be one, may take some comfort from the fact that his hopes would not seem so foolish if this book were being written in the year in which its author was born. In spite of the scandalous episode of the Boer War, it did seem to many intelligent persons, to such men as Gilbert Murray and Norman Angell and Bertrand Russell and Bernard Shaw, in the early part of this century, that something approaching a genuine age of reason was at last in prospect. Their hopes were destroyed by the First World War, a war for which there seems in retrospect to have been no plausible reason, and they have never since been renewed. The politicians who led their far from reluctant peoples into that war were not, in the main, malevolent or even stupid. They subscribed to a set of abstractions, national honour, the glory of empire, the sanctity of secret pacts, without troubling to consider what would result from their concrete application. No more was required of them than that they be rational. We should no longer be surprised that this was an achievement beyond their reach.

7

Citizen Paine

The ill-starred flight of the French royal family on 21 June 1791 found Paine in Paris, where he had gone to supervise the translation into French of the first volume of *Rights of Man*. When Louis XVI was captured at Varennes and brought back to Paris on 25 June, Paine, as a spectator, was mistaken for an aristocrat and threatened with hanging. The reason was that he had failed to adorn himself with a revolutionary cockade. An English-speaking Frenchman identified and rescued him.

Though he was more than ever a cipher, Louis was not immediately divested of his kingship. There were influential Frenchmen, including the Abbé Sieyès, and at that date, even Robespierre, who thought that the new French Constitution should retain the institution of monarchy, however limited its powers. Paine did not oppose them so long as Louis appeared willing to co-operate with the National Assembly, but after Louis, by his attempted escape, had shown himself not to be sincere, Paine felt it to be his duty to convert France also to Republicanism. He founded a Republican Club, which, according to Moncure Conway,[1] contained only four other members, the philosopher Condorcet, no longer using his title of Marquis, Achille Duchâtelet, and possibly also Brissot and the journalist Nicolas Bonneville. The society started a journal *Le Républicain* but only one number appeared. It contained a letter by Paine in which he made his customary point that monarchy and hereditary succession cannot be reconciled with the principles of elective representation and the rights of man.

Paine returned to England in response to an invitation to attend a

---

[1] *Life of Thomas Paine*, vol. I, p. 311.

celebration, at the White Bear Inn in Piccadilly, of the second anniversary of the fall of the Bastille. In fact Paine thought it prudent to absent himself and the landlord of the White Bear also came to think it prudent not to admit the celebrants. At a meeting which did take place at the Thatched House Tavern on 20 August, under the chairmanship of John Horne Tooke, the company subscribed to a manifesto, written by Paine, in which he congratulated the French on their revolution, and outlined some of the reforms that he was to advocate in the second volume of *Rights of Man*.

We have seen that Paine dedicated the first volume of *Rights of Man* to George Washington and on 22 July sent him a present of fifty copies, with a letter in which he expatiated on the success which the book had enjoyed, especially in Ireland. Washington took nine months to reply to Paine, giving the duties of his office as a reason for the delay, and acknowledging in a postscript a gift of twelve copies of the second volume. The tone of Washington's letter is cordial but Conway suggests that part of the reason for the delay may have been Washington's desire at that time to remain on good terms with the British government and his fear that it may have objected to Paine's book.

In fact, the British government gave no sign of showing any interest in the first volume of Paine's *Rights of Man*. Neither political party had any great affection for Burke, and the occasion for repelling Paine's attacks on hereditary monarchy was hardly opportune, when George III had recently been found insane. Paine lived quietly in London at the home of his young friend Thomas Rickman, conversed with his radical acquaintances, and busied himself with the composition of the second volume.

He always wrote quickly and the book was delivered to Chapman, its prospective printer, by 1 February 1792. Chapman, however, considered the book too dangerous to publish, and it was once again Jordan who brought it out on 17 February. On this occasion, however, Pitt, who had no personal hostility to Paine, but was not in favour of a British revolution, even if he was in the best position to lead it, decided that the second volume of *Rights of Man* was too subversive to be ignored. In May, the government took out a summons against both Jordan and Paine on the basis of a Royal Proclamation against seditious writings. Jordan pleaded guilty and was allowed to drop out of the case when Paine took sole responsibility for the book. The letters which he wrote at the time to Sir Archibald Macdonald, the Attorney-General, to Henry Dundas, the Secretary for the Home Department, and to Lord

Onslow, the Lord Lieutenant of the County of Surrey, who had organized a meeting to manifest approval of the Royal Proclamation, show that he believed himself to be legally entitled to publish arguments in favour of improving the British Constitution and that he was not afraid of standing trial for his opinions. He appeared in court on 8 June 1792 and was disappointed when his trial was postponed until December.

The trouble was that Paine misjudged the strength of the British government's determination to silence and discredit him. He had some reason for feeling secure. His portrait had just been painted by George Romney. Some 200,000 copies of the combined *Rights of Man* had been sold, yielding Paine a profit of more than a thousand pounds, which he characteristically donated to the Society for Constitutional Information. How could proposals, so plainly designed for their advantage, fail to appeal to the mass of the British people?

A very fair question, but one that Pitt was also capable of posing, and Pitt had power. Paine's works were burned in the market place of Exeter. His person was burned in effigy at Staines, Leeds, Camberwell, Bristol, Chelmsford and probably elsewhere. It is unlikely that these popular demonstrations were altogether spontaneous. They did, however, tend to show that Paine's assumption that England was ripe for revolution, on the French model, was over optimistic.

How far he had overrated his security soon became clear. On 12 September he made a fiery speech at a meeting of a society of the 'Friends of Liberty'. On the following evening, he was about to leave a friend's house, where he had been regaling the company with an account of this speech, when William Blake, who alone of the guests had the intelligence to see that Paine had put himself into imminent danger, said to him 'You must not go home, or you are a dead man.' His earnestness convinced Paine, who at once set out for Dover, accompanied by a Mr Frost, who somehow knew which was the safest route for them to take, and by Achille Audibert, who had come to London to persuade Paine to accept an invitation from the department of the Pas-de-Calais to be its representative in the Convention. The party had some trouble with a customs officer at Dover but Paine overawed him by showing him letters which he had received from various eminent persons, including George Washington. The order to arrest Paine reached Dover just twenty minutes after the departure of the ship which was carrying him to France.

There was no doubt that the French would welcome him. He was, in fact, one of the nineteen foreigners on whom the French Assembly had conferred the title of French citizen. The others included Priestley, Bentham and Wilberforce, and the American statesmen, Washington, Hamilton and Madison. These favours were bestowed in the month of August 1792, during which the French Revolution took a decisive turn.

The events of August can be traced back to the rash declaration of war by the French Assembly on 20 April 1792 against Austria and Prussia. The enemy under the command of the Duke of Brunswick was confident of victory and underrated both the military skill and the loyalty to their new government of the French army. He did not invade France until the end of July and though he captured the fortress of Longwy on 23 August and Verdun on 2 September he was defeated in an artillery battle at Valmy on 20 September and retired to the frontier.

In the meantime, however, the news that the enemy forces were approaching Longwy aroused both fear and anger in the working population of Paris. On 10 August, encouraged by the Jacobins, they overthrew the municipal government of Paris and set up a new revolutionary commune at the Hôtel de Ville. The Tuileries was stormed and the King and his family took refuge with the Assembly, which immediately capitulated. It handed the King over as a prisoner to the Commune and called for elections to a National Convention for the purpose of revising the constitution.

The elections took some weeks to be carried out and in the meantime there occurred the first manifestation of the Terror, on a large scale, the so-called September massacres. Throughout the five days from 2 September to 7 September eleven hundred persons, imprisoned in Paris on suspicion, were put to death. More than two hundred of them were priests. The Church had already suffered from the confiscation of its lands which were designated as security for the paper notes which the government issued in increasing quantities, the so-called *assignats*.

The property qualification which had previously been in force was abandoned for elections to the Convention in favour of universal male suffrage. Even so, only one tenth of the number of possible electors exercised their right to vote. Of the 749 deputies whom the Convention contained, 285 had been members of one or other of the previous assemblies. Not more than two hundred were extreme revolutionaries, but they prevailed over the more numerous Moderates, who were more lax in their attendance. The only foreigner to be elected, besides Paine, was the Prussian, 'Anacharsis' Clootz. Paine was chosen for the departments of Oise, Puy-de-Dôme and the Somme but he remained faithful to the Pas-de-Calais, receiving an ovation when his ship docked at Calais, followed by an official ceremony, in which his election was confirmed. He reached Paris on 19 September, two days before Louis XVI was officially deposed.

In spite of the frequency of Paine's visits to Paris, it would appear that he neither spoke nor even understood the French language, with the result that the letters and speeches which he addressed to the Convention were couched in English and rendered into French by a translator or interpreter. This did not prevent the Convention from including Paine in a committee appointed in October to draft the new constitution. The other members of the committee were Sieyès, Brissot, Pétion, Vergniaud, Gensonné, Danton, Barère and Condorcet. We shall see that the work of this committee was nullified by the turn of events. Of all its members, only Sieyès adroitly, Paine, as we shall see, more narrowly, and Barère, who succeeded Robespierre as head of the ferocious Committee of Public Safety, survived the Terror.

The first question of importance to occupy the Convention, after Paine's election to it, was whether Louis XVI should be put on trial. Paine was of the opinion that he should be tried, and defended it in a letter which he wrote to the President of the Convention in November 1792. His main argument was that the trial would reveal the depth of the conspiracy on the part of 'the despots of Europe' to make war on France and the extent to which Louis participated in it.

After Louis had been tried and found guilty, the Convention had to decide what penalty he should suffer. A strong party, led by Marat, was in favour of his being put to death. Paine firmly opposed this motion. Addressing the Convention on 15 January 1793, he argued that while Louis's trial had helped to prove that the monarchical system was abominable, Louis himself was not a bad man; had he not had the misfortune to inherit the Crown he would have made a respectable citizen; that he deserved some credit for the help that France had given America in its revolt from England; that the French Assembly was itself to blame for not forcing him to abdicate after his flight to Varennes; that so long as he was alive his brothers would not put themselves at the head of a band of exiles who might become a more serious threat under a more active leadership; and finally, that Robespierre himself had made an eloquent speech in the Constituent Assembly in favour of the abolition of the death penalty in France. In the case of 'Louis Capet', Paine proposed that the sentence of banishment be pronounced against him and his family, to take effect at the end of the war. Until that time he should be kept in prison.

Notwithstanding Paine's protest, for which he gained over three hundred supporters in the Convention, Marat's party prevailed, by a fairly narrow majority, when the vote was taken on 18 January. On the following day, Paine again spoke, pleading that the King's execution at least be delayed until the question could be reconsidered by the Assembly which would be chosen after the acceptance of the Constitution which the National Convention had been elected to frame. His principal argument was that the news of the King's execution would make a bad impression upon the United States of America, which was at that moment France's only ally. He again failed to carry the Convention with him, with Marat first accusing the interpreter, quite unjustly, of mistranslating Paine's speech, and then asserting that Paine was opposing the King's execution only because he was a Quaker. Robespierre, without disavowing his objections to capital punishment, sided with Marat, on the ground that, since it had remained a lawful penalty, the King deserved to suffer it, and on 21 January 1793 Louis XVI was guillotined.

Meanwhile Paine had been tried in his absence before a special jury at the Court of the King's Bench, Guildhall, on 18 December 1792, the charge being that of seditious libel. He had further provoked the government by having *Rights of Man* reprinted in cheap editions and by publishing *Letter Addressed to the Addressors on the Late Proclamation*, a pamphlet in which he defended his opinions against those who had chosen or had been induced to proclaim their support for the Royal Proclamation and on which the charge against him was based. Once again the popular sale of *Rights of Man* contrasted with the ubiquity with which Paine was burned in effigy. Though he was courageously defended by his chief counsel, Thomas Erskine, who made a powerful appeal to the English tradition of free thought and speech, there was never any doubt about the verdict. The jury found Paine guilty, and he was sentenced by the Judge, Lord Kenyon, to become an outlaw. He never again attempted to set foot on English soil.

Paine's conviction was followed in England by a campaign against his abettors. Printers who had brought out editions of *Rights of Man* or *Letter Addressed to the Addressors*, or both, were imprisoned, for periods varying from three months to four years, and fined from twenty to two hundred pounds. According to Conway, upon whose work I am now relying, a Mr Fische Palmer was sentenced to seven years' transportation for distributing Paine's works and a Mr Thomas Muir to fourteen years' transportation for advising people to read them. So far was Paine himself from responding in kind that when British citizens got into trouble with the authorities in Paris he consistently came to their rescue.

The text of the Constitution which the committee to which Paine had been appointed was engaged in drafting was prefaced by a Declaration of Rights, said to be the work of Paine and Condorcet. It contained thirty-two clauses, beginning with the statement that 'the natural rights of man, civil and political, are liberty, equality, security, property, social protection and resistance to oppression'.[1] Liberty is defined, in the familiar way, as 'the right to do whatever is not contrary to the rights of others', and its preservation is said to depend on 'submission to the Law, which is the expression of the general will'. Equality is said to consist 'in the enjoyment by everyone of the same rights', security in 'the protection accorded by society to every citizen for the preservation of his person, property and rights', and the right of property is 'every man's being master in the disposal, at his will, of his goods, capital, income and industry'. Several clauses are devoted to the Law, which is required to be equal for all, not retroactive, and wholly authoritative. Freedom of thought, freedom of speech, unrestricted freedom of the press, freedom in the exercise of religion, freedom to engage in any kind of 'labour commerce or culture', freedom to compete for 'all public positions, employments and functions' are all upheld. What is forbidden is for a man to sell himself, as opposed to his services and his time: 'his person is not an alienable property'. All members of society are equally in need of education and society owes it to them to provide it. There have to be taxes, but only 'for the general welfare and to meet public needs', and all citizens have the right to join in assessing them either personally or through their representatives.

Finally, the social guarantee of the rights of man is said to rest on the national sovereignty, which is 'one, indivisible, imprescriptible and inalienable', and since 'all heredity in offices is absurd and tyrannical' the Constitution itself is always subject to the right of the people to reform and alter it.

I do not know how much Condorcet contributed to the drafting of this document but in almost everything that I have described or quoted one seems to hear the voice of Paine. There would appear to be nothing in it which contravened the principles for which the French Revolution had so far been understood to stand, but Robespierre objected to it on the unexpected ground that it failed to mention 'The Supreme Being',

[1] *Writings of Thomas Paine*, vol. III, pp. 128ff.

which he thereupon identified with Nature. He also complained that it allowed too much scope for commerce.

Whatever Robespierre's reverence for the Supreme Being, as he conceived it, what may have been his principal motive for attacking Paine's and Condorcet's Declaration of Rights, and the constitutional proposals, to which it was the preamble, was the fact that these proposals represented the views of the Girondins, so called because many of them came from the department of the Gironde, as opposed to the members of the Mountain, so called from the position which they occupied in the meeting place of the Convention, who followed the lead of Robespierre and Marat. The Girondins tended to be middle-class, relatively prosperous, and relatively free from the domination of the common people in Paris. The Montagnards, on the other hand, defended the interests and expressed the aspirations of the Parisian working class. They largely overlapped with the Jacobins, who owed their name to their membership of a club which met in a former Dominican convent, said to be Jacobin because the original home of the Dominicans in Paris was in the Rue Saint-Jacques.

The Constitution, drafted chiefly by Condorcet, was presented to the Convention in February 1793 but discussion of it was deferred until April and never in fact took place. The reason for this lay not so much in the machinations of the Montagnards as in the fact that a crisis had again arisen in the affairs of France. There had been royalist insurrections in the provinces, most seriously in the Vendée, and the country was at war with England, Holland, Spain, Austria and Prussia. After being forced to evacuate Belgium, General Dumouriez, the commander of the French northern army, deserted to the enemy and attempted to lead his army towards Paris, with the intention of restoring the monarchy. The bulk of his army, however, refused to follow him, owing mainly to the vigilance of General Hoche, and Dumouriez took refuge with the Austrians.

Paine refers to this episode in a letter written on 20 April to Thomas Jefferson, who had returned to America as Secretary of State for Foreign Affairs. Paine has not yet heard of Dumouriez's failure, but does not express anxiety about the fate of Paris, since he believes that the enemy powers are not acting in concert and that the worst that they will do is re-establish the Constitution of 1791, in which the King was a figure-head, rather than restore 'the old Monarchy'. At the same time he confesses to his disappointment over the course that the Revolution is taking. 'Had this revolution been conducted consistently with its principles, there was once a good prospect of extending liberty through the greatest part of Europe: but I now relinquish that hope.' In consequence, he proposes to return home. 'I shall await the event of the proposed Constitution, and then take my final leave of Europe.' In fact he remained in France for another eight and a half years.

Conway, in his life of Paine, confuses the abortive Paine–Condorcet Constitution with a Montagnard Constitution, drafted by Hérault de Séchelles, and approved by the Convention towards the end of June. The main differences between them were that whereas the former advocated the strengthening of the Executive Council by having it directly elected and made independent of the Assembly, whose members were to be chosen indirectly in two stages, the Montagnard Constitution proposed that ministers were to be subordinate to the National Assembly, to which elections were to be conducted on the basis of universal male suffrage with the requirement of an absolute majority. Only the choice of candidates for the Administration was to be left to the Electoral Colleges. In addition, it was proposed that a right to a livelihood be guaranteed for everyone, that there should be popular education, and that any declaration of war should be subjected to a referendum.

This liberal constitution was approved by an immense majority of the nearly two million voters who exercised their right to ratify it, but it never came into operation. The reason for this was that power had already passed into the hands of the Jacobin Committees, especially the Committee of Public Safety, dominated by Danton, Barère and the financial expert, Cambon. It was this Committee and its successor, appointed in July to put down revolts in the provinces, together with the Committees of General Defence and General Security, backed by the Revolutionary Tribunal, that were responsible for the growth of the Reign of Terror during 1793. The figures are not impressive by modern standards. According to one of the popular histories of the French Revolution, written by Albert Mathiez and published in 1922, the trials in Paris between 6 August and 1 October resulted in twenty-nine death sentences, nine sentences of deportation and twenty-four acquittals, there being also a hundred and thirty cases in which it was decided that there were no grounds for prosecution. Between 1 October and 1 January 1794, out of three hundred and five persons who were put on trial, one hundred and ninety-four were acquitted, twenty-four sentenced to deportation or imprisonment, and no more than one hundred and seventy-seven condemned to death. It is, however, to be noted that these included Marie-Antoinette, Philippe-Egalité, the father of the future King Louis-Philippe, and, what was most important to Tom

Paine, twenty-one of the leading Girondins. Condorcet went into hiding but was recognized as an aristocrat by an innkeeper in a village called Bourg-la-Reine and died in its police station.

The repression in the provinces was more severe. M. Mathiez estimates that the rebellion in the Vendée claimed some six thousand victims, of whom about two thousand were put to death by drowning at Nantes, and that up to two thousand persons were executed in the suppression of a revolt in Lyons. Discontent throughout the country was mainly caused by a rise in the cost of living, in spite of a 'Maximum' imposed on the price of grain as early as 4 May 1793. Part of the trouble was that it was also imposed on wages.

The Terror consisted not merely in the actual number of victims but in the suspense under which almost everybody lived. It was sustained by the passage on 17 September of the so-called 'Law of the Suspects'. As Mr Mathiez quotes it the law was this:

The following persons shall be reputed to be suspects:

1. those who by their conduct or connexions, their conversations or writings, have shown themselves partisans of tyranny or federalism,[1] and enemies of liberty;

2. those who cannot give satisfaction . . . with regard to their means of subsistence and the discharge of their civic duties;

3. those who have been refused certificates of good citizenship;

4. public officials suspended or dismissed from their posts by the National Convention or its commissaries and not reinstated;

5. such former nobles, together with their families and agents, as have not consistently maintained their attachment to the Revolution;

6. those who emigrated during the period between July 1st 1789 and March 30th 1792 even if they have returned to France . . .

It is not surprising that power thenceforward passed increasingly into the hands of the Jacobin committees or that the number of arrests and executions, especially in Paris, multiplied throughout 1794.

---

[1] Opposition throughout the country to the centralization of power in Paris.

As early as 6 April 1793, the date of the formation of the first Committee of Public Safety, Paine foresaw that something of this sort would happen. Writing then to Danton, who could read English, he said that he was 'exceedingly disturbed at the distractions, jealousies, discontents that reign among us, and which, if they continue, will bring ruin and disgrace on the Republic'. It is not only the intervention of foreign powers, and 'the intrigues of aristocracy and priestcraft' but also the mismanagement of the internal affairs of France that have deprived him of his hope of seeing the accomplishment of European liberty. Henceforward France must keep out of foreign wars and look only to herself. An immediate danger is that of a rupture between Paris and the provincial departments. Citing the precedent of America, and the construction of Washington as its capital, Paine advises Danton to have the residence of the Convention sited at a distance from Paris. He warns Danton also against allowing the central government to fix the price of provisions. If there is any such fixing to be done, it should be left to the municipalities. If the orders go out from Paris, the result will be that the country people will refuse to bring their provisions to market. Here Paine displays exceptional prescience. He also warns Danton against the increase in prices caused by the multiplication of *assignats* and goes on to deplore 'the spirit of denunciation that now prevails', referring especially to the threats directed against his friends, the Girondins.

Paine adds that he has written a letter to Marat over the question of putting Louis XVI to death and he was suspected, unjustly, by Marat of having a hand in Marat's being brought by the Girondins to trial before the Revolutionary Tribunal on the charges of incitement to murder and pillage and planning the dissolution of the Convention, a trial in which he was triumphantly acquitted in April. Thereafter he and Paine appear to have been on neutral terms until Marat's murder by Charlotte Corday on 13 July removed what might have been the principal obstacle to the short-lived supremacy of Robespierre.

Paine always suspected Robespierre of being personally hostile to him, but it seems to have been rather on general principles that Robespierre on 7 June 1793 persuaded the Convention to pass a law which exposed foreigners as such to imprisonment, if their countries were at war with France. In any case Paine and Clootz, *qua* members of the Convention, were held to be exempt. A greater danger to Paine resulted from the spy scare at the end of July, causing Barère to propose on 5 August that all English subjects who had come to France since 14 July 1789 be expelled, and Cambon to strengthen the proposal by the rider that all suspect foreigners be put under arrest. Strictly speaking, neither of these measures applied to Paine, but perhaps as the result of his failure to learn French, it tended to be forgotten that he was technically a French citizen. In fact, we shall see that he himself later found it necessary to maintain that his French citizenship was no more than honorary.

Paine continued to go to meetings of the Convention during the summer but he was a lonely figure there and seldom spoke. After the trial and execution of the Girondins in the last week of October 1793 he ceased to attend altogether. In any case the Convention was losing its importance. The Law of Revolutionary Government, which was passed on 4 December, transferred all power to the Parisian committees.

In the circumstances, it is surprising that Paine made no attempt to leave Paris, especially as he had been denounced in the Convention on 3 October by the arch-terrorist, Amar, for supporting the Girondin Brissot in the attempt to spare the life of Louis XVI. Perhaps he feared that if he tried to return to America the vessel on which he sailed would be waylaid by a British ship, but this would not have applied to an escape to Switzerland, which he could have arranged. He resided in Paris successively at the Philadelphia House, No. 7 Passage des Petits Pères, and at No. 63 Faubourg St Denis, a mansion with a large garden formerly belonging to Madame de Pompadour. While he was living at the Philadelphia House, he completed the first part of his book *The Age of Reason*, on which Conway believes that Paine started working as early as 1791. Conway also produces evidence that a version of this part was translated into French by Paine's friend, François Lanthenas, and submitted in March 1793 to a close associate of Robespierre's, Couthon, who forbade its publication. Paine himself in his preface to the second part of the book stated that he finished the first part just six hours before his arrest on 28 December and contrived on his way to prison to persuade his captors to allow him to call on his friend Joel Barlow, to whom he entrusted the manuscript. Barlow, an American former clergyman, who had been awarded French citizenship not long after Paine, was able to have the book printed in Paris. I shall be commenting on both parts in my next chapter.

Barlow was one of the small circle of friends, mostly English and American, but also including the Frenchmen Brissot and Nicolas Bonneville, with whom Paine spent his time conversing at his house in the Faubourg St Denis. Paine was always addicted to brandy and was often depicted by his enemies as being a drunkard. He himself confessed to his friend Thomas Rickman that 'borne down by public and private affliction, he had been driven to excesses in Paris'. Rickman, however, who came over to stay with him in the summer of 1793, gives an idyllic account of Paine's way of life:

> He usually rose about seven. After breakfast he usually stayed an hour or two in the garden, where he one morning pointed out the kind of spider whose web furnished him with the first idea of his constructing his iron bridge; a fine model of which, in mahogany, is preserved in Paris. The little happy circle who lived with him will ever remember those days with delight: with these select friends he would talk of his boyish days, play at chess, whist, piquet, or cribbage, and enliven the moments by many interesting anecdotes: with these he would play at marbles, scotch hops, battledores, etc, on the broad and fine gravel walk at the upper end of his garden, and then retire to his boudoir, where he was up to his knees in letters and papers of various descriptions. Here he remained till dinner time; and unless he visited Brissot's family, or some particular friend, in the evening, which was his frequent custom, he joined again the society of his favourites and fellow-boarders, with whom his conversation was often witty and cheerful, always acute and improving, but never frivolous. Incorrupt, straightforward and sincere, he pursued his political course in France, as everywhere else, let the government or clamour or faction of the day be what it might, with firmness, with clearness, and without a shadow of turning.[1]

Apart from Paine's connection with the fate of Louis XVI, it is not at all clear what his political activity was during the fifteen months that he remained at liberty. There is no evidence that he had anything to say about the final abolition of feudal rights without compensation, which was decreed on 13 July 1793, the decree against hoarding, which was made a capital crime on 26 July, the introduction of military conscription on 23 August, or the change in the autumn to the Revolutionary Calendar, renaming the twelve months of the year, making them each consist of thirty days with five intercalary days and six in leap year. He must surely have approved of the abolition of feudal rights, disliked the terroristic implications of making hoarding a capital offence, and most probably had ambivalent feelings about the introduction of conscription, his commitment to liberty of conscience

[1] Quoted in Conway, *Life of Thomas Paine*, vol. II, pp. 67–8.

conflicting with his perception that only the creation of a citizen army could protect France from her many foreign enemies and so preserve the increase in liberty which he still believed that the Revolution had brought to France. This view receives some support from the fact that as late as 20 October 1793, after the fall of the Gironde, the elevation of the Committee of Public Safety, the passing of the Law of Suspects, and the execution of Marie-Antoinette, he still does not repudiate the French Revolution or wish that the measures of which he disapproves be frustrated by military defeat. Writing to Jefferson on that date he says that he sees no prospect either 'that France can carry revolution into Europe on the one hand or that the combined powers can conquer France on the other hand'.[1] Believing that each side wishes for peace, though neither will ask for it, he expresses the hope that Congress will send Commissioners, including Jefferson himself, to negotiate a truce. There is, however, no evidence that he seriously expected this hope to be fulfilled.

Meanwhile Washington, entering on his second term as President of the United States, was inclined to repent of his alliance with France and anxious to improve his relations with Great Britain. In this policy he was strongly abetted by Gouverneur Morris, the American Ambassador in Paris, and it is to the machinations of Gouverneur Morris that Conway plausibly attributes the chief cause of Paine's arrest. Whether or not Gouverneur Morris was a confirmed Royalist, as Conway asserts, he undoubtedly had a stronger sympathy for Britain than for revolutionary France, and he also harboured a personal dislike and jealousy of Paine. There had been various incidents which fostered his jealousy, such as the fact that a number of American sea-captains, who had been detained at Bordeaux in order to prevent their goods reaching England, owed their liberation to Paine and not to him, and the fact that Paine was the first to be informed of the appointment of Genêt as French Ambassador to the United States. As it happened, this appointment turned to Morris's advantage, since Genêt was soon dismissed because he was held to have meddled improperly in the question whether Spaniards should be expelled from the region of the Mississippi, a project of some of the leading citizens of Kentucky, which had been admitted to the Union on 1 June 1792, and Morris was able to fasten the responsibility for Genêt's blunder upon Paine.

Paine never knew that Gouverneur Morris was intriguing against him and was inclined to lay the blame on the Committee of Public

---

[1] *Writings of Thomas Paine*, vol. III, p. 134.

Safety, which since 27 July 1793 had included Robespierre. The case against Robespierre rests on a single sentence discovered in one of his notebooks after his death: 'Call for a decree, accusing Thomas Paine, in the interest of America as much as that of France.' This leaves no doubt that Robespierre was a party to Paine's arrest, but the reference to the interest of America suggests that he had been duped by Morris. He and Paine were, indeed, political opponents but there is no evidence that he bore Paine any special animosity or even that he thought him a dangerous ally of the Girondins. Admittedly, taking my lead from Conway, I am disposed to think that this is another instance of an enduring tendency to malign Robespierre. Robespierre, though inflexible in his commitment to the Revolution, was not the arch-terrorist that he is popularly taken to have been. 'He tried to save Danton and Camille Desmoulins, and did save seventy-three deputies whose deaths the potentates of the Committee of Public Safety had planned.'[1] It was not his addiction to Terror but the alarming increase in his personal authority that caused the events of the '9th Thermidor', the abolition by the Convention of the Paris commune and the denunciation of Robespierre, Saint-Just and Couthon, on 27 July 1794, resulting in their execution on the following day, and the reorganization of the Committee of Public Safety three days later, after 115 of their supporters had been subjected to the guillotine.

By this time Paine had been in the Luxembourg prison for seven months. We have not yet fully explained how he came to be there. The two reasons appear to have been his involvement with the Girondins and the suspicion of his being a British citizen and consequently an enemy alien. It was the absence of any doubt on the second point that caused the inclusion of the Prussian 'Anacharsis' Clootz, Paine's fellow foreigner in the Convention, in the group of Girondins who were sent to the guillotine. Though Paine had stronger claims to being considered an American or even a French citizen than to being attached, despite its having made him an outlaw, to the country of his birth, he was denounced on Christmas Day by the terrorist Bourdon de l'Oise for absenting himself from the Convention since Brissot and his followers had ceased to be members of it and, more mysteriously, for having 'intrigued with a former agent of the Bureau of Foreign Affairs'. The agent was identified by Paine as a M. Otto, the French Foreign Minister's secretary, who acted as interpreter when Paine replied to some questions of Barère's about the abortive Constitution which

---

[1] *Life of Thomas Paine*, vol. II, pp. 78–9.

Paine had helped to draft, the possibility of obtaining supplies from America and the utility of sending Commissioners there. After Paine had been denounced it was moved by Bentabole, a member of the Committee of General Security, that foreigners be excluded from every public office during the war, and Paine was arrested and imprisoned on 28 December.

The news of Paine's arrest provoked Major Jackson of Philadelphia and seventeen other Americans, residing in Paris, to send a letter to the Convention, referring to Paine as their countryman, recollecting the services which he had rendered to America, praising him as an apostle of liberty, asking for his release and offering to take him back to his and their country, while standing surety for his good conduct for the short time that he would remain in France. They described themselves, and by implication Paine also, as friends and allies of the French Republic.

This petition was buried in the files of the Committees of Public Safety and General Security. It did, however, draw an answer from Vadier, the President of the Convention. Without disputing the assertion that Paine had served the cause of the American Revolution, Vadier remarked that Paine had not understood the revolution which had regenerated France. More significantly, he referred to Paine as a native of England and consequently subject to the measures of security prescribed by France's revolutionary laws.

We are left with a suspicion that if Gouverneur Morris had taken a stronger stand on Paine's American citizenship he could have obtained his release from prison: but this he was content not to do. Conway has unearthed an exchange of disingenuous letters between Morris and the French Foreign Minister Deforgues, in which each of them ends by describing Paine as a French citizen, thereby justifying his liability to suffer under French law, but oddly overlooking the fact that one of the grounds for his arrest was that he was an enemy alien. Not only that but Morris wrote a long letter to Jefferson in March 1794 saying, truly so far as it goes, that he had asked for Paine's release as an American citizen, but that the French authorities insisted on detaining him on the score of his friendship with Brissot as well as other crimes which Morris did not specify, unless the drunkenness which he attributed to Paine was counted among them. In this way he prevented the American government from acting independently on Paine's behalf.

Believing, as he then did, that Robespierre was chiefly responsible for his arrest, Paine sent an appeal to the Convention on 7 August, ten days after Robespierre's fall. Most of the other prisoners in the Luxembourg who had been sent there on Robespierre's orders had already been released and Paine could not understand why he was still detained. He refers in the first paragraph of his letter 'to the very dangerous illness I have suffered in the prison of the Luxembourg': the second ends with the characteristic exclamation 'Ah, my friends, eight months loss of liberty seems almost a life-time to a man who has been, as I have been, the unceasing defender of Liberty for twenty years'.[1] Having gone on to denounce Robespierre, he points out that when he left the United States in 1787 he promised his friends that he would be returning the following year, that it was the hope of seeing a revolution happily established in France and extended to other countries that kept him away for 'more than seven years', that such action on his part entitled him to something better than imprisonment, and finally that so far from being a foreigner, in the sense that would make him liable to arrest, he had been invited into France by a decree of the National Assembly and remained a citizen of the United States. This letter was intercepted by Paine's enemies who remained on the Committee of Public Safety and never reached the Convention. If it had, I think it probable that Paine would have been released.

How narrowly did he escape the guillotine? Writing in 1796 he attributed his survival to the violent fever from which he suffered in the summer of 1794. The prison doctor, Marhaski, who was favourably disposed towards him, may have protected him. It may have been assumed that he was anyhow on the point of death. In his old age, he supplied Rickman and others with a more romantic version of his escape. It is worth quoting, even if it does not irresistibly command belief:

One hundred and sixty eight persons were taken out of the Luxembourg in one night, and a hundred and sixty of them guillotined next day, of which I knew that I was to be one; and the manner I escaped that fate is curious, and has all the appearance of accident. The room in which I lodged was on the ground floor, and one of a long range of rooms under a gallery, and the door of it opened outward and flat against the wall; so that when it was open the inside of the door appeared outward, and the contrary when it was shut. I had three comrades, fellow prisoners with me, Joseph Vanhuile of Bruges, since president of the municipality of that town, Michael and Robbins Bastini of Louvain. When persons by scores and by hundreds were to be taken out of the prison for the guillotine it was always done in the night, and those who performed that office had a private mark or signal by which they knew what rooms to go to, and what number to take. We, as I have said, were four, and the door of our room was marked, unobserved by us, with that number in chalk: but it happened if happening is the proper word, that the mark was put on when the door was open and flat against the wall, and thereby came on the inside when we shut it at night; and the destroying angel passed by it.[1]

As the weeks passed after Robespierre's downfall and Paine remained in prison, he was at last moved to suspect Gouverneur Morris. Having learned that James Monroe, subsequently President of the United States from 1817 to 1825, had arrived in Paris to replace Morris, Paine sent him a letter in which he enclosed a copy of the letter which he had sent to the Convention and went on to describe Morris as 'my inveterate enemy'. Believing, rightly, that Monroe was well disposed towards him, he expected to be released within a few days, but this did not happen. Increasingly bewildered, he wrote a long 'memorial' to James Monroe on 10 September and a series of letters throughout October, reiterating the arguments in favour of his release and suggesting to Monroe the means by which he could effect it. The reasons for the delay were first that Morris contrived to let a month pass before making it known to the French that he had been recalled and allowing Monroe to present his credentials and secondly that Monroe hesitated to intervene on Paine's behalf without some authorization from his government. On 2 November 1794 he received a letter from Edmund Randolph, who had replaced Thomas Jefferson as Secretary of State for Foreign Affairs, instructing him to protect any American citizen who was innocent of the offence with which he was charged, chose to regard this as applying to Tom Paine, wrote at once to the Committee of General Security, and in two days' time obtained Paine's release.

By that time Paine was exceedingly ill, half-frozen, half-starving, and with an abscess in his side. It was only through the care of Mr and Mrs Monroe, who took him into their house, that he survived. They gave him a room to himself and it was in his confinement there not as a prisoner but as an invalid that he wrote the second part of *The Age of Reason*. He completed it in time for a pirated edition of the whole work to be published in October 1795.

[1] *Life of Thomas Paine*, vol. II, pp. 131–2.

At one time it was believed in England that Paine had been guillotined and it was while he was living with the Monroes, in whose house he remained for eighteen months, that he had the pleasure of reading a pamphlet which purported to report the speech that he had made upon the scaffold. Its first sentence contained the words 'I am determined to speak the Truth in these my last moments altho' I have written nothing but lies all my life'. The date assigned to Paine's execution was 1 September 1794. It is extraordinary how much the English government continued to dread the influence of Paine's liberal ideas.

It was otherwise in France, even though the excesses of Robespierre and the Parisian committees had brought about a conservative reaction. The surviving Girondins were re-admitted to the Convention on 8 December 1794, but Paine was treated as a special case, receiving his invitation on the previous day in a speech delivered by Thibaudeau:

It yet remains for the Convention to perform an act of justice. I call for the re-admission of one of the most zealous defenders of liberty – Thomas Paine. I speak for a man who has brought honour to our time by his energetic defence of human rights, and the glorious part that he played in the American Revolution. Decreed a naturalized Frenchman by the legislative Assembly, he was nominated by the people. It was only by an intrigue that he was driven out of the Convention, on the pretext of a decree which debarred foreigners from representing the people of France. There were only two foreigners in the Convention: one is dead and I speak not of him but of Thomas Paine, who made a powerful contribution to the establishment of liberty in a country which is allied with the French Republic. I demand that his membership of the Convention be restored to him.[1]

Conway accuses Thibaudeau of self-contradiction, on the ground that he describes Paine as a naturalized Frenchman in one sentence and as a foreigner in the next. It seems to me, however, that the 'pretext' to which Thibaudeau refers may have been understood by him as that of counting Paine as a foreigner when he was not. This reading becomes more plausible when it is remembered that the foreigners in question were enemy aliens and that Paine was deemed to be a British citizen. His own view of his citizenship, as we have seen, was that it was neither British nor French but American, presumably

[1] *Life of Thomas Paine*, vol. II, p. 153.

from the time that the American Declaration of Independence made this possible for him. He consistently maintained, at least after his arrest, that the decree which made him eligible for membership of the Convention fell short of naturalizing him but entitled him to regard himself as an honorary French citizen. His motives may have been both his attachment to America and the belief that his being no more than an honorary French citizen made him less vulnerable to Robespierre.

The next amends made to Paine by the French, on 3 January 1795, took the form of his being placed first on the list of those to whom the Committee of Public Instruction awarded pensions for services to literature. Chénier, who spoke for the Committee, referred to Paine as 'this philosopher, who opposed the arms of Common Sense to the sword of Tyranny, the Rights of Man to the Machiavellism of English politicians; and who, by two immortal works, has deserved well of the human race, and consecrated liberty in two worlds'.[1] Paine was pleased by this description of him, but refused the pension even though he needed the money.

Not long after the rehabilitation of Paine, the Convention passed a decree the purpose of which was to give some practical effect to the Treaty of Friendship and Commerce which still subsisted between France and the United States. No doubt there had been a leakage of the steps that George Washington was taking to link the United States more closely with England. I shall be commenting presently on Paine's bitter reaction to this move. When Monroe learned of the decree, he wrote to the Committee of Public Safety, suggesting that a copy should be taken to America 'by some particularly confidential hand', and that the most suitable person to send on this errand would be Thomas Paine. He would travel immediately from Bordeaux on an American ship, and his departure would be kept a secret to avoid British interception.

In reply the Committee welcomed Monroe's approval of the decree but rejected the employment which he had devised for Paine on the ground that 'the position he holds will not permit him to accept it'. Since Paine held no official position beyond his membership of the Convention, it is not clear why the Committee objected to Monroe's proposal. Perhaps they suspected that Paine would not be well received by Washington: perhaps they believed, most probably rightly, that if he went to America he would see no point in returning to France, and still valued his presence in Paris on account of his friendship with the

[1] ibid., p. 154.

American Minister, if for no other reason. They were able to retain
him so long as they wished, because he needed a passport from the
Convention in order to leave France.

The Reign of Terror had discredited the Constitution of the
Montagnards and in 1795 a committee of eleven persons, not actually
including the agile Abbé Sieyès but not unresponsive to his influence,
was appointed to draft a new Constitution. Their report was presented
on 23 June by Boissy d'Anglas, and their proposals finally accepted on
22 August. Thibaudeau who was also on the committee declared that
its purpose was to find 'a middle way between royalty and demagogy',
and what this middle way consisted in was the exaltation of property.
French soldiers who had 'served one or more campaigns in the cause of
liberty' were allowed to be citizens but otherwise citizenship was
restricted to men over twenty-one years old, born in France, resident
there for a year and paying direct tax. The sting lay in the last clause for
only owners of property paid direct tax. The implication was made
brutally clear in a September number of the *Gazette de France*:

> In all ordered associations, society is composed solely of property
> owners. The others are only proletarians who, ranked in the class of
> supernumerary citizens, wait for the moment which allows them to
> acquire property.

In fact the new Constitution was even less democratic than this
would suggest, for not all citizens were qualified to vote. To be an
elector one had to be over twenty-five years old and to possess an
income equivalent to the proceeds of two hundred days' work. The
Legislators whom these electors chose were distributed among ten
Assemblies. Legislation was to be proposed by a Council of Five
Hundred, whose members had to be at least thirty years old, and its
proposals were to be accepted or rejected by a Council of Elders,
consisting of two hundred and fifty persons over the age of forty, who
were required to be either married men or widowers. Since it was feared
that the elections might yield a royalist majority, it was stipulated that
at least two thirds of those elected should have been members of the
previous Convention. It was then to be left to these bodies to elect an
executive consisting of five persons, the so-called Directory. One third
of the members of the councils and one of the directors were to retire in
1797, the councillors being re-eligible, but the director not for a period
of five years. Presumably, the idea was that the executive should not
become too powerful. Thereafter elections on the same principles were
to take place annually.

The first members of the Directory were elected and took office on 26 October 1795. To mark the fulfilment and underline the implications of the new Constitution the Place de la Révolution in Paris was renamed the Place de la Concorde. The original choices of the legislature were Sieyès, Barras, Reubell, La Révellière and Letourneur, but Sieyès prudently declined to serve and was replaced by Carnot, not an ardent Republican but a scientist and a brilliant military organizer, who more than anyone else was responsible for the early victories of the French revolutionary armies. In April 1797 the colourless Letourneur was replaced, in the royalist interest, by the Marquis de Barthélemy. The Directory was, however, dominated by the Republican triumvirate of Barras, Reubell and La Révellière, with Barras, the patron of Napoleon Bonaparte, and a lover of Josephine, in the leading role.

Thomas Paine was far from disapproving of the Directory or of the Constitution which gave it power. On the contrary in a pamphlet in which he defended the 'Coup d'état of the 18th Fructidor', alternatively the 4th September 1797, when Barras and his associates called in the army to defeat a conspiracy, arising out of the election of Royalists to the legislative assemblies, and to procure the banishment, among many others, of Carnot and Barthélemy, Paine declared that 'A better *organized* constitution has never yet been devised by human wisdom.'[1]

Even so, he did not give it his entire approbation. The one great fault that he found with it was that it deprived those without property not only of the right to vote but even of their citizenship. In the speech which he made to the Convention on 7 July 1795, on his first appearance there since his imprisonment, he argued, unanswerably, that this was inconsistent with the three first articles of the Declaration of Rights, on which the French Revolution originally depended.[2] More particularly, he showed that the distinction between the payment of direct and indirect taxes on which so much had been made to turn was merely superficial:

> The land proprietors, in order to reimburse themselves, will rack-rent their tenants; the farmer, of course, will transfer the obligation to the miller, by enhancing the price of grain; the miller to the baker, by increasing the price of flour; and the baker to the consumer, by raising the price of bread. The territorial tax, therefore, though called *direct*, is in its consequences, indirect.[3]

[1] *Writings of Thomas Paine*, vol. III, p. 345.
[2] See above p. 85.
[3] Conway, ibid., pp. 281–2.

Paine had no difficulty in showing that the line drawn between direct and indirect taxpayers was similarly loose in its application to merchants and manufacturers, so that it did not even serve as an accurate measure of wealth.

Even if it had so served, he would have taken exception to it, since his principal contention was that when it came to citizenship or the right to vote, there should not be any sort of property qualification. In a pamphlet entitled *First Principles of Government* which he published early in July 1795, in the hope of influencing the National Convention, he restated his belief that there were in the end only two principles of government, the hereditary and the representative, and relied on his familiar arguments in favour of the representative principle. He then went on to say that we should not trouble to inquire into its origin or its justification. It originates in the natural right of man. 'It appertains to him in right of his existence, and his person is the title deed.'[1] As will have been noted, this is rather a simplification of his earlier views. He now puts forward the dubious argument that since 'it is impossible to discover any origin of rights otherwise than in the origin of man, it consequently follows, that rights appertain to man in right of his existence only, and must therefore be equal to every man'.[2] Curiously enough, the more obvious deduction which could no longer have occurred to Paine, that natural rights are a fiction, leads to the same conclusion: for zero is equal to itself.

This does not invalidate the point that Paine is principally concerned to make. He states it as follows:

> The true and only true basis of representative government is equality of Rights. Every man has a right to one vote, and no more, in the choice of representatives. The rich have no more right to exclude the poor from the right of voting, or of electing and being elected, than the poor have to exclude the rich; and whenever it is attempted, or proposed, on either side, it is a question of force and not of right. Who is he that would exclude another? That other has the right to exclude him.[3]

Put less rhetorically, the conclusion is that neither has the right.

This is the kernel of Paine's pamphlet. He makes the obvious point that wealth or the lack of it is 'no proof of moral character' and

---

[1] *Writings of Thomas Paine*, vol. III, p. 265.
[2] ibid., p. 271.
[3] ibid., p. 268.

advances the practical argument that a high property qualification which excludes the majority of the people from any share in government will provoke them to revolt. Unfortunately, subsequent history has shown this to be false. Paine ends by attributing 'the violences that have since desolated France, and injured the character of the revolution' to the failure of the Convention to establish the Constitution of 1793, and adds what ought to be but is not always, especially in contemporary Britain, recognized as a truism, namely that 'an avidity to punish is always dangerous to liberty'.[1]

Neither this pamphlet nor the speech for which it was intended to provide a background had any influence upon the audience to which it was addressed. With the dissolution of the Convention of 1793, and its replacement by the Assemblies, which I have described, Paine's insistence that he was not a French but an American citizen debarred him from taking any further part in the government of France. Nor was he active in French politics behind the scenes. In a preface to the French translation of his pamphlet *Agrarian Justice*, which was published in 1797, he briefly condemned both the Socialist conspiracy of Babeuf and the royalist conspiracy which succeeded it, but neither the coup d'état of 22 Floréal, otherwise 11 May 1798, in which the Directory annulled ninety-eight elections where the return of right-wing candidates displeased them, nor the coup d'état of 18–19 Brumaire, that is, 9–10 November 1799, which abolished the Directory and brought Bonaparte to power as First Consul, abetted by the irrepressible Abbé Sieyès, evoked even a pamphlet from Paine. When Bonaparte returned to France, after his campaign in Italy, he is reputed to have flattered Paine by telling him that a statue of gold ought to be erected to him in every city of the universe.[2] Later he drew Paine into the plans that he appeared to be making for invading England, consulting him about the design of the ships which could be used to convey his troops. When Paine discovered that this threat to England had never been more than a feint to distract attention from Bonaparte's naval expedition against Egypt, he felt that he had been personally ill-used, but he did not relinquish his belief that Bonaparte's army was fighting in the cause of liberty, and he was able to share his friend Jefferson's admiration for the First Consul's educational and legal reforms. The transformation of General Bonaparte into the Emperor Napoleon I can hardly have pleased him but there is no record of his protesting against it in print.

[1] ibid., p. 277.
[2] See A. O. Aldridge, *Man of Reason* (Lippincott, 1959), p. 267.

In so far as Paine wrote anything of importance in the years that he was still to remain in France, it referred to English affairs. I have already listed the social reforms which he advocated in *Agrarian Justice*,[1] costing them with the same care as he had shown in the second part of *Rights of Man*. The guiding principle of this work was that 'the earth, in its natural uncultivated state . . . was the common property of the human race'.[2] A work which aroused greater interest was a pamphlet entitled *The Decline and Fall of the English System of Finance*, which Paine published in April 1796. It supported his old objections to the increase in the circulation of paper money with the argument that it brought down the value of gold and silver. If this had not happened in England so quickly as in America and France it was because of the English funding system, whereby the capital of the National Debt was retained by the Bank of England. Nevertheless Paine predicted that the steep rises in taxation resulting from the need to pay for the wars in which England was repeatedly engaged would soon have their inflationary effect; and he was justified in so far as the Bank of England suspended the exchange of its notes for gold in 1797. Nevertheless in evaluating Paine's attack on paper money, we need to remember the fact, which I have already mentioned,[3] that the purchasing power of the pound had fallen only in the ratio of 1.39 to 1 between 1791 and 1939 and that it is only in the past fifty years that the country has suffered from runaway inflation.

Paine's pamphlet was widely read in France and translated into many other European languages. Richard Carlile, in his Life of Paine, which came out in 1819, gives William Cobbett as his authority for stating that Paine assigned the profits which it brought him to the relief of the prisoners who were held in Newgate for debt.

When he left the Monroes Paine went to stay with his old friend the journalist Nicolas Bonneville and his family. The Monroes themselves, having been recalled, returned to America in the spring of 1797 and Paine intended to accompany them but got no further than Le Havre because, as he wrote to Jefferson, 'there were British frigates cruising in sight'. He wrote regularly to Jefferson, who became the third President of the United States in 1803, succeeding John Adams whom Paine distrusted as a potential despot, as well as a friend to England rather than France. By this time Paine was probably supporting the Bonnevilles, since Nicolas Bonneville had been sent to prison in 1799

---

[1] See above p. 107.
[2] *Writings of Thomas Paine*, p. 329.
[3] See above p. 102.

for describing Bonaparte as 'a Cromwell' and though soon released had had his journal suppressed. Paine's wish to return to America was supported by Jefferson and at last in 1802 the short-lived peace of Amiens made it safe for him to undertake the voyage. He set sail from Le Havre on 1 September, with the faithful Thomas Rickman speeding him on his way, and landed at Baltimore on 30 October.

After fifteen years' absence he may well have expected to receive a warm welcome from the citizens of the Republic which he had done so much to bring into existence. If so, he failed to take account of the fact that in the meantime he had published *The Age of Reason*.

8

The Age of Reason

As late as the beginning of this century, Theodore Roosevelt, the twenty-sixth President of the United States, chose to refer to Thomas Paine as a 'filthy little atheist'. He was mistaken on all counts, not least on the third. So far from being an atheist, Paine was an ardent deist: indeed his principal motive for hurrying to finish the first volume of his treatise on religion, *The Age of Reason*, before his arrest, was his fear that, in spite of Robespierre's Festival of the Supreme Being, the anti-clericalism of the French Republicans was leading them into atheism. What he was not, and with good reason, was a Christian. He made a special point of attacking Christianity because, in one form or another, it was the official religion of the countries in which he had lived, but, as we shall see, he was equally opposed to any religion which could, in his view, only have the effect of setting up a barrier between human beings and what he believed to be the benevolent deity who had created them.

The two volumes of *The Age of Reason*, though composed within a year of one another, differ considerably both in length and content. Though the first contains seventeen chapters and the second only two, entitled respectively 'The Old Testament' and 'The New Testament', the first is much the shorter, occupying sixty-three pages in Conway's edition of Paine's writings, whereas the second occupies one hundred and ten pages. As for the difference in content, while the first contains some sharp comments on the grosser absurdities of Christian theology, it is mainly devoted to pleading the cause of deism. The second volume has little to say directly in defence of deism, but mounts a sustained attack first on the Old Testament as purporting to be the word of God and second on the New Testament as purporting to establish the divinity of Jesus Christ.

The major reason for this difference is that Paine considered it to be of primary importance to defend deism against the threat of atheism and believed that he had achieved this in his first volume. A minor reason is that when he wrote the first volume he rather surprisingly lacked access to any copy of the Bible, so that in quoting from it he had to rely upon his memory. This did not lead him seriously astray. When he wrote the second volume, he was in possession of a Bible, no doubt supplied to him by the Monroes. As a result, one might have expected the second volume to be an improvement on the first, but in fact it goes the other way. For once he had the Bible in his grip, the procedure which Paine adopted was to go through the whole of the Old and New Testaments, book by book, pointing out the absurdities and contradictions which they contain, the unflattering picture which they give of the deity and his chosen people, and the ridiculous interpretations which Jewish and Christian apologists have put upon them.

The consequence of this approach is that the second volume of *The Age of Reason* is not likely to be of much interest to the modern reader who, if he makes use of his reason, will find very little in either Testament that he is able to regard as literally true, except perhaps for some brutal and pathetic episodes in early Jewish history. What makes the position worse is that Paine, having rightly identified the Bible as primarily a specimen of mythology, does not go on to appraise it as a work of art. For example he can find nothing better to say about the book of Ecclesiastes, which at least in the Authorized English translation is hauntingly poetic, than that 'it is written as the solitary reflections of a worn-out debauchee'.[1] The only parts of the Bible for which he has a good word are the 19th Psalm because of the deistic implications of its opening verse: 'The Heavens declare the glory of God, and the firmament showeth his handiwork', and, surprisingly, the book of Job. I say, surprisingly, because Paine regarded the god in whom he believed as a benevolent being, and the misfortunes which God is represented in the book of Job as allowing Satan to inflict upon Job, merely in order to test his faith, are indications, if not of positive malevolence, at least of a suspicious and ruthless insecurity, which is characteristic more of a tyrant than of a wholly powerful and benevolent deity. It is true that Job is said to have been eventually rewarded for his steadfastness by being endowed with more offspring and more animals than Satan had been permitted to destroy, but Paine had too much

---

[1] *Writings of Thomas Paine*, vol. IV, p. 127.

common sense to believe that virtue is made proportionate to property in this world, and while he did believe in an after-life, it was not a life in which the material losses which a good man might have suffered were compensated in kind, since he did not think of the after-life as physical: for instance, he characterizes the notion of the resurrection of the body as 'a miserable conceit'.[1]

One reason why Paine may have excluded the book of Job from his general condemnation of the Bible is that he did not believe that it belonged there at all. He considered it to be a book of Persian or Chaldean origin, older in date than the Pentateuch, and translated into Hebrew at some date after the Jews returned from their captivity in Babylon. Paine's grounds for this view are set out at length in his answer to the Bishop of Llandaff, Richard Watson, whose *An Apology for the Bible*, published in 1796, had been a tolerably sympathetic rejoinder to *The Age of Reason*.

Put concisely, Paine's arguments were that Job is not a Jewish name, that Uz, where he was said to live, is not in Jewish territory, that there is no reference in the book to any Jewish law or ceremony, that the Jewish commentator, Aben-Ezra, had asserted that the book had been translated into Hebrew from another language, that Spinoza had expressed the belief that Job was a Gentile, that Origen speaks of the book as older than Moses, that in the Old Testament, as opposed to the New, Satan does not appear as a separate personage, all the evils which it records being perpetrated or commanded directly by God, that Job is represented as adoring and submitting to God but not as praying to him, and finally that the book contains 'astronomical allusions' which would be consistent with the learning of 'Persian magi', 'but foreign to the relatively illiterate Jews'.[2]

So far as Paine was concerned, the fact, if it be one, that the Book of Job had a Gentile origin should not have appeared a strong reason for excluding it from the biblical canon, since he rightly holds the same to be true of the two mutually inconsistent accounts of the world's creation which figure in the book of Genesis and, again rightly, finds pagan sources for every feature of the Christian myth. Admittedly, not all his attributions are well justified. For instance, I think it unlikely that the legend of Satan's revolt against God, immortalized by Milton, is historically connected with the Greek myth of the war waged by the race of giants against Zeus, or that the confinement of one of the giants to Mount Etna foreshadowed Satan's confinement in Hell.

[1] *Writings of Thomas Paine*, vol. IV, p. 285.
[2] ibid., pp. 272ff.

However, the way in which Paine embroiders on these assumptions is effective.

> The Christian mythologists, after having confined Satan in a pit, were obliged to let him out again to bring on the sequel of the fable. He is then introduced into the garden of Eden in the shape of a snake, or a serpent, and in that shape he enters into familiar conversation with Eve, who is in no way surprised to hear a snake talk; and the issue of this tête-à-tête is that he persuades her to eat an apple, and the eating of that apple damns all mankind.[1]

Paine goes on to argue, very plausibly, that the Christian mythologists allow Satan not merely to emerge from his pit, in order to serve God's purpose of persuading Eve and, through Eve, Adam to disobey their creator, but to enjoy at least for a considerable time what well may be regarded as a victory over God. Not only did these mythologists fail to return Satan to his pit, or bury him under a mountain, after his original mission was accomplished, but 'they bribed him to stay. They promised him ALL the Jews, ALL the Turks by anticipation, nine-tenths of the world beside, and Mahomet into the bargain. After this,' says Paine, 'who can doubt the bountifulness of the Christian Mythology.'[2]

But the mythologists go further. Since God is represented as punishing not just the one serpent but the whole class of serpents for the temptation of Eve, condemning them to go on their bellies and eat dust, it follows, if God is presumed to be just, that the adoption of the disguise was Satan's own device, to which God feared that he might again resort. But what if God is also presumed to be omniscient? In that case he must have penetrated Satan's disguise, with the consequence that his punishment of serpents was unjust. Faced with this inconsistency in the myth, Paine chooses to interpret it as depriving God, at least temporarily, of his omniscience. Thus he is able to say of the mythologists:

> Not content with this deification of Satan, they represent him as defeating by stratagem, in the shape of an animal of the creation, all the power and wisdom of the Almighty. They represent him as having compelled the Almighty to the *direct necessity* either of surrendering the whole of the creation to the government and sovereignty of this

[1] ibid., p. 29.
[2] ibid.

Satan, or of capitulating for its redemption by coming down upon earth and exhibiting himself upon a cross in the shape of a man.

Had the inventors of this story told it the contrary way, that is, had they represented the Almighty as compelling Satan to exhibit *himself* on a cross in the shape of a snake, as a punishment for his new transgression, the story would have been less absurd, less contradictory. But instead of this they make the transgressor triumph, and the Almighty fall.[1]

In fairness, it should here be said that it is nowhere stated, or even implied, in the book of Genesis that the serpent who brought about the downfall of Adam and Eve was Satan in disguise. Indeed, we have already remarked that the only book of the Old Testament in which Satan makes a personal appearance is the book of Job and that this was one of the reasons which Paine himself gave for excluding that book from the canon. I have no doubt that the author or authors of that part of the book of Genesis in which sin is attributed to Adam and Eve had been influenced by the Zoroastrian belief in an eternal struggle between a good spirit of light and an evil spirit of darkness; yet, in spite of some inconsistencies, it is sufficiently clear that the tendency of the Bible as a whole is to express belief in the supremacy of a God who, in the New Testament at least, is held to be good.

But, even if we dismiss Satan from the scene, what a strange story it is, stranger indeed than if we had allowed Satan to remain. For now we are faced with the question why an all-powerful and wholly beneficent deity should have burdened his human creatures with a disposition to sin. The stock answer is that he showed his beneficence by bestowing on them the gift of free will: it was only their own fault if they misused it. But even if the requisite notion of free will is coherent, which I doubt, and even if we refrain from asking the question what causes men to make bad choices, we can surely still ask why any of the possible choices needed to be bad. Why should not all the alternatives be beneficial? If I leave a child free to choose from a number of presents, I do not express my love for him by making sure that some of them are harmful.

Let us, however, let this objection pass, and let us not waste time on dissecting the pointless story of the Virgin Birth or analysing a theory of personal identity which permits God, the son of God and the Holy Ghost to be both three persons and only one. In whatever way he did it,

---

[1] *Writings of Thomas Paine*, vol. IV, pp. 30–31.

why was it necessary that God should turn himself into a man at all? The orthodox answer is that he displayed his great love for his creatures by suffering the agony of crucifixion and so expiating the original sin of Adam and Eve, which they mysteriously handed on to their descendants. Since he himself imposed the penalties for this sin, it is not easy to understand why he did not simply annul them. This would have been a loving act, and it would have had the advantage of applying to the whole human race, instead of making their salvation depend upon the late arrival and limited spread of Christianity, whereby most of them, according to the versions of Christianity that prevailed in Paine's lifetime, and even now are far from being extinct, at least run a serious risk of being eternally damned.

Moreover, the most serious of the penalties which Adam and Eve were supposed to have incurred through their disobedience was that of their eventual death, and this has not been abrogated. The crucifixion of Jesus has not made us immortal. It is true that the sayings attributed to him imply that there will be life after death, but this is by no means an assurance of universal bliss: it would appear that most persons are forced to remain in limbo, and that many are doomed to eternal suffering. The description of 'Gentle Jesu, meek and mild', which is commonly presented for our acceptance, does not fit the rather irascible character whom the Evangelists quite frequently portray. 'Forgive your enemies' is a good moral principle, but it is not one to which Jesus is represented as consistently adhering.

I do not press this point because it would take us too far afield to consider how far a coherent description can be extracted from the Gospels of a Jewish preacher, in whose actual existence it would be reasonable to believe. The gravamen of Paine's charge against Christianity is not that Jesus is himself a figure of legend, or even that he was not divine, which in fact there is no good evidence that he ever claimed to be, but rather that the principle in which the religion is grounded is morally objectionable. The principle in question is that of vicarious atonement. As Paine puts it, 'the theory or doctrine of redemption has for its basis an idea of pecuniary justice, and not that of moral justice.' 'If,' he continues,

> I owe a person money, and cannot pay him, and he threatens to put me in prison, another person can take the debt upon himself and pay it for me. But if I have committed a crime, every circumstance of the case is changed. Moral justice cannot take the innocent for the guilty even if the innocent would offer itself. To suppose justice to do this, is

to destroy the principle of its existence, which is the thing itself. It is then no longer justice. It is indiscriminate revenge.[1]

For my own part, I am inclined to go still further than Paine. The idea that those who have caused suffering should themselves be made to suffer for it is, indeed, emotionally appealing. I find myself wishing that persons who have indulged in torture, especially the torture of children, should undergo retribution, not merely as a means of reforming them or deterring others, but retribution for its own sake. At the same time, my reason tells me that the notion of purely retributive punishment is not defensible. Somehow we have acquired the idea that wrongs are righted if harm is done to the person who perpetrated them; in some cases they can be: a thief, who has not got rid of it, can be obliged to return stolen property; but these cases are exceptional. If the thief is not in a position to make restitution, it is not clear how putting him in prison benefits his victim. There may be good utilitarian reasons for punishing murderers; but whatever form their punishment takes, and whatever effect it has, it does not have the effect of bringing the victim back to life. If pain is an evil, the infliction of more pain does not wipe the evil out. There is no such thing as squaring the account. Two wrongs do not make a right.

I am not the first person to reason in this fashion and I dare say that others who agree with me so far have sometimes found it difficult to follow the argument where it leads them. I am bound to admit that I often do so myself. My reason and my emotions come into conflict and my reason does not always win. I sometimes find myself wishing harm to others, either reacting to what I take to be a personal affront, or else more honourably out of moral indignation. It adds to the confusion, that at least in the second type of case, I cannot bring myself to be ashamed of my feelings, though I believe that the actual exercise of vengeance would be beyond me. This is not an objection to violence as such, for instance in self-defence or in the interest of a cause which one believes to be just. It is the shady concept of retribution, and the depth of one's emotional commitment to it, that are mentally disturbing.

I have been drawn into a digression, besides hovering on the fringes of a philosophical problem which I do not know how to solve. One thing which is clear to me, however, is that whichever view one takes of retribution in general, there is no justification of any sort for the principle of vicarious atonement, and this fact, as Paine perceived, is itself sufficient to demolish the claim of Christianity to be even a beneficent myth.

[1] *Writings of Thomas Paine*, vol. IV, p. 43.

At the time that Paine wrote *The Age of Reason*, the view of orthodox Christians was that the Bible was the word of God. For example, in the case of the Old Testament, it was believed that God dictated the books of the Pentateuch to Moses and the book of Samuel to Samuel, and that it was through divine inspiration that Solomon wrote his Proverbs and David his Psalms. As might be expected, Paine has no difficulty in discrediting all these attributions. His principal and decisive argument is that persons are not the authors of books which record in the past tense events that happened long after their deaths or actually consist in the deaths of the putative authors themselves. This applies in the case of both Moses and Samuel. There are Proverbs which refer retrospectively to Solomon and at least one of the best-known Psalms was evidently written after the Jews had returned from their captivity in Babylon, which occurred more than four hundred years after King David's death.

Admittedly, the fact that these books were not written by the authors to whom they were long attributed does not entail that the persons who did compile them were not divinely inspired. Paine makes much of the fact that the decision as to which books definitely constituted the Bible, as opposed to those that were apocryphal, was not taken until the fourth century AD and then at least to some extent by lot, but even this is not formally inconsistent with its being in its roundabout way the work of God. A stronger argument, assuming the conception of the deity that was shared by Paine and his opponents, is that if the Bible in its entirety were the word of God all of the statements in it must be true; but this at least is not logically possible since many of them are mutually inconsistent in the Old Testament as well as the New.

Another point on which Paine and his adversaries agreed was that God was morally good, but, as Paine repeatedly points out, this is not the conclusion that one would naturally draw if one took everything that was asserted of God in the Old Testament to be literally true. Or rather, it is not the conclusion that one would draw if one believed that such things as the barbarous treatment by the Jews of the captives that accrued to them in warfare were not only truly reported by God's own amanuenses, but also enacted in accordance with his instructions or at any rate with his approval. The line that Paine takes is that these barbarities were in fact committed by the Jews, but that they were not sanctioned by God.

Could we permit ourselves to suppose that the Almighty would distinguish any nation of people by the name of *his chosen people*, we must suppose that people to have been an example to all the rest of

the world of the purest piety and humanity, and not such a nation of
ruffians and cut-throats as the ancient Jews were – a people who,
corrupted by and copying after such monsters and imposters as
Moses and Aaron, Joshua, Samuel and David, had distinguished
themselves above all others on the face of the known earth for
barbarity and wickedness. If we will not stubbornly shut our eyes
and steel our hearts it is impossible not to see, in spite of all that
long-established superstition imposes upon the mind, that the
flattering appellation of *his chosen people* is no other than a LIE which
the priests and leaders of the Jews had invented to cover the baseness
of their own characters; and which Christian priests sometimes as
corrupt, and often as cruel, have professed to believe.[1]

Never mind if Paine's description even of the ancient Jews is not
altogether fair. Even he may not have been exempt from the prejudice
against the Jewish people which was widespread among his contemporaries and is not yet extinct. What is much more remarkable is
Paine's failure to notice that the very existence of barbarity and
wickedness which he attributes to the Jews presents a threat to his own
religious beliefs. The problem of evil is just as much a problem for deists
as it is for Christians, at least so long as the deists believe, as Paine did,
that their Supreme Being is wholly benevolent as well as all-powerful. I
also find it curious that while Paine addresses arguments, which we
shall presently examine, to support his belief in a Creator, he takes the
benevolence of this deity for granted. To put it more precisely, he looks
for no further proof than the accomplishment of the Creation. But while
Christianity may be a myth, the existence of human suffering is not.

For the most part, Paine is content to accept the books of Kings and
Chronicles, so far as they are mutually consistent, as historically
accurate, except when they record such untoward events as Elijah's
transportation by a whirlwind into Heaven. Neither has he much of
interest to say about the Old Testament prophets, beyond pointing out
that of all of them only Isaiah and Jeremiah are mentioned in the
historical books. The name of Jonah does occur in Kings but is not
connected with the book of Jonah, which Paine, solely on internal
evidence, chooses to regard as a Gentile satire.

There is perhaps one point worth noticing in Paine's rapid review of
the prophetic books. The phrase 'Behold, a virgin[2] shall conceive, and

---

[1] *Writings of Thomas Paine*, vol. IV, pp. 114–15.
[2] In the original Hebrew, the word can be taken to mean no more than 'young
woman'.

bear a son', occurring in the fourteenth verse of the seventh chapter of the book of Isaiah, had frequently been construed as a prediction of the Virgin Birth of Jesus Christ. Merely by examining the context in which the phrase appears, Paine is able to show that it is represented as a promise, reputedly given by Isaiah to Ahaz, King of Judah, that he would receive a sign from the Lord, assuring him of victory over the Kings of Syria and Israel who were allied against him. Isaiah had no difficulty in producing a child who was said to satisfy the necessary condition. It is only from the book of Chronicles that we learn that Ahaz was nevertheless defeated, his capital, Jerusalem, pillaged, a hundred and twenty thousand of his subjects killed, and two hundred thousand carried into captivity.

Paine deals more summarily with the New Testament than with the Old. Without the benefit of the biblical scholarship which began to flourish in the nineteenth century, he succeeds in making a good case for the view, now generally accepted by scholars of all persuasions, that the gospels were not written by the persons whose names they bear or compiled until many decades after the dates which they assign to the events that they claim to report. Apart from stressing the improbability of the entire story, and the absence of any corroborating evidence from contemporary sources, Paine relies mainly on the discrepancies in the four accounts of its principal episodes. Thus the Annunciation is not mentioned at all in the books ascribed to Mark and John and different accounts of it are given in Matthew and Luke. It is only in Matthew that Herod is represented as ordering the murder of all male children under two years of age, causing Joseph and Mary to flee with the infant Jesus into Egypt. Paine considers it worth remarking that John the Baptist, who was also under two years of age, survived the order, but his adversaries might retort that there is no evidence that Herod's order was carried out with total efficiency. This would, however, be a dangerous argument for them to use since such a proceeding would be likely to attract notice and there is no independent evidence that it ever took place at all.

The author of Matthew is again the odd man out when it comes to reporting the details of the crucifixion and the resurrection. He alone writes of an earthquake accompanying the crucifixion, of there being darkness over all the land from the sixth to the ninth hour, of the opening of graves and the emergence from them of saints, all of them phenomena which might have been expected to have attracted public notice. More importantly, the author of Matthew alone reports that the Jews persuaded Pilate to set a guard upon Jesus's sepulchre and alone introduces another earthquake when an angel rolls back the stone from the door of the sepulchre and then sits upon it. The other Evangelical writers agree with him about the presence of angels though there is no general accord about their number and position, any more than there is about the identities of the women who visited the sepulchre and the times at which they did so.

Paine pays similar attention to the discrepancies in the gospel accounts of the posthumous appearances of Jesus to his disciples and the place and manner of his ascension into Heaven. Since his criticism is based upon a selection of the internal evidence, which it is open to anyone to peruse, I do not think it necessary to enter into all its details.

The only other parts of the New Testament of which Paine takes any notice are the Epistles of Paul. Here, again lacking the knowledge acquired through modern scholarship, he fails to identify these epistles as the earliest of Christian sources or to acknowledge the decisive part that Paul played in the diffusion and the doctrinal content of Christianity. This allows him to say that

> Whether the fourteen epistles ascribed to Paul were written by him or not is a matter of indifference; they are either argumentative or dogmatical; and as the argument is defective and the dogmatical part is merely presumptive, it signifies not who wrote them.[1]

The only point on which he explicitly joins issue with Paul concerns Paul's taking resurrection to be evidence of immortality. Paine's counter-argument is that the evidence goes the other way: 'If I have already died in this body, and am raised again in the same body in which I have died, it is presumptive evidence that I shall die again.'[2] This depends upon the assumption, which Paul presumably did not accept, that resurrection entails reincarnation: moreover if the idea of reincarnation makes any sense at all, which is open to dispute, it can accommodate immortality, so long as an infinite series of reincarnations of the same creature is allowed to be a possibility.

Paine's final assessment of Christianity is very harsh:

> Of all the systems of religion that ever were invented, there is none more derogatory to the Almighty, more unedifying to man, more repugnant to reason, and more contradictory in itself, than this thing called Christianity. Too absurd for belief, too impossible to convince,

[1] *Writings of Thomas Paine*, vol. IV, pp. 180–81.
[2] ibid., p. 177.

and too inconsistent for practice, it renders the heart torpid, or produces only atheists and fanatics. As an engine of power, it serves the purposes of despotism; and as a means of wealth, the avarice of priests; but so far as respects the good of man in general, it leads to nothing here or hereafter.[1]

I do not know what to say to this. I do not find Christianity credible, but I am not sure that it is a more absurd myth than the religion of Zoroaster. Undoubtedly it has bred many fanatics, but so have the Hindu religions, and so has Islam. It would be difficult to find a more obnoxious cult than that of the Aztecs, of which human sacrifice on a large scale was an integral part. Even so, Christianity might be considered worse if its threat of damnation is understood to imply a probability of eternal suffering. Perhaps few Christians nowadays take such a literal view of Hell but many have done so in the past. I suppose that if one takes full account of the persecution of heretics, the frequency and savagery of the religious wars which Christianity had engendered, the harm caused, especially to children, by the pernicious doctrine of original sin, a case could be made for saying that the world would have been better off without Christianity. All the same, it is ridiculous for Paine to assert that it has never done any good at all. Quite apart from the magnificent music, painting and literature which it has inspired, many people have found comfort in believing it, and it has caused many people, however irrationally, to lead admirable lives. The truth is that it is futile to attempt to draw up balance sheets of this kind. There is just no telling what the course of history would have been if Constantine in the fourth century AD had chosen to make Mithraism or the cult of Isis, rather than Christianity, the official religion of the Roman Empire or if Julian the Apostate, a much finer character, had been able at a slightly later date to rehabilitate the pagan gods.

For my own part, since I do not count secular humanism as a religion, I abjure any religious belief, but this was far from being true of Thomas Paine. His hatred of Christianity, his determination to bring all its faults to light, arose from his conviction that the widespread influence which it commanded was a disservice to religion. God should be worshipped directly as the Creator of the Universe. We have no need of any intermediaries. As for our knowledge of him it can come to us only through his works:

> We have only a confused idea of his power, if we have not the means of comprehending something of its immensity. We can have no idea

[1] ibid., pp. 189–90.

of his wisdom, but by knowing the order and manner in which it acts. The principles of science lead to this knowledge; for the Creator of man is the Creator of science, and it is through that medium that man can see God, as it were, face to face.[1]

Paine's confession of faith in the first chapter of *The Age of Reason* is short and moving:

> I believe in one God and no more: and I hope for happiness beyond this life.
>
> I believe in the equality of men, and I believe that religious duties consist in doing justice, having mercy, and endeavouring to make our fellow creatures happy.[2]

After going on to say that he does not believe in the creed proposed by any church that he knows of, Paine ends with the simple statement 'My own mind is my own church.'[3]

Paine's moral sentiments are unexceptionable. What remains in question is his deism itself. Does he supply us with any good reason for believing that God exists?

The arguments which he briefly put forward were not new. They were what Immanuel Kant in his *Critique of Pure Reason* had called 'The Cosmological Proof', and 'The Physico-Theological Proof', more popularly known as 'The Argument from Design'. Kant refuted both of them. It is, however, unlikely that Paine had heard of Kant, though *The Critique of Pure Reason* was published in 1781. Paine did not read German, and the book was not translated into English until 1855. He could have read David Hume's *Dialogues Concerning Natural Religion*, which was published in 1779, three years after Hume's death, but there is no evidence that he did so.

Paine's rendering of the Cosmological Proof is extremely brief.

> The only idea man can affix to the name of God, is that of a *first cause*, the cause of all things. And, incomprehensibly difficult as it is for a man to conceive what a first cause is, he arrives at the belief of it from the tenfold greater difficulty of disbelieving it.[4]

---

[1] *Writings of Thomas Paine*, vol. IV, p. 191.
[2] ibid., pp. 21–2.
[3] ibid.
[4] ibid., p. 47.

After adding, irrelevantly, that there is more difficulty in conceiving of space and time as not coming to an end than their coming to an end, Paine goes on to assert that everything of which we are aware, including oneself, 'carries in itself the internal evidence that it did not make itself'.[1]

The fact that nothing, whether organic or inorganic, makes itself is then supposed to lead us, compulsively, 'to the belief of a first cause eternally existing, of a nature totally different to any material existence we know of, and by the power of which all things exist; and this first cause, man calls God.'[2]

The flaws in this argument are obvious. If one starts with the premiss that everything has a cause, one cannot consistently arrive at the conclusion that there was a first cause; for a first cause, by definition, is something that does not have a cause. Even if it were the case, which I doubt, that every object displayed internal evidence that it did not make itself, it would not follow that something else made it; it might not have been 'made' at all. Presumably Paine held this to be true of God, but there again he succumbs to the contradiction of starting with the premiss that everything is made by something else and concluding with the existence of an unmade maker. He could, indeed, have avoided the contradiction by limiting his premiss to the proposition that everything physical is made by something else, but since the argument would then carry the implication that the maker was physical in its turn, it would have left him with no warrant for a transition to a purely spiritual first cause. This was, in fact, the mainstay of Kant's argument. He held that the concept of causality applied only to constituents of the phenomenal world: it lost its meaning when it was extended to an object that was supposed to transcend space and time.

One may, however, ask whether this was a supposition that Paine actually made. It is customary for deists, as indeed for persons adhering to any religion that incorporates belief in a Creator, to describe him as eternal but I have not discovered any arguments in favour of this proposition, or even any explanation of what it is supposed to mean. The one point that seems clear is that if there was an act of creation is must have taken place at some instant in time. I think that we have to agree with Kant that the notion of even a single descent into time on the part of a being who exists outside time is not intelligible. Suppose then that we construe eternal existence as equivalent to existence at every moment of time, perhaps with the implication that this series of

[1] ibid.
[2] ibid.

moments has neither beginning nor end. This very nearly brings the Creator into his universe, except that he is not endowed with spatial properties. We are left with the picture of a series of physical events accompanied by and, more importantly, preceded by an infinite series of purely psychical events. Let us grant, for the sake of argument, that this picture is intelligible. Then the question arises why the physical events are thought to require these predecessors. Since causality alone would not carry us beyond the physical series, the answer must be that the physical events are thought to furnish some overall explanation of the physical world. In this way the cosmological argument gives way to the argument from design.

I implied earlier that it was surprising to find Paine concerning himself only with the question whether space and time would ever come to an end, since the doctrine of creation, which he wished to uphold, bore rather on their having a beginning. The position which we have attributed to him, in an attempt to make his deism coherent, is that space had a beginning, in the sense that there was a time when space had not yet been created, but that time itself had not. The idea of there being series which are infinite in both directions, inasmuch as they lack both a first and last term, is familiar enough in mathematics: the series of fractions intervening between two cardinal numbers provides a simple example. Its application to time, however, is more dubious. The propositions that time had a beginning and that it did not are both easy to formulate. Either there is just one event that precedes every other, or there is no such event: for every event there is an event which precedes it. The trouble is that if one asks which of these propositions is true, our imaginations falter. Neither proposition is verifiable on its own. At best, one or other forms part of a scientific theory which as a whole accords better than its rivals with our current stock of observations. Currently, the theory which appears to be most strongly supported is one that allows for there having been a first event. I hope to have made it clear that this is not a first cause, in any sense that would have been acceptable to Paine.

I turn now to the argument from design. It is confidently supported throughout the first volume of Paine's book by references to Newtonian mechanics, especially in its dealings with astronomy, and to the successful applications of geometry to physical phenomena. The operation of the lever is one example. William Paley's *A View of the Evidences of Christianity*, which has become the standard text in the exposition of the argument from design, was not published until 1794, but it went beyond Paine only in laying greater stress upon the adaptation of means to ends in the structure and behaviour of organisms and in developing an analogy with human artefacts. These additions do nothing to weaken the objections already raised by Kant and Hume.

Kant's objection once again is that there is no legitimate transition from empirical phenomena, however much their orderly arrangement may impress us, to the existence of a designer beyond the reach of our experience. We have no reason to suppose that things in the natural world are not capable on their own account of exhibiting the order and harmony and the obedience to universal laws that we discover in them. Hume, after putting into the mouth of one of the characters in his *Dialogues* a very strong statement of the argument from design, on the theme that 'The curious adapting of means to ends, throughout all nature, resembles exactly, though it much exceeds, the productions of human contrivance' with the consequence that 'the Author of nature is somewhat similar to the mind of man: though possessed of much larger faculties, proportional to the grandeur of the work, which he has executed',[1] supplies another character, Philo, with a set of objections which, to my mind, are even more convincing. I should add that I am in fundamental agreement with Hume's view that all causal judgements need to be ultimately based on regularities that occur within our experience.

Assuming this to be so, Philo has no difficulty in showing that the argument of his opponent, Cleanthes, is no stronger than an argument from analogy. But then, if we assume that like effects have like causes, which is a crucial move in Cleanthes's argument, we have no warrant for concluding that the Universe was planned by an infinite eternal incorporeal Being, since we have no experience of anything of this sort. Human artefacts are constructed by persons who are physically embodied and do not live for ever.

Viewed in this light the analogy is too strong to suit the apologist for deism, but in another aspect it is too weak. There is no denying that, in addition to human artefacts, the world contains many natural objects which resemble artefacts in that they or their parts perform some function, to which they are more or less well adapted. But this is not enough for the deist. He needs to show that the universe as a whole is like a machine: at least that there is some purpose which it serves. The world as a whole is no more like a machine than it is like an animal or vegetable organism, and there is no evidence whatsoever of there being any purpose which it serves.

[1] David Hume, *Dialogues Concerning Natural Religion*, ed. Norman Kemp Smith (Bobbs Merrill, 12th ed. 1977), p. 143.

Philo is represented as making two further points of importance. The first is that if the features of the physical world which are thought to call for explanation are referred back to 'a similar universe of ideas',[1] why should we stop there? Why should not the series of ideas itself stand in need of explanation? It is obvious that this point is not weakened but only obscured if 'the universe of ideas' is deified.

The second point is a variant of the first. Experience has shown us, as Philo is made to say, that 'matter can preserve that perpetual agitation, which seems essential to it, and yet maintain a constancy in the forces, which it produces'.[2] Why then should it be thought incapable, without any supernatural assistance, of giving rise to 'all the appearing wisdom and contrivance which is in the universe'?[3]

In fairness to Paine it should be said at this point that his reading of Newton had led him to the conclusion that 'the natural state of matter, as to place, is a state of rest'.[4] For there to be motion there has to be an external cause. I take the reference to be to Newton's concept of force. In my own opinion, the use of the term 'force' in physics is misleading, in so far as it suggests that something more 'active' is involved than relative changes of position. However this may be, there is no warrant in science for taking the causes of motion to be anything other than physical and I should want to take the further step of analysing these causes in terms of natural laws. Here, particularly, I should be at odds with Paine. 'Everything,' he writes, 'which has hitherto been discovered, with respect to the motion of the planets in the [solar] system, relates only to the laws by which the motion acts and not to the cause of motion.' And a little later he differentiates between the motion of matter on earth, in its states of decomposition or recomposition, and 'the motion that upholds the solar system [which] is of a entire different kind, and is not a property of matter'. I hope that I have said enough to show that even if this conclusion were acceptable, which I do not grant, it would not warrant the ascription of such motion to a supernatural cause.

These last quotations have been taken not from *The Age of Reason* but from a lecture entitled 'The Existence of God' which Paine delivered in January 1797 at the first public meeting in Paris of the Society of Theophilanthropists which Paine had helped to found in the previous September. Perhaps it is because the lecture is primarily devoted to recommending the study of natural philosophy as an antidote to

[1] *Dialogues Concerning Natural Religion*, p. 162.
[2] ibid., p. 183.
[3] ibid., p. 184.
[4] *Writings of Thomas Paine*, vol. IV, p. 241.

atheism and contains no onslaught upon Christianity that Conway regards it as an early work, dating perhaps from the middle 1770s, when Paine was writing for the *Pennsylvania Magazine*, and polished up for the occasion. Not that Paine ever gave up his view that mathematics and the natural sciences should be taught in schools, rather than the Latin and Ancient Greek which dominated the curriculum, at least in the more prestigious establishments, not only in Paine's day but well into this century. Paine's objection to this practice is bluntly stated in the first part of *The Age of Reason*.

> As there is nothing new to be learned from the dead languages, all the useful books being already translated, the languages are become useless, and the time expended in teaching and in learning them is wasted.[1]

Consequently, he proceeds to argue, the study of these languages should be abolished.

Having myself received a predominantly classical education, and believing that I derived some benefit from it, I should feel obliged to attempt to rebut Paine's argument if I had actually continued the study of the classics. As it is, there are so many who are much better qualified than I to take up Paine's challenge that I am content to leave the task to them.

A remark, made by Conway, that Paine's lecture to the Theophilanthropists was based on Newton's letters to Bentley, in which Newton himself postulates a divine power as necessary to explain planetary motion, is one on which I do feel obliged to comment. There is no balking the fact that many intelligent thinkers have been deists, Voltaire as well as Paine, Newton indeed more nearly Christian. It has been suggested to me[2] that it was rational to be a deist until Darwin developed his theory of evolution. I cannot accept this suggestion, since, if my arguments are valid, deism would not supply us with an explanation for any natural phenomena, and I do not think it rational to accept a wholly vacuous hypothesis. At the same time, I acknowledge that a neo-Darwinian explanation of adaptive behaviour in terms of a well fortified theory of natural selection at least tends to diminish the initial attraction of the argument from design.

Though he remained a member of it, the Theophilanthropical

---

[1] ibid., p. 56.
[2] By my former colleague Richard Dawkins; see his admirable *The Blind Watchmaker* (Longman 1986).

Society developed in a way that cannot have been entirely welcome to Paine. Its members took to singing humanitarian and even theistic hymns and to sponsoring ethical readings from the Bible, as well as from Chinese, Hindu and Greek authors. Not that Paine did not intend his deism to sustain morality but what he took to be its scientific basis was more important to him.

The Theophilanthropical Society ceased to exist in Paris as a consequence of the Concordat which Napoleon Bonaparte concluded with Pope Pius VII in July 1801, reinstating Catholicism in France. Napoleon is reported to have said that he himself did not believe that such a person as Jesus Christ ever existed, but if the people were superstitious, he saw no point in thwarting them. Paine revived the Theophilanthropical Society in New York and its journal *The Theophilanthropist* appeared for a short time after his death. The Society was a forerunner of the South Place Ethical Society which holds its meetings in London in Conway Hall, very suitably named after the American Moncure Conway, to whom we have seen that we owe so much for our knowledge of the life and works of Thomas Paine.

The Age of Reason did not provoke the same hostility in England as the *Rights of Man*. Even so a bookseller called Thomas Williams who had sold one copy of it was tried before a special jury in 1797 on a charge of blasphemy and sentenced by Lord Kenyon to a year's imprisonment. On this occasion, Thomas Erskine appeared for the prosecution, evoking a letter of protest from Paine, in which he claimed, truly, that if he criticized the Bible it was from religious motives.

Indeed, whatever logical objections there may be to Thomas Paine's deism, one cannot but admire the force and courage of his attack not only on Christianity but on any form of religious superstition.

9

The Last Years

It was not only *The Age of Reason* that should have made Paine doubtful about his welcome in the United States. George Washington had died in 1799, but his memory was still revered, and Paine had done his utmost to besmirch it, though not, it must be said, without some provocation. As we have seen, he had served under Washington in the American War of Independence, Washington had shown good will towards him and had endeavoured, not wholly without success, to induce the States to grant him some financial recompense:[1] they had corresponded on friendly terms before Paine took refuge in France. So Paine was convinced both that Washington appreciated what he had done for America and that he considered him a personal friend. His suprise, therefore, turned into violent indignation when Washington, whom he truly believed to have the power to secure his release from the Luxembourg prison, not only appeared to have made no effort to do so, but failed to communicate with him in any way at all. He became even angrier when Washington continued to ignore his existence after Monroe had made use of a letter from the Secretary of State, Randolph, to intervene with the French authorities in Paine's favour. As a result on 22 February 1795, Washington's sixty-third birthday, Paine wrote him a reproachful letter, which Monroe persuaded him not to send. Some eighteen months later he included this letter in a long and bitter 'Letter to George Washington' which he published as an appendix to his *Memorial Addressed to James Monroe*.

The substance of this first letter can be fairly briefly summarized. It begins with Paine's saying that he writes with reluctance since 'it is

[1] See above pp. 50–51.

always painful to reproach those one would wish to respect'. He then
argues at some length that Washington showed ingratitude in allowing
him to languish in a French prison.

> I do not hesitate to say that you have not served America with more
> disinterestedness – or greater zeal, or more fidelity, than myself, and
> I know not if with better effect.

Why then had Paine been so badly treated? Because he was an
opponent of Washington's foreign policy. Gouverneur Morris was
wholly unfit to be the American Ambassador to France and neglected
his duties. But 'if the inconsistent conduct of Morris exposed the
interest of America to some hazard in France, the pusillanimous
conduct of Mr Jay in England has rendered the American government
contemptible in Europe.'[1]

The Mr Jay in question was John Jay, who had in 1789 been
appointed the first Chief Justice of the Supreme Court of the United
States. He had been sent to England to discuss the question of the
freedom of the seas, and had committed the American government to
what Paine regarded as a cowardly and dishonourable treaty of
neutrality, which conceded to England the right to capture American
ships which might be carrying supplies to France. To allow a foreign
government to make war upon the commerce of America 'was
submission and not neutrality'.[2]

Paine concluded his letter by expressing his regret that Washington's
conduct had deprived him of the pleasure which he used to derive from
the memory of their former friendship.

It appears to have been the narrowness of Paine's escape from death,
as the result of the illness which he contracted in prison, that caused
him actually to send Washington a shorter but more personal and
bitter letter in September 1795. He there writes that only his illness,
from which he has not yet fully recovered, has prevented him from
returning to America, that if he had returned he would have insisted on
Washington's showing him copies of any letters, containing references
to him, that Washington had written to Morris, Monroe or anyone else,
that as things were he desired to have copies of any such letters sent to
him, that his discovery that Robespierre had denounced him 'in the
interests of America as well as of France' had caused him to believe that
Washington had connived at his arrest and consequently that he would

---

[1] *Writings of Thomas Paine*, vol. III, pp. 230–35.
[2] ibid., p. 234.

continue to think him treacherous until Washington gave him cause to think otherwise.

Washington never replied to this letter, which was not sent to him directly but under cover to Benjamin Franklin Bache. There is evidence that the letter was read by Timothy Pickering, who had succeeded Edmund Randolph as Secretary of State, and Conway suggests that Pickering, no friend to Paine, may have withheld the letter from Washington, without explaining how Pickering came to be in a position to intercept it. In any case Conway admits that Washington had come to care less for Paine not because of *The Age of Reason*, since Washington was himself a deist, but because of his commitment to a policy which Gouverneur Morris had persuaded him that Paine was trying to frustrate. This policy, to which Paine was indeed opposed, though he was hardly in a position to frustrate it, was that of making a commercial treaty with England in return for England's surrendering the six military posts that she still maintained in America.

This was not an indefensible policy, but it did favour England at the expense of France and in the published 'Letter to George Washington', dated 30 June 1796, and incorporating the two letters from which I have been quoting, Paine contrived to embarrass Washington by reproducing a letter that Washington had written to the Committee of Public Safety of the French Republic, submitting to its wish to have Gouverneur Morris recalled, commending Monroe as Morris's successor and referring to the French Republic as 'the great and good friend and ally of the United States', at a time when Jay was secretly negotiating the English treaty. Paine, whose fervent Republicanism preserved his hostility to England at all costs and his loyalty to France, in spite of the sufferings which he had undergone there, devoted a considerable portion of his letter to showing how America's nominal alliance with France had been compelled by Washington to dwindle into neutrality or worse, while 'Jay's treaty of surrender' gave a monopoly of 'the rights of American commerce and navigation' to England.

For the rest, Paine's letter consisted chiefly of a recapitulation of the services which he had rendered to the United States and a bitter attack on the character and conduct of George Washington. The following is a typical extract:

As my citizenship in America was not altered or diminished by anything I had done in Europe . . . it was the duty of the Executive department in America, to have made (at least) some enquiries about me, as soon as it heard of my imprisonment. But if this had not been the case, that government owed it to me on every ground and principle of honour and gratitude. Mr Washington owed it to me on every score of private acquaintance, I will not now say, friendship; for it has some time been known by those who know him, that he has no friendships; that he is incapable of forming any: he can serve or desert a man, or a cause, with constitutional indifference; and it is this cold hermaphrodite faculty that imposed itself upon the world, and was credited for a while by enemies as by friends, for prudence, moderation and impartiality.[1]

Paine carries his indictment of Washington to the point of alleging that whereas Washington's 'egotism' leads him to speak as though the American Revolution was 'all his own doing', his actual contribution was very small. He had no share in the political part and his military achievement was conspicuous only for his 'constancy'. He was, indeed, nominally Commander in Chief but of the military campaigns which he actually conducted that of 1776 was a failure, those of 1775, 1778, 1779 and 1780 achieved nothing except the taking of Stony Point by General Wayne. The crucial defeat of General Burgoyne at Saratoga in 1777 was effected by General Gates, the Southern States were liberated by General Greene, and the defeat of Lord Cornwallis in 1781 mainly due to French ships and money brought to America by Colonel Laurens and Paine himself. Washington is given no credit for any of those achievements.

Paine's letter ends with the reaffirmation of the evil consequences to America of Jay's treaty with England and the following diatribe:

This is the ground on which America now stands. All her rights of commerce and navigation are to begin anew, and that with loss of character to begin with. If there is sense enough left in the heart to call a blush into the cheek, the Washington administration must be ashamed to appear. – And as to you, Sir, treacherous in private friendship (for so you have been to me, and that in the day of danger) and a hypocrite in public life, the world will be puzzled to decide whether you are an apostate or an imposter; whether you have abandoned good principles, or whether you ever had any.[2]

At the end of his presidency Washington wrote to a friend, speaking of himself in the third person, 'Although he is soon to become a private

[1] *Writings of Thomas Paine*, vol. III, p. 220.
[2] ibid., p. 252.

citizen, his opinions are to be knocked down, and his character reduced as low as they are capable of sinking it, even by resorting to absolute falsehoods.' As evidence, he then adduces the publication of Paine's letter. He does not, however, specify what were the absolute falsehoods that he took it to contain. One of them may have been the allegation that so far from taking any steps to rescue his old friend from the miserable fate that had befallen him in Paris, he gave Robespierre to understand that he would be rather in favour of his putting Paine to death. I take it that this allegation was, indeed, false to some extent. What is likely to have happened, as we have seen,[1] is that Washington did get Jefferson to ask Gouverneur Morris whether anything could be done for Paine and received the reply that Morris had approached the Committee of Public Safety, on Paine's behalf, claiming him as an American citizen, and had been rebuffed. This still leaves Washington open to the charge that, if he really cared at all deeply for Paine, he would have pressed the matter further. There is also the question how Robespierre came to receive the impression that it would be in America's interest to be rid of Paine. If he obtained it from Gouverneur Morris, was Morris acting on his own account? The truth is probably more complicated. I think it unlikely that Morris was obeying any instruction that Washington had given him. At the same time he believed that Washington shared his enthusiasm for an alliance with England and it might have occurred to him that Washington, by all accounts not a very warm-hearted man, would not have regarded the loss of Paine as too high a price to pay for it, especially since he had been given reason to believe that Robespierre could not be dissuaded from putting Paine to death.

With regard to the English treaty, Washington could reasonably claim that Paine had not been wholly fair to him in representing it simply as an act of disloyalty and ingratitude to France. Paine should at least have admitted that Washington had a motive in securing the removal of English forces from American territory.

I think also that Washington was entitled to resent Paine's belittlement of his contribution to the success of the American Revolution. Paine had written of Washington's 'constancy' as though it amounted to nothing more than his not being a traitor like Benedict Arnold, but this was a travesty of the facts. There were indeed times when Washington seemed to despair of victory, but there were always good grounds for the pessimism that he displayed. The important point is that he never gave in: his constancy was exhibited in his leadership.

[1] See above p. 127–29.

His generalship may have been predominantly Fabian; perhaps his relationship to General Gates resembled that of Eisenhower to General Patton. The fact remains that Fabius brought the Romans victory.

In perspective, Paine does not come well out of this episode. In attacking Washington, he carried his invective too far: there is a trace of jealousy detectable in it. There are, however, excuses to be made for him. He had just passed through a serious ordeal; he was not yet recovered in health; even if he was mistaken in thinking that Washington had been totally indifferent to his fate, he had good reason to believe that this was so. In fact, Washington's attitude was not beyond reproach; however much he was deceived by Gouverneur Morris, he should not so readily have forsaken Paine.

What is of greater interest is the political motive of Paine's outburst. For all the pre-eminence of his part in the American Revolution, Washington did not match Paine in his enthusiasm for representative government as such; he was neither such a foe to England, once the two countries had ceased to be at war, nor did he share Paine's hostility to monarchical government in any form. We have seen that Paine approved of the American Constitution, and did not consider that it unduly favoured the Executive branch. Nevertheless he was aware of the danger of the American President's achieving too close a resemblance to a King.

This danger was made to appear more imminent by the rapid appearance of two main parties in American politics, the Federalists and the Republican-Democrats, one of them, as the contrast in their titles suggests, having a much weaker attachment to Republican principles than the other. George Washington himself is described in books of reference as a Federalist, mainly, I believe, on account of the composition of his Cabinet. Temperamentally, he may have been autocratic, but there is no evidence that he wished to restore hereditary government or tamper with the Constitution in any way that could legitimately give offence to Paine. At most he might be accused of favouring aristocracy; not so much an aristocracy of blood, as an aristocracy of wealth.

The person who aroused Paine's deep suspicion was not so much George Washington, in spite of his denunciation of him, as Washington's Federalist successor, John Adams. John Adams's tenure of the Presidency was limited to a single term, and by the time Paine arrived in America the office had passed into the hands of his friend the Republican-Democrat Thomas Jefferson. The election which Jefferson had won had been very closely contested, and the Federalists remained a powerful political force. Since Paine believed them, rightly, not to be admirers of his *Rights of Man*, and, perhaps unjustly, to be attempting to turn the government of America into at least an oligarchy, he wasted no time over engaging them in literary warfare. He arrived in America on 30 October 1802 and on 15 November of that year there appeared in the *National Intelligencer* the first of seven letters entitled 'Thomas Paine to the Citizens of the United States, And particularly to the Leaders of the Federal Faction'. Five more such letters appeared in the *National Intelligencer* between 22 November 1802 and 29 January 1803, a sixth in the Philadelphia *Aurora*, dated 12 March, and the last in the Trenton *The True American*, dated 21 April 1803. An eighth letter, which appeared in the *National Intelligencer* on 2 February 1803, is sometimes cited as part of this series, but as it consists wholly in a rebuttal of a charge of atheism brought against Paine, in a letter quoted in his reply, by his old friend and ally Samuel Adams, because of *The Age of Reason*, of which Samuel Adams had probably read only hostile accounts, without having read the book itself, it is not at all political.

The first of the political letters aims at little more than announcing Paine's reappearance in the United States and his intention not to ask for or accept any place or office in Jefferson's government. His motive was to protect Jefferson from any guilt by association which might extend to him on account of *The Age of Reason*. Paine also took the opportunity to puff *Rights of Man*, which John Adams and others of his party had criticized. 'It had,' he wrote, 'the greatest run of any work ever published in the English language. The number of copies circulated in England, Scotland and Ireland, besides translations into foreign languages, was between four and five hundred thousand.'[1] Paine goes on to say that he relinquished all his profits to the English people and would have done the same in America if the book had been published there, following the precedent which he had set in the case of his *Common Sense*. 'My reward existed in the ambition to do good, and the independent happiness of my own mind.'[2]

In the first letter there was little invective: in the second there is very little else. Paine's attack is directed against the Federalists in general and John Adams in particular. He does not deny the necessity of a Federal government. On the contrary he claims credit for being the first person to suggest that it be instituted, besides playing a leading part in the process of its establishment. His view was that the danger inherent

[1] *Writings of Thomas Paine*, vol. III, p. 382.
[2] ibid.

in the existence of a centralized executive power would be nullified by the representative system.

What had since happened, according to Paine, was that the Federalists had secretly done away with this safeguard. Under cover of the name they sought to put an end to what it originally stood for, the exercise of the general will, filtered through their representatives, of the citizens of the different States.

> To them it served as a cloak for treason, a mask for tyranny. Scarcely were they placed in the seat of power and office, than Federalism was to be destroyed, and the representative system of government, the pride and glory of America, and the palladium of her liberties, was to be overthrown and abolished. The next generation was not to be free. The son was to bend his neck beneath the father's foot, and live, deprived of his rights, under hereditary control. Among the men of this apostate description, is to be ranked the ex-president *John Adams*. It has been the political career of this man to begin with hypocrisy, proceed with arrogance, and finish in contempt. May such be the fate of all such characters.[1]

Paine goes on to say that he had been suspicious of John Adams ever since the year 1776, when Adams had criticized *Common Sense* for its attack on the English form of government. The implication was that Adams had always been a monarchist, and since Washington was childless had hoped to inaugurate his own dynasty.

Paine offers no further evidence for this accusation, nor does he bring any charges against the Federalist party except their attempting to increase revenue by the imposition of taxes which Jefferson subsequently abolished and their raising a standing army of twenty-five thousand men. Paine argues that at a time when England and France were busy fighting one another, there could not appear to be any need for such an army to defend the United States, and he infers from this that the purpose of raising it was to destroy the representative system. If this inference was correct, it seems strange that the army was not used to keep the Federalists in power.

That Paine's political judgement had been at least temporarily impaired by the unforeseen hostility with which he had been greeted in America on account of *The Age of Reason*, added to the injustice with which he had been treated in France, is shown by his referring in his

[1] *Writings of Thomas Paine*, vol. III, pp. 388–9.

next letter to 'The Reign of Terror that raged in America during the latter end of the Washington administration, and the whole of that of Adams'. Not even the repressive measures taken by Pitt, to prevent the advance of democracy in England, could fairly be described as a Reign of Terror. Apart from this, Paine's letter is entirely devoted to an exposition of his grievances, mainly with reference to his imprisonment in France, but also complaining of the very different rewards that had been adjudged by their countrymen as owing to Washington and himself for their comparable services to the American Revolution.

Of the remaining letters, three of which are filled with further denunciations of the Federalists, and more of Paine's personal reminiscences, in the course of which he reveals that the increase in value during over fourteen years of the small property which he owned in America had made it easier for him to adhere to his principle of working for nothing 'where the happiness of man is at stake', the only one of historical interest is the seventh. Though the last of the series to appear in its final form, it mainly antedates the others, since the greater part of it consists in a reproduction of Paine's proposals for 'Maritime Compact' which had been published in Paris and Washington in 1800. Two or three years earlier Paine corresponded on the question with Talleyrand, the French Minister for Foreign Affairs, and had received praise from Talleyrand for his effort to 'reunite the two Republics in whose alienation the enemies of liberty triumph'.[1]

'Maritime Compact' consisted of a preamble and ten articles which there is no need to reproduce in detail. The preamble declared the intention of 'the undersigned Powers' to enter into an Association for the purpose of establishing the ensuing articles as 'a Law of Nations on the Seas'. The object being to outlaw the English practice of running the maritime commerce of any nation with which it was at war, the first article stated that the rights of nations to enjoy the freedom of the seas in time of peace should be the rights of neutral nations at all times. Consequently, a belligerent nation had no right to interfere with the shipping of a neutral nation, whether by capture and search, detention or blockade, even when it had reason to believe that the neutral ships were conveying supplies to its enemies. Most of the ensuing articles were devoted to specifying the penalties which were to be inflicted on any belligerent nation which infringed this right. They mainly consisted of an embargo on trade with the offender imposed by all the members of the association and the exclusion of its ships from all their

[1] ibid., p. 420.

ports. The tenth article bound the signatories not to supply any of the belligerent powers with military stores or armaments of any kind whatsoever.

Paine reports that he circulated his plan to the ministers of all the neutral nations who were in Paris in the summer of 1800, as well as writing four letters on the subject to Jefferson within the span of just over a fortnight. The response from the neutral powers was very gratifying. Russia, Sweden, Denmark, Portugal and Spain barred English ships from all their ports. All the Italian ports, except Venice, which was controlled by the Emperor of Germany, were similarly closed. Denmark denied England access to the port of Hamburg. Paine expresses the belief that had it not been for the untimely death of the Emperor Paul of Russia, which was designed to head the Association, a Law of Nations, in accordance with his proposals for securing the freedom of the seas, would have been proclaimed and England would have been obliged to conform to it or lose her commerce, and the mischief inflicted on America by Jay's treaty would have virtually ceased.

Paine's letters to Jefferson were written in October 1800. Replying to them in March 1801, Jefferson expressed his agreement with Paine's principles, but would not commit the United States to acting upon them. 'We should avoid implicating ourselves with the Powers of Europe, even in support of principles which we mean to pursue'.[1] In the same letter Jefferson offered Paine a passage back to the United States on an American ship which was being used to enable an emissary of Jefferson's to confer with the French authorities. The report of this offer, which we have seen that Paine declined, had been the source of Federalist attacks upon both Jefferson and Paine. It was alleged that Paine was being given an official status to which he was not entitled and even that Jefferson had given his approval to a scheme of Paine's to promote French interests at the expense of the United States. By publishing Jefferson's letter to him Paine hoped finally to demonstrate that these charges were baseless.

Paine characteristically concludes his letter by contrasting the former Administration which 'rendered itself notorious by outrage, coxcombical parade, false alarms, a continued increase of taxes, and an unceasing clamour for War', with the present Administration which deserves the support of all those who are in favour of 'Peace, moderate taxes, and mild Government'.[2]

[1] *Writings of Thomas Paine*, vol. III, p. 427.
[2] ibid., p. 429.

This letter was sent for publication in the Trenton *The True American* from Paine's old home in Bordentown. After landing in Baltimore he had made his way to Washington where he was well received by the Jeffersons. By this time he had learned that Spain had ceded Louisiana to the French who had closed New Orleans to all foreign shipping, provoking the Federalists to advocate the seizure of New Orleans. Anxious as ever to preserve the alliance of America and France, Paine wrote a letter to Jefferson suggesting that he offer to purchase Louisiana from the French, only to find that Jefferson had already had the same idea. Jefferson duly made an offer to Bonaparte which was accepted in the autumn of 1803. About a year later the French inhabitants of Louisiana delivered a remonstrance to Congress, in which they complained that they had not been granted admission to the Union and that they were being denied their right to add to their ownership of African slaves. Paine published a reply to their remonstrance, in which he argued that it was for Congress to decide when the territory was sufficiently populated to qualify for statehood, but that in the meantime its inhabitants were guaranteed the enjoyment of the same liberty and security as American citizens, and in conclusion that the import of African slaves was not a right but a power, for which they should not dare to ask Heaven, let alone man; he wondered whether they wished to repeat in Louisiana the horrors of the slave uprising in San Domingo.

Paine was vindicated on the first count but not on the second. The inhabitants of Louisiana were in no way harmed by the fact that their State was not admitted into the Union until 1812. On the other hand the moral objection to slavery made little headway in the Southern States even after its formal abolition in consequence of the Civil War.

On his way to Bordentown from Washington Paine stopped in Philadelphia, where he was distressed to find that Benjamin Rush, his old friend and ally in the campaign against slavery, would not speak to him on account of *The Age of Reason*. Paine always maintained that it was a deeply religious book, and I doubt if he ever realized how many of his friends he had offended, besides giving ammunition to his enemies, by dissociating what he took to be true religion from Christianity. It was not just that he was denounced from the pulpit at Bordentown and elsewhere. In March 1803 he planned to go to New York to see Monroe, before Monroe left again for France, and drove, in company with Colonel Kirkbride, to Trenton, intending to board a stage-coach there. When Kirkbride tried to reserve a place for Paine, the owner of the stage-coach refused to allow an avowed deist on board, and the owner of another stage company also refused, saying that his stage and horses had once been struck by lightning and that he was not going to take the risk of its happening again. Paine and Kirkbride found a carriage which took them to a friend's house in Bridgetown, but they were literally drummed out of Trenton by a hostile mob.

For all the unpopularity which his loyalty brought him, in a place where he had previously been respected, Kirkbride never weakened in his friendship for Paine and it was a severe blow to Paine when Kirkbride died in October 1803.

Paine's departure from Paris had left the Bonnevilles in financial straits and they decided to accept Paine's invitation to join him in America. Nicolas Bonneville, however, was still being kept under surveillance, after undergoing a prison sentence, as we have already remarked, for comparing Bonaparte to Cromwell, and he was denied permission to leave France. Perhaps it was feared that, once safely abroad, he would repeat his offence, though why the Emperor Napoleon Bonaparte should object to being compared to Oliver Cromwell is not entirely clear. Nevertheless, though Paine expected Nicolas Bonneville to join him in America, he never did so, and while his eldest son, Louis, was soon sent back to him, he was separated from his wife Margaret and the two younger children, Benjamin and Paine's godson Thomas, until he was able to travel to America after Napoleon's fall.

It would not appear that Paine altogether welcomed the arrival of Madame Bonneville and her children, without her husband, in the summer of 1803. She spoke no English and we have seen that, in spite of all the years that he spent in Paris, Paine never acquired more than a rudimentary knowledge of French. When she arrived he lodged her in his house at Bordentown, having arranged for her to give French lessons, while he himself stayed in New York. The two younger children were sent to boarding schools for which Paine paid. Madame Bonneville soon got tired of living in the country and joined Paine at his boarding house in New York. She was extravagant to the point of causing Paine to issue an official announcement that he was not responsible for her debts, but he seems to have paid them all the same. She did not earn much for whatever French lessons she gave and the cost of keeping her and the children led Paine to put his house at Bordentown up for sale. She kept house intermittently for him at New Rochelle and was there on Christmas Eve 1804 when a man called Derrick who owed Paine a small sum of money fired a shot which shattered the windows of Paine's study. Paine was in the room and was lucky that the bullet did not enter it. Derrick was identified and brought to trial about eighteen months later but Paine did not press charges against him.

Madame Bonneville appears not to have been either an efficient or an enthusiastic housekeeper. In a letter written from New Rochelle to a friend in New York in July 1805, Paine wrote 'It is certainly best that Mrs Bonneville go into some family as a teacher, for she has not the least talent of managing affairs for herself'. The letter is interesting for the light that it throws not only upon Paine's relations with Madame Bonneville, but also on his standard of living. It would seem that Madame Bonneville had left her son, Thomas, behind with Paine and after saying that he will also take in Benjamin 'for his own sake and his father's, but that is all I have to say', Paine continues:

> I am master of an empty house, or nearly so. I have six chairs and a table, a straw-bed, a feather bed, and a bag of straw for Thomas, a tea-kettle, an iron pot, and iron baking pan, a frying pan, a gridiron, cups, saucers, plates and dishes, knives and forks, two candlesticks and a pair of snuffers. I have a pair of fine oxen and an ox-cart, a good horse, a Chair, and a one-horse cart; a cow, and a sow and 9 pigs. When you come you must take such fare as you meet with, for I live upon tea, milk, fruit-pies, plain dumplins, and a piece of meat when I get it: but I live with that retirement and quiet that suit me. Mrs. Bonneville was an encumbrance upon me all the while she was here, for she would not do anything, not even make an apple-dumplin for her own children. If you cannot make yourself up a straw bed, I can let you have blankets, and you will have no occasion to go over to the tavern to sleep.[1]

The question arises why Madame Bonneville chose to remain in America with her two younger children, rather than return to her husband in France, and why Paine encouraged her to do so at least to the extent that he spent more money on their account than he could easily afford. I think that the obvious answer is correct. Paine had lived with the Bonnevilles for five years in Paris, paying nothing for his board on the understanding that they would come to live at his expense in the United States; if he had not much money, Nicolas Bonneville had even less; Paine was very fond of the children: it was reasonable for him to hope that Nicolas would soon be permitted to emigrate; Madame Bonneville may not have been a good housekeeper but she was by all accounts an attractive woman.

[1] *Life of Thomas Paine*, vol. II, pp. 354-5.

Was she Paine's mistress? The fact that she was over thirty years younger than he does not rule out this possibility, but there is not much reason to think it actual, beyond the fact that she was his principal legatee. She spent little time in New Rochelle and for the most part they lived in separate houses in New York. It was indeed implied by James Cheetham, the editor of a New York journal called *The American Citizen*, who published a *Life of Thomas Paine* in 1809, the year of Paine's death, that Thomas Bonneville was Paine's natural son, but when Madame Bonneville sued him for libel she had no difficulty in winning her case.

James Cheetham is of interest, not only because his book provided ammunition for those persons who wished to discredit Paine retrospectively on political or religious grounds, but also because it was admiration for Paine's *Rights of Man* that originally brought him from England to America. They quarrelled when Cheetham ventured to edit an article which Paine had sent him for publication. Paine claimed also to have discovered that Cheetham, who had been posing as a supporter of Jefferson, was using his journal to attack him.

Most of the information which Cheetham used to denigrate Paine had been supplied to him by William Carver, another friend of Paine's who turned into an enemy. Carver was a veterinarian and a shopkeeper in New York who introduced himself to Paine claiming to have been a young farrier in Lewes while Paine was an exciseman there. Paine wrote in friendly terms to Carver from New Rochelle and boarded in his house in New York in 1806. It was while staying with Carver in July 1806 that Paine had an apoplectic stroke, from which he never fully recovered. They quarrelled over money which Carver said that Paine owed him for his board, while Paine complained that Carver had not taken proper care of him. Carver, in his turn, alleged that he had found Paine living in a state of filth in New Rochelle.

Carver was also partly responsible for the rumour that Paine became a drunkard in his later years. After Paine had left his house in 1807, he informed two young English visitors that Paine had been in the habit of drinking a quart of brandy a day. Later, however, when questioned by a friend of Paine's he withdrew the charge. It is possible that Paine drank more than usual when he was enfeebled by his stroke. We have, indeed, already remarked that he was addicted to brandy throughout most of his adult life but there is no evidence that he ever became an alcoholic, except possibly for a brief period in France,[1] and Conway was able to collect a convincing amount of testimony that he was no more than a moderate drinker in the last years of his life.

[1] See above pp. 125–6.

While we are on the subject of the aspersions cast on Paine's private life, I should say that I do not think that there is any unfavourable inference to be drawn from his will. He did leave a sum of money amounting probably to less than two thousand dollars in all to Madame Bonneville absolutely, but such wealth as he possessed consisted primarily in his ownership of the farm at New Rochelle, and he directed that the proceeds of its sale should go, apart from two or three small bequests, half to be divided between Thomas Rickman and Nicolas Bonneville, and half to Madame Bonneville, in trust for her children Benjamin and Thomas. Apart perhaps from Rickman, he had no closer friends than the Bonnevilles. He had no family of his own; it is unlikely that he would have felt any obligation to leave money to a wife from whom he had been separated for so many years, but in any case she had pre-deceased him.

Madame Bonneville was Paine's literary executor and she has to be assigned some motive for destroying part of this legacy. The trouble is that we do not know what the manuscripts and letters were that she destroyed. The explanation offered by Moncure Conway is that she became a Roman Catholic, and that she destroyed writings to which she objected on religious grounds. But while it is true that she became a Roman Catholic, it is not easy to see what Paine could have written which would have been more objectionable to her than *The Age of Reason*, which she could not disavow: nor did she ever lend her authority to the rumour, which was spread by some of his enemies, that he underwent a death-bed conversion to Christianity. At the most she may have declined to publish some of the material which Paine is said to have assembled for a third volume of *The Age of Reason*, intended mainly as a rejoinder to its critics. If she destroyed private letters, it could just as well have been because they showed less rather than more affection for her than she wished to make public; another possibility is that they did not always show Paine at his best, since we do know that she cared about his reputation, so much so that she declared her intention of writing a biography to confute his slanderers. We shall see that she supplied some information to William Cobbett, but the evidence which would take us beyond that point is lost. When Nicolas was at length free to leave France they lived for a time together in America and then returned to Paris where they set up a bookshop. Nicolas died in 1828 and in 1833 his widow joined her son Benjamin who was stationed in St Louis, having become a brigadier general in the United States army. When his duties took him away from St Louis he put all his library, including the papers which his mother had entrusted to him, in store.

The warehouse burned down and all the papers were destroyed. Madame Bonneville lived until 1846, is said to have become increasingly devout, and made no further effort to vindicate Thomas Paine.

Among the papers which were lost in the fire were most probably parts of an autobiography which Paine told Henry Yorke, an Englishman who visited him in Paris in 1802, that he was intending to write, as well as the material that Paine had compiled for a third volume of *The Age of Reason*. A fairly good indication of what this volume would have contained is to be found in the so-called Prospect Papers, a set of fifteen very short essays which Paine contributed in 1804 to a New York monthly magazine, called *The Prospect: A View of the Moral World* and edited by Elihu Palmer, a former Presbyterian minister who had been converted to deism, and so much admired Paine as to describe him as 'probably the most useful man that ever existed on the face of the earth'. Palmer died in 1804 and his widow came to Carver's house to nurse Paine when he suffered his apoplectic stroke there in 1806. The poor accommodation which was allotted to her was one of Paine's grievances against Carver. Paine left Mrs Palmer a hundred dollars in his will.

The Prospect Papers cover a variety of topics, from the Tower of Babel to the gloom of a Sabbath-day in Connecticut, but as a whole they do no more than underline and illustrate by further examples points that *The Age of Reason* had already made. The concluding paragraph of an essay comparing the religion of deism with the religion of Christianity sets out concisely what the whole series is designed to prove:

Here it is that the religion of Deism is superior to the Christian Religion. It is free from all those invented and torturing articles that shock our reason or injure our humanity, and with which the Christian religion abounds. Its creed is pure, and sublimely simple. It believes in God, and there it rests. It honours Reason as the choicest gift of God to man, and the faculty by which he is enabled to contemplate the power, wisdom and goodness of the Creator displayed in the creation; and reposing itself on his protection, both here and hereafter, it avoids all presumptuous beliefs, and rejects, as the fabulous inventions of men, all books pretending to revelation.[1]

---

[1] *Writings of Thomas Paine*, vol. IV, p. 322.

A point not made in *The Age of Reason* occurs in a letter written by Paine in 1806 to Andrew Dean, who had rented part of Paine's farm at New Rochelle. After referring to the Bible as 'a book of lies and contradictions' he allows that 'the fable of Christ and his twelve apostles' is the least hurtful part. At the same time, he maintains that everything told of Christ, including his reported resurrection at sunrise on the first day of the week, has reference to the sun. The fable is 'a parody on the Sun and the twelve signs of the Zodiac, copied from the ancient religions of the Eastern world'.[1] This suggestion is ingenious, but I am not qualified to say whether it is historically sound.

In a pamphlet addressed 'to the Ministers and Preachers of all Denominations of Religion', and published in 1807, Paine undertook a rather laborious examination of a number of passages in the Old Testament which had been treated, chiefly in the book of Matthew, as prophecies of events occurring in the life of Jesus Christ. Paine has no difficulty in showing that the interpretations in question do not withstand critical scrutiny. The examination of these alleged prophecies was preceded by a short essay 'On Dreams', the main point of which was to argue that dreams, dismissed as periods of madness, are not prophetic, and succeeded by a short account of Paine's beliefs concerning a 'future state'. His opinion is

that those whose lives have been spent in doing good, and endeavouring to make their fellow-mortals happy, for this is the only way in which we can serve God, *will be happy hereafter*: and that the very wicked will meet with some punishment: but those who are neither good nor bad, or are too insignificant for notice, will be dropt entirely.

On the face of it, this would seem to imply that rather few people would be gratified or burdened with a future life, though Paine presumably included himself among them, as one who had occupied himself in trying to benefit his fellow men. He gives no grounds for his opinion beyond saying that it is consistent with his idea of God's justice and with the reason that God has given him.[2]

A pamphlet of more interest than Paine's repetitious assertion of his religious views is one that he addressed in 1804 to the people of England. It outlined the project of a French invasion which Paine hoped that the people of England would support. The original plan,

[1] ibid., p. 423.
[2] ibid., p. 420.

which was discarded by Bonaparte in favour of his assault on Egypt and perhaps never seriously envisaged by him, was that a thousand 'gun-boats', propelled by oars, each with 'a twenty-four or thirty-six pounder at the head, and a field-piece in the stern', and each carrying a hundred soldiers, should start from Belgian and Dutch ports and land on the flat sandy coasts of the counties of Essex, Suffolk, Norfolk and Lincolnshire. These gun-boats would most probably cross in safety, not only because they could use their artillery to drive off the English fleet but because the expedition could choose to start after a storm when the English fleet would have been blown off, or in a calm or in a fog, and when they had reached their destination, after thirty-six hours' rowing, the shallowness of the coast would protect them from capital ships. Napoleon was to have commanded the expedition and Paine was to have accompanied him. Though he does not say that the invitation would be renewed, I think it reasonable to assume that this was his belief. The justification for the invasion would be England's breach of the treaty of Amiens by her retention of the strategically important island of Malta.

It is not clear how much resistance Paine expected the invasion to encounter. He is in no doubt that in any event the French would be victorious and he expects that the result would be an English revolution and the replacement of the English monarchy by a system of representative government, with a Constitution principally devised by himself. Though he had left France, distrusting Bonaparte, he now writes of him in glowing terms:

> France has now for its chief the most enterprising and fortunate man, either for deep project or daring execution, the world has known for many ages. Compared with him, there is not a man in the British government, or under its authority, has any chance with him. That he is ambitious, the world knows, and he always was so; but he knew where to stop.[1]

And then Paine goes on to speak of the improvement of agriculture, manufacture and commerce that Bonaparte had brought about in France. When he penned this encomium, Paine had not yet learned that Bonaparte had become the Emperor Napoleon. It is a little surprising that the transformation of France into an Empire did not weaken his attachment to its cause, at least in its conflict with England.

[1] *Writings of Thomas Paine*, vol. IV, p. 453.

The concluding paragraphs of the pamphlet are worth quoting, if only as an illustration of Paine's political tenacity:

> If the present eventful crisis, for an eventful one it is, should end in a revolution, the people of England have, within their glance, the benefit of experience both in theory and fact. This was not the case at first. The American revolution began on untried ground. The representative system of government was then unknown in practice, and but little thought of in theory. The idea that man must be governed by effigy and show, and that superstitious reverence was necessary to establish authority, had so benumbed the reasoning faculties of men, that some bold exertion was necessary to shock them into reflection. But the experiment has now been made. The practice of almost thirty years, the last twenty of which have been of peace, notwithstanding the wrong-headed tumultuous administration of John Adams, has proved the excellence of the representative system, and the NEW WORLD is not the preceptor of the OLD. The children are become the fathers of their progenitors.
>
> With respect to the French revolution, it was begun by good men and on good principles, and I have always believed that it would have gone on so, had not the provocative influence of foreign powers, of which Pitt was the principal and vindictive agent, distracted it into madness, and sown jealousies among the leaders.
>
> The people of England have now two revolutions before them. The one as an example; the other as a warning. Their own wisdom will direct them what to choose and what to avoid, and in everything which regards their happiness, combined with the common good of mankind, I wish them honour and success.[1]

Paine's attachment to America and his pride in the part which he had played in securing its independence were cruelly rebuffed in 1806 when he was denied the vote in an election at New Rochelle, on the ground that he was not an American citizen. The chief inspector, Elisha Ward, who turned Paine away from the polling station, was described by Paine in a letter to his old friend Jock Barlow as belonging to a family of Tories who had hidden behind the British lines during the Revolution. The reason which Ward and his fellow inspectors gave for their decision was that Gouverneur Morris did not claim Paine as an American when Paine was imprisoned in Paris and that Washington

[1] ibid., pp. 455–6.

approved of Morris's inaction. We have, in fact, seen that both these propositions were false, while noting that neither Morris nor Washington exerted themselves to obtain Paine's release. Paine was sufficiently indignant to think of prosecuting Ward and his colleagues. Among other things, he tried to obtain attested copies of the correspondence between Randolph and Monroe by which his release was effected. He also wrote to George Clinton, Jefferson's Vice President, asking him to testify to the contribution which Paine's writings had made to the success of the American Revolution. If Madame Bonneville is to be believed, Paine either failed to obtain these pieces of testimony, or they were judged insufficient: for she wrote that Paine took his case to the Supreme Court of New York and lost. It should, however, be added that no record of the case has yet been discovered.

Paine suffered another disappointment when an appeal which he made, successively to Jefferson and to Clinton, for more financial reward for the services he had rendered, and compensation for the money he had spent in the cause of the Revolution, was referred by them to Congress and rejected. Since the terms of his will show that Paine had not been reduced to penury, one might suspect that he became avaricious in his old age. However, I think it more likely that he wanted the money from the American government chiefly as a concrete proof that his importance as a progenitor of the United States was still appreciated. That he was not at all disposed to regard himself as a back number is proved by his writing to Jefferson in January 1806 with the proposal, which Jefferson courteously declined, that he be sent as a special envoy to France. Undiscouraged, he renewed his proposal in March, and Jefferson, who always treated him with respect, again displayed tact in replying that his services were not required.

It was not only with respect to foreign affairs that Paine still aspired to exercise influence over American politics. His last political pamphlet, which was printed in 1805, was addressed to the citizens of Pennsylvania concerning a proposal to call a convention to consider the reform of the State's Constitution. The proposal, which came to nothing, was supported by Paine on the ground that the current Constitution of Pennsylvania, which had come into force in 1790, was inferior to its predecessor of 1776. Its inferiority consisted in its being less democratic. Paine revived his former argument[1] against a bicameral legislature. He considered that the power of veto allotted to the Governor and the patronage which he was permitted to exercise gave

[1] See above pp. 100–1.

him a dangerous resemblance to an English king, and he also more subtly advocated the principle of settling civil disputes by arbitration rather than having them brought before the courts.

If this was the last political pamphlet that Paine is known to have published, his activity as a journalist continued unabated so long as his health lasted. Until his quarrel with Cheetham he was a regular contributor to *The American Citizen*. From March 1807 and for the remainder of the year he wrote articles and editorials for the *Public Advertiser*, under the direction of the printer Jacob Frank. It was in this journal that he published the last of his known writings, an attack on the Federalists for their hostility to France, combined with a denunciation of Cheetham as a 'British Hireling'. Earlier, before he forsook *The American Citizen*, he had made a similar attack on a man calling himself Stephen Carpenter, who had advocated that the United States join England in a war against France and Spain. Paine sought to discredit Carpenter by saying that he was in fact an Irishman called Cullen, the son of the keeper of a box-office at a Dublin theatre.

One of the charges brought by the Federalists against Jefferson was that he had failed to fortify New York against a British attack. While pooh-poohing the idea that New York stood in any such danger, Paine took advantage of this opportunity of maintaining the superiority of gun-boats, constructed according to his formula, over contemporary ships of the line. His argument was soon to be invalidated by the conversion of battleships from sail to steam.

From 1806 onwards Paine continued to live in New York. After leaving Carver, he boarded with the painter John Wesley Jarvis, who had painted a portrait of him, at the age of sixty-seven. A replica of it by Charles W. Jarvis, dated 1845, came into the possession of Moncure Conway, and supplied him with a misleadingly flattering frontispiece to his biography. Except that the nose appears longer, the Jarvis portrait, which is now in the National Gallery of Art in Washington, depicts a face little changed from the one shown in Shaw's engraving of the Romney portrait of Paine at the age of fifty-five. The original of the Romney is lost, as is a second portrait of Paine that Jarvis is known to have painted, probably while Paine was staying at his house.

After leaving Jarvis, with whom, however, he remained on good terms, Paine took rooms first in the house of a baker and then at an inn, before moving in July 1808 to the house of a family called Ryder in Greenwich Village. He paid them ten dollars a week until February 1809, when the rent was doubled because by then he needed so much attendance. In May when he knew himself to be dying he persuaded

Epilogue

The prejudice against Paine's deism did not vanish with Paine's death. In 1819 Richard Carlile and his wife were sent to prison in England, he for three years and she for two, and fined £1,500 and £500 respectively, for publishing Paine's works. In spite of undergoing further prison sentences, Carlile persisted in his attempts to publicize not only Paine's religious but also his political views. How successful he was is shown by the fact that the leaders of the Chartist movement which covered the decade of 1838–1848 appended their Charter to an edition of Paine's *Rights of Man*.

They were justified in doing so, since their demands for manhood suffrage, equal electoral districts, annual parliaments, voting by ballot, payment of Members of Parliament and absence of a property qualification for them to become Members, had, with the exception of the ballot, all been advocated by Paine. Unfortunately, the Chartist movement petered out, and their demands for equal electoral districts and annual parliaments have not yet been met, though the others have. In the case of annual parliaments this is just as well.

The defeat of the Chartists may explain why Paine had very little political influence throughout the remainder of the nineteenth century, and even in the first quarter of the twentieth. Three favourable biographies of him by Richard Carlile, his friend Thomas ('Clio') Rickman and William Sherwin appeared in 1819. An American free-thinker, Gilbert Vale, published a Life of Paine in 1841, but it was not until 1892 that Moncure Daniel Conway brought out his admirable two-volume *Life of Thomas Paine* to be followed by his four-volume edition of *The Writings of Thomas Paine* of which the first two appeared in

1894 and the others in 1899. Since *Common Sense* and the *Rights of Man* are independently available as Penguin Classics and *The Age of Reason* in the Thinkers Library, no inference needs to be drawn from the fact that I have used Conway's work in preference to the later edition of Paine's writings by Philip S. Foner (1945), which is recommended by the Thomas Paine Society. I shall be referring to the emergence of this society later on.

My present concern is to show how little attention was paid to Paine in the aftermath of his death. The year 1819 is exceptional because it was in that year that William Cobbett disinterred Paine's corpse and brought it back to England. Cobbett, who had emigrated to America in 1792, had been shocked by Paine's attack upon George Washington and had himself come to Washington's defence in a pamphlet which he published under the pseudonym of Peter Porcupine. He had read the mischievous life of Paine which George Chalmers, using the pen-name of Francis Oldys, had published in 1791 and incorporated its malice in his own brief sketch of Paine. However, his opinion of Paine changed almost immediately to admiration when he read Paine's pamphlet *The Decline and Fall of the English System of Finance*, and although there is no evidence that the two men ever met, they had friends in common and in 1818 Cobbett announced his intention of writing a life of Paine. He went so far as to obtain a quantity of material from Madame Bonneville but made no serious attempt to fulfil his undertaking.

Cobbett's loss of interest in his proposal to write Paine's life was matched by a loss of interest in the disposal of Paine's physical remains. After exhibiting them proudly on their arrival at Liverpool and failing to arouse enough enthusiasm to raise funds for a monument to be erected to Paine, he took them south and kept them in a box. After Cobbett's death in 1835 his son included them in an auction sale of his father's effects, but the auctioneer refused to put them up for sale. Cobbett's son appealed to the Lord Chancellor, who ruled that Paine's bones should not be regarded as a marketable asset. According to Conway they then somehow came into the possession first of a day labourer and then of a furniture dealer in London, who presumably removed them from the 'empty coffin', with a silver plate bearing the inscription 'Thomas Paine died June 8th 1809, aged 72', which a gentleman at Guildford owned in 1849. Five years later the Reverend R. Ainslie, a Unitarian clergyman, claimed to own 'the skull and right hand of Thomas Paine'. There is evidence that the remains of Paine had been in the possession of various persons in the interval, but it is not known how the skull and right hand came to be detached from the rest of the skeleton nor what subsequently became of them.

Audrey Williamson, who published a painstaking but excessively discursive life of Paine in 1973, supplies a few additional details. She writes of Paine's skull as having been acquired at some stage by a Brighton phrenologist. Though she fails to mention the Reverend R. Ainslie, she asserts, quoting Conway as her authority, that Paine's hand and skull were examined by a professor of the Royal College of Surgeons, who described Paine's hand, on account of its smallness and delicacy, as 'the hand of a female'. On her own account, she refers to a rumour that Paine's 'main skeleton' was buried in 1849 in the churchyard of Ash, a village in the neighbourhood of Cobbett's house in Guildford, but she quotes no source for the rumour or any evidence for its truth.

Our ignorance of the final disposal of his corpse is something that Paine shares with Voltaire and Rousseau. What he does not share, as I have already said, is the constancy of their fame. In the latter half of the nineteenth century he was better remembered in the United States than in England. The monument to him which was erected in New Rochelle in 1839 was repaired and rededicated in 1881 and a bronze bust unveiled in 1889. A portrait of Paine was accepted for Independence Hall in Philadelphia in 1875 and a marble bust in 1905. These honours were paid to him in recognition of the part that he played in the American Revolution, rather than as a mark of the acceptance of his political programme. *The Age of Reason* also assisted the development of free-thinking in the United States, as indeed it did in England, though there the diminution of religious belief, putting such deism as Paine's itself at risk, owed more to the growth of the science of geology and, as we have remarked, to the development of Darwinism.

That the political works of Paine should never have exercised much posthumous influence in the United States is not surprising, in view of the poor showing that has always been made there by any approach to Socialism. What is more remarkable is their failure to play any conspicuous part in the recovery of English radicalism from the defeat of the Chartists or even in the Republican movement which was gathering momentum in the nineteenth century until the longevity of Queen Victoria and the amatory indiscretions of Sir Charles Dilke snuffed it out. It may be the case that Disraeli claimed to be reviving the doctrine of Tom Paine when, as Chancellor of the Exchequer in Lord Derby's Conservative government, he was primarily responsible for carrying through the Second Reform Bill of 1867. But while the Bill did extend the franchise by reducing the property qualification, it fell a long way short of fulfilling Paine's aspirations. So much so that no mention of Paine occurs in the index of Lord Blake's monumental life of Disraeli, any more than it occurs in Sir Philip Magnus's comparable biography of Gladstone. Neither did the Fabians make a hero of Paine, though they did put up a commemorative tablet to him in 1892 at an inn in Lewes which he frequented. The White Hart Hotel at Lewes was the venue in 1904 for what was described as 'The First Paine Celebration in England' but the celebration was for Paine's anti-Christian rather than his political standpoint. Bertrand Russell, who had written a letter of apology for his inability to take part in the celebration, contributed an essay on 'Thomas Paine' to a volume entitled *Great Democrats* which appeared in 1934, but the flavour of its attitude to Paine is indicated by its being reprinted many years later in an expanded version of Russell's *Why I Am Not a Christian*, which was originally published in 1927.

Very much the same applies to Bernard Shaw. Rather surprisingly, the anniversary of Paine's death was commemorated in 1909 both in Thetford and in London, and *The Times* found space for a special article, mainly appreciative of Paine, in which he was truly described as 'the most famous native of the little borough town of Thetford'. This gave Shaw occasion to remark on the importance of the principle of toleration in the course of his attack upon censorship which occupied his very long preface to the text of his minor play *The Shewing-Up of Blanco Posnet*. On the other hand, in the index to his major political work, *The Intelligent Woman's Guide to Socialism and Capitalism*, which was published in 1928, the name of Thomas Paine does not appear. Paine is indeed mentioned in Shaw's *Everybody's Political What's What*, which was published in 1944, but not primarily as a politician. *Rights of Man* is overlooked but it is said that people used to be transported for reading Paine's *The Age of Reason*. The two other passages in which Paine's name occurs are not entirely consistent. In one it is implied that 'our rulers' are still being taught at schools like Eton and Harrow, Rugby and Winchester that 'Deists like Voltaire, Rousseau and Tom Paine were villainous atheists';[1] in another that whereas 'in the nineteenth century, Shelley, Tom Paine, and Mary Wollstonecraft were ostracized as enemies of God they are now famous for their public virtues'. Shaw, however, goes on to say 'But in private they behaved scandalously.' The point which he is concerned to make is that this is no longer held

---

[1] G. B. Shaw, *Everybody's Political What's What* (1944), p. 147.

against them, but it would seem to be a proposition which he himself accepts. We have seen that in Paine's case at least there is no good reason for thinking it true.

The rejection of Paine in the nineteenth century was exemplified in the hostile account of his character which Leslie Stephen contributed to the *Dictionary of National Biography*, of which Stephen was the first editor. This evoked rejoinders from Moncure Conway and the formidable Rationalist J. M. Robertson, and Stephen had the grace to admit that he had been misled.

The only Fabian Socialist, if he can fairly be so described, to do full justice to Paine in the early part of this century is H. N. Brailsford, who devoted a chapter to him in his book *Shelley, Godwin and Their Circle*, which was first published in September 1913. The conclusion of Mr Brailsford's essay appears to me so apt and eloquent that I intend to purloin it for my own peroration.

The rehabilitation of Thomas Paine, which has increasingly gained momentum since the conclusion of the Second World War, is due almost entirely to the work of one man, Joseph Lewis, the American publisher and free-thinker, who lived from 1889 to 1968. Though he enjoyed no success either with his book *Thomas Paine, Author of the Declaration of Independence*, or with his play about Paine, *The Tragic Patriot*, which he wrote in 1947 and 1954 respectively, he had managed as early as 1936 to persuade the Popular Front government of Léon Blum to erect a statue of Paine in the Parc Montsouris, Paris, which was dedicated in 1948. He was also able to raise money for the erection of a statue of Paine, which was dedicated in 1950 in Morristown, New Jersey. Lewis published a monthly journal which was given the title of *The Age of Reason* in the 1950s and he was the organizer of the Thomas Paine Foundation in the United States. Independently, a Thomas Paine National Historical Association had come into being in 1906, and in 1910 had reconstructed Paine's cottage at New Rochelle not far from its original site.

In the year that Lewis died the United States issued a postage stamp on 29 January to commemorate Paine's birthday, two hundred and thirty-one years earlier, but the Foundation did not survive. In the meantime, however, Lewis had helped to raise money for a statue of Paine to be erected in Thetford. Previously there had been only a bronze plaque, paid for by American airmen who had been stationed near Thetford in the Second World War. The statue, situated in a dominant position outside the office of the Town Council, was unveiled on 7 June 1964. A vigorous if rather contorted work, sculpted by Sir

Charles Wheeler, at one time President of the Royal Academy, it suffered from being defaced by local vandals and the covering of gold paint which now protects it is excessively bright. Tom Paine is represented with a quill pen in his right hand and in his left a copy of *Rights of Man*, upside-down and with the lettering awry. A Conservative councillor resigned in protest at its erection, on political, however, rather than aesthetic grounds.

The political dispute over the erection of the statue had one good effect in that it led to the founding of The Thomas Paine Society of which Michael Foot became and remains the President and R. W. Morrell the Secretary. The Society issues a quarterly bulletin and a newsletter twice a year. Whereas the two hundredth anniversary of Paine's birth had achieved little more notice than a dinner at the Guildhall in London, the Society saw to it that the two hundred and fiftieth anniversary, in 1987, was widely acclaimed. There were meetings at Sheffield, Leicester and Nottingham, an exhibition displayed at the library of Alford in Lincolnshire, where Paine had been a customs officer, and a celebration luncheon and a festival of liberty at Thetford, where there was also an exhibition at the Ancient House Museum of works by and about Paine and objects relating to him, the most interesting being a set of metal tokens which were put into circulation at the time of his trial in 1792. With one exception, all of them were hostile, varying in their invective and having in common the depiction on one of their faces of Paine hanging on a gibbet.

Not quite so much attention was paid to this anniversary in the United States, but a dinner organized by the Thomas Paine National Historical Association took place in New Rochelle. Three hundred persons were charged for their attendance and the proceeds served to modernize and extend New Rochelle's Thomas Paine Memorial Museum. A message was sent by President Reagan in which he paid tribute to Paine for the famous passage in his Crisis letter beginning 'These are the times that try men's souls',[1] a letter that 'provided invaluable inspiration for the men of the Continental Army at a time when the American Revolution seemed in danger of being crushed'. The President went on to quote Paine's dictum 'Those who expect to reap the blessings of freedom must, like men, undergo the fatigue of supporting it', and deftly hinted at its contemporary application. He chose to overlook Paine's onslaught on Christianity, or possibly it had escaped his notice.

[1] See above p. 45.

There is no safe decision procedure for subjective conditionals in history and I should not venture to assert that but for Tom Paine the American States would never have been united or made themselves independent of Great Britain. There is, however, no doubt that his *Common Sense* and other early writings were major causal factors in the actual development of the American Revolution. It would perhaps not be fair to say that he took his political philosophy from Locke, since he claimed never to have read him, but he occupied the same theoretical position. What he did was to give Locke's principles a more radical application. We have seen that his gallant attempt to guide the course of the French Revolution was unsuccessful, and while in the first volume of *Rights of Man* he enjoys a logical triumph over Burke, the Conservatives who think of Burke as supplying them with a political warrant are perhaps not greatly susceptible to logic. The second volume is remarkable for its blueprint of a Welfare State, but I doubt if either the New Dealers in America or the politicians who built up the Welfare State in Britain were consciously influenced by it. As for *The Age of Reason*, its deism needs a stronger defence and its way of discrediting the Bible appears old-fashioned, though I suspect that it is still capable of making converts, especially among younger readers.

I conclude that the importance that has recently accrued to the memory of Thomas Paine is mainly symbolic. Democracy is a term to which governments of almost any type are now obliged to pay lip-service. Except that he did not go beyond manhood suffrage, Paine genuinely believed in it. He thought that all men without exception should have as large a say as was practically possible in the management of their own affairs, and he combined this with a recognition of the need for society to take responsibility for those of its members who were not in a position to fend adequately for themselves. Conversely, he repudiated unearned privilege. He was willing that men should battle for their rights, but assumed that once they had obtained them they would be bound to perceive the futility of war. There are very few people who would openly reject these propositions, but it is only to a very limited extent that they have ever been translated into practice. That is my reason for saying that the importance attached to Paine's ideas is mainly symbolic, though I hope to have made it clear that I myself take them seriously. It should also be added that his scientific claims were not at all chimerical. As a designer of bridges, he has an honourable place in the history of architecture.

Index